THE LIFE OF
# DALE CARNEGIE
## AND HIS PHILOSOPHY OF SUCCESS

Carlos Roberto Bacila

THE LIFE OF DALE CARNEGIE AND HIS PHILOSOPHY OF SUCCESS

Original Title: A Vida de Dale Carnegie e sua Filosofia de Sucesso

.

© 2013, by Carlos Roberto Bacila

ISBN: 9781549957017

Translated by Tracy Smith Miyake

Photo "About the Author" by Cheila Fernanda Noé Bacila

# TABLE OF CONTENTS

# INTRODUCTION

This book is dedicated to Fernando Amarante, who Dale Carnegie certainly would have been honored to know.

I thank Dale Carnegie for all he has done for me and for my friends, in the past, present and future.

I also thank my dear friends, near and far. Our friendship runs both ways. You have helped me to write this book; now it is my turn to do the same, if you please!

Also thanks to all the animals, all the plants, all the beings, living or not, and all the forces that we perceive, but do not comprehend.

Thank you!

Dear reader, this book is for you. It was written over thirty years' time, and tells the true story of a real -life enchanter. I hope you get as much as you can out of it. Certainly that is what Carnegie would have wanted for you, and definitely what I wish for you: Much Success!

Carlos Roberto Bacila

# FOREWORD

In the spring of 1953, Dale Hill was presenting a Dale Carnegie course in San Francisco, at the Sir Francis Drake Hotel. Everyone was concentrating on the goals of the course and the materials to be covered when they were suddenly interrupted by a beautiful woman of about thirty years, who entered the room and said in heavily accented English: "I'm sorry to interrupt you, but when I saw the great name of Dale Carnegie in the paper, I had to come." Then she related, to everyone's horror, that she had been a prisoner in a concentration camp during World War II. She and twenty-six other prisoners had been beaten, humiliated and tortured, and suffered greatly the whole time they were imprisoned. But someone in that hell hole had a copy of *How to Win Friends and Influence People*. William Longgood described what these hostages of an enemy army, who had practically given up on living, did with the book: "They never stopped reading it. And the book was passed from one to another. Each person read the tome dozens of times until the book fell apart. She said the book gave them hope, and saved everyone's sanity. Tears fell down her face, and she left the meeting."[1]

Those who know a little about the influence of Dale Carnegie's books are not surprised by occurrences like this one, which greatly moved everyone in that San Francisco lecture room that day. Carnegie's books *How to Win Friends and Influence People* and *How to Stop Worrying and Start Living* inform, touch, and enable his readers to this very day. The greater public is familiar with the Dale Carnegie training course, which is conducted around the world and known for its guaranteed quality. Another of Carnegie's important contributions was the development of the notion of support groups, which have helped millions of people, whether ill or stigmatized or compulsive, to work together to find solutions to the problems that torment them. However, there is a hidden side of Dale Carnegie that can be better understood philosophically, an approach that enables us to better understand his huge success and the great repercussions of his work, as well as to understand the true extension of his thoughts. Similarly interesting is the life of the man himself, who was one of those fascinating people who practiced exactly what he preached, and lived a life entirely compatible with his philosophy, a philosophy that has yet to be completely unveiled, and all of its consequences yet to be understood. While many thinkers look for traces of the most authentic American philosophy in the works of renowned, well-quoted philosophers, it may be that Dale Carnegie, a man who did not follow the conventional academic path, is exactly the source of the true lost philosophy: the philosophy for life.

Dale Carnegie was on familiar terms with kings and queens, presidents, legendary entrepreneurs and well-respected scientists, but he also knew how to interact with the most neglected souls: beggars, people with special needs, the poor, and so many other stigmatized people. When he created a common language for all, a universal path to success and personal influence, Carnegie showed that the accumulation of wealth and noticeable prowess was accessible to any and all. But in order to attain these gains, he developed something bigger, a background philosophy that was strong enough to be functional, which paid respect to other people as complete beings, a philosophy which not only meets every social, economical and political need, but is always respectfully attached to diversity; a philosophy of learning how to grow materially and spiritually. It reflects in practically everything that follows Carnegie, from the books labeled "self-help", to the courses that guide participants towards personal and professional excellence, oratory and a new language for mutual understanding. Further, I decided to expose the method that Dale Carnegie used to study, write and work: a method that surpasses traditional ways of writing doctoral theses and instead teaches how to reach for and attain bold personal goals.

Is there a common link among all these areas? That is what we will see in this work.

Carlos Roberto Bacila

# HOW DID I WRITE THIS BIOGRAPHY?

It was July, 2008 and very hot in the United States. I called the Dale Carnegie Institute in New York. The secretary picked up, and when I said my name, she already knew what it was about. "Ms. Johnson will receive you tomorrow at ten".  I cannot overstate how lucky I was to have met Brenda Leigh Johnson, one of the Dale Carnegie Group's directors. I sat down at the director's table and tried to explain, in my poor English, that I knew and respected the work of Dale Carnegie. His books are among the best-sellers of all time, even decades after publication; and let's not forget the Course, a success with one hundred years of tradition. And yet I suspected that his philosophy was more consistent than what the critics had pointed out. That is to say, I believed that there was much more to Dale Carnegie than simply the label he received from the critics as 'the predecessor of self-help books'. I knew deep down that more thorough research could benefit diligent readers and participants in  the Dale Carnegie Course much more, verifying a perspective that had not yet been recognized, a philosophy open to discussion. Besides this, other readers not yet familiar with Carnegie's work, perhaps avoiding stigmatized 'self-help reading', could reconsider their position, if the scientific or philosophical character of his work were recognized and verified. I was unsure of where this search would lead me, but this was a very personal project that had  an immeasurable value for me, not only because Carnegie's literature had so greatly influenced my teaching and my own life, but also because after defending and publishing my doctorate in law, I found myself working on a new project without any academic pressure, driven only by my own conscience.

Brenda listened to what I had to say, and gave me a CD-ROM about the Dale Carnegie Institute, a film about his life and some other materials that were wonderful for me. I did not think she would do anything for me, as I was an unknown person with no references, no recommendations, who simply knocked on the doors of the Institute and asked for favors. I could have been a journalist trying to stir up mud about the stalwart Institute... I could have been an irresponsible sensationalist... But, for reasons unknown to me, I deserved her trust... And what did Brenda do? She invited me to visit the Dale Carnegie Museum, which houses relics of one of the most important American writers (after this, I would visit two more museums holding relics of Carnegie's life, in the towns of Warrensburg and Belton, both in the state of Missouri). Brenda was waiting to drive me to the museum the next morning when my train arrived in Hauppauge, a pleasant small town near New York City where the administrative headquarters of the Dale Carnegie Institute as well as the museum are currently located. I was thrilled. For years I had read and reread Dale Carnegie's most important books. I admired the author as if he were an old friend, because his frank, direct style of writing draws the reader close to the writer's convictions. But I had never imagined that on a beautiful sunny morning, I would be observing objects that had belonged to the great Dale Carnegie himself. Brenda showed me typewriters, glasses, letters and postcards that he had written to his dear mother. Pens, chairs... one of the chairs in the collection had belonged to Abraham Lincoln and was acquired by Carnegie when he was writing his biography of that influential president. I saw family snapshots, initial drafts of books that one day would be worldwide successes but were preserved as simple outlines that were yet to become legend. I was overcome with emotion every time Brenda pointed out details that she, as a careful director, knew with precision. We shared hours of unforgettable dialogue. We went to lunch, and Brenda introduced me to her husband and son. I was moved by such cordiality, but also was well aware of my responsibility. I knew that this was just the beginning of a research project that already had great meaning to me, but that without a doubt could mean so much to others like me, who had been fortunate enough to come into contact with such a genius and master as Carnegie and his work.

What was at stake? The life work of the people who worked at the Dale Carnegie Institute for more than ninety years developing oratory and personal and professional relationship techniques. A course that trained over six million people, enabling them to develop abilities and manifest previously hidden professional talents. I owed and continue to owe these people respect, at the very least. As a result, I always kept in mind the stakeholders in this project: the beneficiaries of Carnegie's work (a multitude of people), the professionals at the Dale Carnegie Institute (because, in a way, Carnegie's thoughts influenced their professional lives) and, of course the people that would see the other side of Carnegie.

But the strongest word that comes to me in defining my encounter with Brenda is, without a doubt, gratitude. She received a foreigner as if he were an old friend. I was overwhelmed by my feelings, but I also felt obligation and the extension of my responsibility.

How to take the first step? How to begin a project about a single life and yet also the project of a lifetime? This question was always in my mind. I wanted to write about a life and a thought, a biography that, for me, possessed very eloquent meaning, and I had to share it with the world. The answer showed itself in a surprising manner. Dale Carnegie, the person whose life and philosophy would be the center of my studies for the next years, was himself no stranger to biography. His biography of Abraham Lincoln, perhaps the most distinguished of all United States presidents, is a jewel, a pearl that draws the reader close to lesser-known facts about the great statesman. We will dedicate a whole chapter to commentary on this classic book, exploring the depth and, at the same time, the simplicity with which Carnegie conveys accounts that at that time were still largely unknown about the commander-in-chief who guided the country through the Civil War. Besides his work *Lincoln the Unknown,* Carnegie also wrote a fascinating book that analyzes and assembles the biographies of forty of some of the most influential personalities, revealing aspects of their lives and intellects that constitute true life lessons.

In this work, titled *Biographical Roundup; Highlights in the Lives of Forty Famous People,* the first subject portrayed is George Bernard Shaw, whose life curiously resembled Carnegie's. Shaw left school after only five years, and was poor throughout his youth. From an early age he had to work to help support his family. In his first job, he earned four dollars and fifty cents a month. Between the ages of sixteen and twenty, he was a cashier in an office, and made eight dollars a month. But as a child he had already learned to love art, music and literature. At seven, he read Shakespeare, Dickens and Dumas, among others. But he also suffered through a miserable existence for years before attaining his dream of becoming a writer. Nevertheless, when he attained success, he flooded the world with his writings and received millions in royalties, to the extent that he gave away the thirty-five thousand dollars he received with his Nobel Prize for Literature. But before this success, Shaw's submissions had been refused so frequently by the publishers to which he sent the manuscripts that any other person would have given up. Also notable is the inferiority complex that haunted him.[2] This description of Shaw greatly resembles Carnegie's own life, especially each one's tireless persistence and dedication to attaining their dreams.

Carnegie's biographical studies went above and beyond the norm, because he worked on the radio for years talking about the lives of very special people, and also because wrote countless articles in newspapers that were practically biographies of the rich and famous. As some of these distinguished people were still alive at the time, Carnegie did long interviews with them to learn their secrets to success. One of these interviewees was W. C. Fields, one Hollywood's greatest artists, who Carnegie described as looking like he had just stepped out of a Dickens novel. Before becoming a celebrity, though, Fields had to sweat just to make it from one day to the next. When still a teenager, things were so dire that he pretended to drown in the sea so that his friends could sell hot dogs to the crowd that had gathered to watch in horror. His life was very tough. The hardship began when, at the tender age of eleven, he had a disagreement with his father; Fields had left a shovel on the ground, and his father stepped on it and hurt himself. The resulting argument became so intense that Fields ended up running away from home, and remained homeless until he was sixteen. His eyes brimmed when he talked about this stage of his life.[3]

Sinclair Lewis, another Nobel Prize winner, led a similarly fascinating life. Before becoming a huge success, Lewis wrote six unexceptional books; it was only for his seventh novel, *Main Street,* that he that he received worldwide attention. Over seventeen years, Sinclair restyled the book three different times; he worked an entire year before tossing it all away, writing and rewriting the material. Here we find another similarity to Carnegie: writing and rewriting was a part of Lewis' routine. Lewis also had a hard life before becoming famous; he worked hard for six months and only sold one single joke for the grand sum of two dollars. Once, Carnegie asked Sinclair Lewis what advice he would give to young writers; Lewis replied at once that he did not have any advice to give anybody. I highly doubt this. I believe that Lewis would have a lot of advice for people. However, the person who asked him about advice and lessons, Dale Carnegie, also had a lot to teach us, specifically at this point, how to write biographies.

Fortunately, especially with regards to Lincoln's biography, Carnegie described the method he used to write it, a magnificent guide which highlights the need to become more and more involved with the theme, to treat it seriously and raise it to an unequaled level of analysis. Thus, in trying to take a lesson from the author of such a great biography, I followed Carnegie's lead, visiting places that were part of Dale Carnegie's own personal, emotional and professional life. In doing so, I frequented the beautiful New York Public Library on Fifth Avenue and 42$^{nd}$ Street, where he spent countless hours times studying and researching topics. I went to the 125$^{th}$ Street YMCA in

Harlem, where in 1912 he founded the most traditional oratory, human relations, sales and personal development course that the world has ever seen, one that continues to improve to this day, and which has just celebrated a hundred years. I also visited both universities that had rejected his applications to be a professor of rhetoric before Carnegie was able to begin his course at the YMCA. Today, American universities recognize the Dale Carnegie Course as transfer credits, just as valid as university courses. I visited the area where he first lived after arriving in New York, a humble apartment in Hell's Kitchen. I visited the first property he bought, in Queens, where he settled and stayed even after his success..

After many visits in New York, my next destination was the state of Missouri, where it all began... In Missouri, I found not only dozens of places and impressive relics that bring to life Dale Carnegie's saga, but also very kind people that were always helpful in any research about their native son.

Carnegie had written letters and articles for over seventy newspapers in the United States; this prolificity allowed me, through patient research, access to valuable texts that he wrote, true gifts of literature. These works complemented his writings with examples, explanations and even research that he conducted to crystallize some of his principles, similar to *backup material in* speech and writing or, even better the *reserve power* we will discuss in the chapter about his book *Public Speaking and Influencing Men in Business.* Nothing that I wrote could ever replace Carnegie's incomparable works; what I can do is research his life and philosophy, and better understand how Dale Carnegie brought so many new things in the area of human relations, and why his life contributes so significantly to personal development. In this sense, I believe Carnegie's texts, letters, notes, rough drafts, pictures, and relics spread all over the world will give his readers, course graduates, or any people interested in learning a valuable acquisition when it comes to Carnegie's intellectual legacy and the example of his life.

This was a good start. My path was laid out in front of me, although I certainly could not see all the twists and turns in front of me that I would need to go over step by step and confront, exactly as Carnegie had taught when writing a biography. Suddenly, I had an amazing and inexplicable feeling that some greater force was guiding me and talking to the Universe around me. Maybe it was all related to Dale Carnegie's own life and philosophy. For a moment, I had the feeling that while trying to take a picture, I too was a part of the scenery. In reading the book, the reader will come to understand what I am trying to say.

Returning to New York, I visited St. Patrick's Cathedral on Fifth Avenue, which Carnegie had attended for many years. He considered himself a protestant, but visited churches of all creeds and prayed respectfully. In this magnificent cathedral, he sought peace and tranquility in his life, and received the strength he needed to go on with his mission. In this same sanctum I prayed for two things: first, to be successful in my work portraying one of the greatest people the world has even known. Secondly, well, I asked to find a better hotel than the one where I was staying.

## THE POWER OF DALE CARNEGIE'S BIOGRAPHY

Last night I went to a bar where friends gather to talk and smoke cigars over coffee. Francine[4], a very cultured doctor, told me about Alfonso, a wealthy yet disenchanted friend of hers. Alfonso was advanced in age, had no close personal relationships, lacked the will to do anything, and even worse, didn't have a single friend as a traveling companion. What to do when one nears the end of life? Francine questioned the lack of sense in life, and its certain end, deploring the situation of people that slave away at badly paid jobs (such as day laborers), or even worse, those who work jobs they cannot stand, like the emergency room doctor who dreads being on call, or the police officer who equally despises carrying out his duties.

— *Francine, - I contemplated – Each person has to figure out what they like the most, whether they are fifty-two or seventy, even if they need to return to cherished moments in their childhood to do so.*

— Persistent, Francine retorted – *But by then it is too late. You have kids in college, bills to pay, how can you escape this vicious cycle?*

— *They need to establish a plan to change their lives –* I told her– *but it's necessary to have strong will and tenacity to reach one's goals. I have a challenge for your friend Alfonso, and for your hypothetical day laborer, doctor and police officer as well. The challenge is this: read ten biographies about people you really admire. If, in the end, these people do not change their minds, I will share your disenchantment and give up.*

Francine got to thinking... Why read biographies?

I believe in the intrinsic power of biography, because it shows that the great personalities of history triumphed over hardship and difficulties, and sometimes over problems we have trouble even imagining. Most recently, I read the biography of the great Hollywood actor Jack Nicholson. When he acted in *Easy Rider* in 1968, young people immediately identified with the movie and Nicholson became very popular. The movie gave value to those people "with no destination"; that is to say, those who moved along the fringes of social conventions, whose path more closely resembled soaring freely towards boundless horizons. Nicholson followed up on this publicity with a strong acting style and was always well respected by the critics. He was probably the best-paid actor to work on a short movie role: he worked on *Batman* for four months and received an initial sum of eleven million dollars. Just the profit on the movie's initial returns brought him another sixty million.[5] But any viewer who watches his magnificent performance as the Joker can be sure that his success was the result of impressive preparation; the director Tim Burton commented that Nicholson went deeper into his profession than any other actor. Before Batman, Nicholson prepared intensely for his role as the devil in *The Witches of Eastwick,* his biographer described him as reading Dante's *Inferno*, studying Gustave Dore's paintings, consulting text by St Thomas Aquinas, even taking violin lessons to represent his character most accurately[6] What do we conclude from this? That intense and dedicated work brings success. Another thing we can learn from Nicholson's biography is about his poverty before stardom; there were days when he didn't know where his next meal was coming from.[7] But the actor learned even from this; in his biography, Nicholson referred to his childhood and his humble roots as training for struggle: struggle against not only poverty, but also against bad arguments, fancy dialogues, or talentless producers.[8]

Biographies are true recipes for life. I have read over a hundred of them and can assure you that learning from them is a given. It is as if we have a great master to teach us how to win and how to avoid the master's own mistakes. Obstacles are frequently common. The destiny of those great people who influenced the world was not announced from the moment of their births, but built day after day on the endless denials they heard and disregarded. Funnily enough, this biography of Dale Carnegie could be a real solution to Francine's dilemma, because these kinds of problems were a staple of Carnegie's life. When we hear Debbie Bond, a Dallas Cowboys cheerleader, talk about Carnegie, we can hear her sincerity: "I tell people about Dale Carnegie all the time because he changed my life"[9.] We know that Carnegie changes the lives of those who read his books and attend his Course, but why? Where does such power come from? What is the secret of Dale Carnegie?

Maybe one of his secrets was learning from others, from their lives and biographies. He greatly valued what well-known people did and said, and tried to study their methods. At the beginning of his life, he learned simple things like gestures and vocabulary from orators so that he could apply them to his speeches.[10] Later on, he stated that this was not the best way to learn oratory, and he practically reinvented the art of public speaking. He noticed how his boss, one Rufus E. Harris, signed his full name without lifting the pen off the paper. Carnegie started signing his own name like this because he believed that was the formula to success. As he grew older, he started to discover more important facts in biographies, facts much more decisive than mimicking gestures and signing one's name. He started to harvest the essential from biographies. From this essence he moved one step forward and developed his own methods. In this way, he took individual techniques and transformed them into highly valued rules for general use. This personal growth brought him to create 'support groups', as we now call groups for work, study and missions, but also which are for people addicted to drugs, alcohol, gambling, etc. He also developed a new notion of public speaking, one clearer and more efficient than the classic, more pompous style. In doing so, he literally changed the way that ideas are brought to the public. He produced practical rules for doing one's job, conducting business, connecting to people, attaining prestige and making friends. But we should also emphasize his discovery of methods to control anxiety and attain better mental health. He was the pioneer of self-development courses and books.[11] Soon, the life that Dale Carnegie built was also worthy of study on its own merits, and his own biography deserving of study. At sixty, Carnegie said something that summarized his way of studying and expanding his principles: "I will tell you a secret that will make it easy for you to speak in public immediately. Did I find this in a book? No. Was it taught to me in college? No. I had to figure it out gradually, and slowly, through years of trial and error."[12]

It is common to hear that humanity's great achievers are people who were born with a special talent, a gift, that enables such people to succeed so triumphantly. Accordingly, people like Alexander the Great, Joan of Arc, Al Pacino, Albert Einstein, Marie Curie, Pelé, Mother Theresa of Calcutta, and Sammy Davis Jr. are or were fated people, as they carried this gift of magnificent realization inside themselves since birth. Frankly, I believe that the great personalities are not born, but made by Nature. Surely there must be a strong sense of self-determination, a free will that drives one to sail in deep water, just as Ishmael needed to embark on the Pequod to learn the ways of the sea and free himself from a heartless routine and a boring and mediocre life. Ishmael was searching for something bigger, the fulfillment of an ideal or the very discovery of this ideal; it is necessary, though, to know exactly what you will find in this tempestuous sea, or at least try to find out.

In the intersection between the endlessness of the sea and the strongest human self-determination, we find Dale Carnegie, in whose name how to walk in dignity is taught every day. But for him to become the outstanding personality that he became, he needed to travel a long road, and to struggle with adversity, while confronting incomprehensible opponents in nature and society. Keeping one's footing on such a difficult path is impressive enough, but transforming oneself into a  motivator, a life and business counselor, and a presenter of ideas to society is a different matter.  It is imperative that we unveil his steps, try to learn even more, understand beyond his fantastic books his attitude on how to walk the long road that is life. Even further, it is necessary to understand why and how Carnegie could and still can influence, in the past and the present, millions and millions of people. Some of the people he impacted are famous writers that reflect the influence they received through Carnegie. But what about the other millions of people that continue to be influenced by his philosophy? What are were the consequences of this influence on religion, work, letters, behavior and other areas? The dimensions are staggering. Yet there is still room for an equally important discussion, which refers to the enforcement and development of a philosophy that adapts best to the American way of life: pragmatism. If anyone interpreted, promoted and used the philosophy of Pierce and James, it was certainly Dale Carnegie.

Sometimes we find an idol or a hero, someone who is very dear to us because of their inspiring feats. Other times, we admire someone for their courage and determination. There are times, however, when we find in someone such strong qualities that they seem be to be beyond human. We observe more carefully and see that they exceed our imagination. As a result, we start to see in this person a true guide to light our path. Of course, we hope that everything about this master is perfect. But we forget that the master, too, walks around and finds his own obstacles. When people from Carnegie's era saw any sign of weakness or flaw in him, they raised their voices furiously to attack him. Even so, if we compare Dale Carnegie's life to the lives of present-day "heroes"... well, these "heroes" could learn a lot from him: lessons in humility, character, patience, wisdom, dedication to personal growth... The word 'dale' means 'valley'. Maybe nature chose this name to say that someone would come to guide people to walk between mountains, in a beautiful meadow crossed by a stream. This guide would take people through the valley so they could fend for themselves while hiking in the mountains. If this is true, Dale Carnegie came to talk to us and explain, during a tranquil stroll in the valley, what is needed to move forward and conquer the enormous mountains of life. Many poems were written about the wonder that is the Universe; Dale Carnegie wrote a manual about how to enjoy it gently, managing this magnificent force that is Nature, the friendly smile.

Carnegie developed ideas from the intellectual and philosophical pantheon, from Marcus Aurelius to Hebert Spencer, from Epictetus to Immanuel Kant. But the curious thing is that he makes all philosophies measure up to his standards of applicability. As a result, his quotations are not just woolgathering, or a demonstration of erudition, but are included to truly serve the reader. We can say that he channels learning towards practice and efficiency, and as a result, he is a proponent of Pragmatism, as we will soon see.

Overall, he uses a simple, objective, practical, attractive style that is above all useful to the reader. If the word self-help could be applied to only one category of books (a concept with which I do not agree, for I believe every book – scientific, popular, novels, philosophical, criticism – can help the reader), I believe it would best suit all those kinds of books that can benefit the reader. How many books were written in order to demonstrate the author's erudition, or refinement, or just to showcase the author, but do not contain any prerogative to help the reader, or to stimulate them toward personal, scientific or spiritual growth?

Writing with clarity requires not only competency, but also an immense will to respect the reading public. We can confirm that Carnegie possessed an enormous capacity for writing well as well as a great will to reach his public, benefiting their lives and inspiring every step for the seekers. As for wanting the best for his readers, this is consistent with the principles he preached. His honesty can be seen in his kind and warm written words. As for the content of his vocabulary, always followed by rich examples and singular quotes, I attribute to it two particularities of Carnegie. First, the education he received, which evidently cannot be credited solely to the courses he attended, but which came especially from a deep desire to learn, to read, to observe and to think. Carnegie was, without a doubt, a brilliant self-educated person. He devoured novels, biographies, philosophical texts and anything else that could contribute to his classes and writings. As he tried to find his way and develop his own style, he read a lot and researched, and this gave him the abilities of a spectacular writer.

Secondly, I consider that the success of Dale Carnegie's writings and the dynamic and profundity of his practical thoughts are owed to his impressive life experience. Let's be clear, no one can produce knowledge by having a life free from turbulence. Jack London, one of the most amazing writers I know, would not have written *War*[13] or *The Sea-Wolf*[14] had he not passed through a hard and intense life of struggle. Herman Melville, author of *Moby Dick*[15], would not have described the impetuous and metaphoric voyage of the *Pequod*, piloted by the obstinate Ahab and the idealistic Ishmael, if Melville himself hadn't heard real sailors' own stories, nor stories of whales that, tired of being hunted, started to sink ships.[16] We would never have met *Papillon: the man who escaped Hell*[17] if Henri Charrière had not endured the bitterness of prison. Who knows, if he had lived a frivolous life, he might have only ended up a spoiled boy from one of the more festive neighborhoods of Paris. We certainly would not have had the monumental biography of Sammy Davis Jr.[18] if he had not been poor, discriminated against, humiliated, nor suffered countless hardships in his life. There is no escaping it: hardships in life transform the human being, creating a singular story and making the person into a magnificent warrior. Many times we may think that we are at the very bottom of the well, although it seems almost endless (although sometimes we may have to sink even deeper before we hit the bottom), but we do not consider it an experience necessary to strengthen our muscles and intellect. To create a true warrior spirit, one needs persistence, the will to fight, vigor, patience, and the strength to overcome obstacles. We only understand the dimensions of the storm after it passes, when we see the sun shine, the calmness return. Dale Carnegie's work overflows with intense experiences of life, nightmares, martyrdom and suffering that, on those merits alone, made his real characters triumph. But that was not all; Dale Carnegie himself passed through sinister storms, but he was able to assimilate and transform these vicissitudes into energy and glory. Without a doubt, the intense experiences of his youth gave him a unique and vital vision of the world. He also belongs to the category of people who were shaken by destiny. Another interesting aspect in his work was the fact that he valued those people who are usually stigmatized by society. He was not influenced by stigmas, which is a fantastic virtue. It is not unusual for us to be deluded by social rules that penalize those people who are different from the norm in any way.[19] It is truly fascinating how Carnegie positively explored objective data that are belittled by many who ignore the issue; physical disabilities, different behaviors, poverty and so many other characteristics that have long been stigmatized through history became, for Carnegie, opportunities for personal development and even contemplation.

The intention of this book is to unveil the fascinating life of Dale Carnegie, an existence that brought him to masterfully describe the true meaning of practical life, the feeling that comes from reaching our goals as well as the methods to achieve them, and the mechanisms for efficient human relations. In his body of work, we learn much more than how to make friends, influence people, stop worrying and speak in public; we meet a fabulous person who shows us, through the example of his life and creative genius, how to manifest our ideals and how to transform philosophy into reality. After all, reaching freedom, for example, is similar to leaving a dark building, opening the door, seeing the bright colors of trees and flowers, hearing birdsong, breathing  fresh air, seeing people walk by on the sidewalk, leaving the dark building where we live. Carnegie shows us this: how to leave the dark building and find life. Is it worthwhile to become familiar with his life and philosophy? I will leave that answer to the reader.

# CHAPTER 1

## LIFE ON A FARM IS NOT ALWAYS ROMANTIC

*Until today you attached yourself to certain things for fear they could not be replaced. Just for today, imagine how life would be if you received something better than what you held on to so far.*

(Iyanla Vanzant)

On a beautiful sunny morning, Mister Carnagey arrived at the farm with a little box for Dale, with something hidden inside. Like any child, Dale was curious: *What do you have there, Father?* James Carnagey pulled apart the paper covering the box and heard a howl. Dale peered in and saw a yellow ball of fur, his new puppy. James had paid fifty cents for it, but not even a million dollars would bring as much happiness as that puppy did. The dog received the name Tippy. For five years Tippy was Dale's companion and great friend. They grew up together as brothers and even more, as true friends. At the end of the day, right after Dale had had dinner and washed his plate, there was Tippy, alert, waiting for Dale, greeting him with barks and jumps. When Dale came back from school dejected, he would forget all his disappointments at school, because his return was a magical moment. The happiness that emanated from that little golden animal was contagious. But one night, the unexpected happened: not ten steps away from Dale, Tippy was struck by lightning and killed. Many years later, Dale would recall that event as the great tragedy of his childhood.[20] That was a life lesson, only one of many that life brings; a life lesson for a boy from Missouri.

The state of Missouri sits in the Midwest of the United States, on the border between the colonized east and the beginning of the old "Wild West": what was considered during the nineteenth century to be the roughest region of the country, the Far West, no-man's-land.[21] Life out west was arduous and survival was hard; the plains suffer through arctic winds from Canada, cold that can kill cattle and people, and then heat that bakes almost every crop. The vegetation was low and sandstorms were constant. Homesteading through government grants began in 1862, and between 1865 and 1890 the West was completely open to settlement. Some settlers met tragic ends, perhaps most famously the Donner Party that succumbed to snow and hunger on their way to California in 1847. [22] The trek from Missouri to Sacramento could take as long as one hundred and forty days.[23] Missouri seems to have been influenced by the Wild West as well as by the North and South. At the end of the 1860's, Missouri's population increased by fifty percent, making it the fifth largest state in the Union with two million inhabitants.[24]

James William Carnagey was a very poor man with a sixth-grade education who made his living by working in the fields and breeding livestock, earning twelve dollars a month as a farmhand. Jim, as he was known, had moved to a farm in Missouri on his father's advice.[25] His parents lived in Illinois and, when the family got too big, Jim's father suggested that Jim try to get a piece of land in Missouri and settle there. Jim followed his father's suggestion and rented a place with a farmer in Maryville. It was there that he met his future wife.

Mrs. Lynch was responsible for introducing Amanda Elizabeth to Jim. Amanda taught in a school next to Mrs. Lynch's farm, and asked if she could board with Mrs. Lynch, as she lived quite far from the school. At first Mrs. Lynch refused, but Amanda was very persistent and promised she could cook and sew. After some hesitation, Mrs. Lynch said: "Well, if you can bake and you can sew, and you'll be willing to help out, I'll take you."[26] But Mrs. Lynch did more than that. After Amanda came to live with her, Mrs. Lynch told her that there was a young man named Jim Carnagey that also lived there. Amanda smiled and commented that he was probably no relation to Andrew Carnegie. They met and both came to the conclusion that they were made for each other. Eventually, Jim was able to buy a farm. On January 1, 1882[27], James Carnagey and Amanda Elizabeth Harbinson were married at Amanda's parents' home in Pickering, Missouri. She took the name Amanda Elizabeth Carnagey. When she met Jim, Amanda was a Sunday school teacher in a Methodist church. The Methodist church was founded in England by John Wesley in the eighteenth century and derives from Martin Luther's Protestantism as well as from Calvinism; its founding principle is the daily, systemic and "methodical" glorification of God. Good deeds must be permanent, and one cannot relax one's faith regardless of any positive outcomes.[28] Amanda also supported the Temperance movement, and thought highly of Carry Nation and her war on the demon alcohol.[29] Carry Nation was a woman of such strong personality and fearlessness that despite being beaten, kicked, whipped and hit with bats until her bones were broken, she did not give up her fight against the consumption of alcoholic beverages, even invading saloons to break liquor bottles with her hatchet. But Carry Nation's campaign bore fruit soon after her death in 1911, when Prohibition became the law of the land through the signing of the 18th Amendment, which prohibited the sale, manufacture and transport of alcohol. To be fair, another factor that encouraged the adoption of Prohibition in 1919 was Jack London's book *John Barleycorn*. Looking back now, we can note two interesting coincidences about Carry Nation and the Carnagey family. The first is that all of them were buried in the same cemetery, in the city of Belton, Missouri. The second one was that Carry Nation spoke and acted with such grit and determination that she would likely have made any battle-hardened general shake in his boots. In 1937, when talking about his own life, Carnegie recounted one of Carry Nation's exploits, describing her fight against alcohol in a bar in Wichita, Kansas on January 21, 1901: *She rushed in through the swinging doors, waved her hatchet in the air and shouted: '-This is the arm of God. I have come to save you men from a drunkard's hell.' The customers fled out of the side door. The bartender ducked behind a table, while Carry Nation threw beer bottles at the mirrors and smashed in the heads of whiskey barrels with her hatchet. In a few minutes the place looked as if it had been struck by a Kansas cyclone.*[30] Years later, Carnegie would develop a speaking style based on enthusiasm and firm conviction. Carnegie's greatest example of enthusiasm was likely his mother Amanda, a fantastic woman who was strongly influenced by Methodist thinking and especially by Carry Nation. Despite the severity of these viewpoints, Amanda exuded leadership and a dynamic that would end up influencing her children. First born was Clifton, who later would graduate in psychology and work in Kansas City[31], despite being considered a bit too unstable to keep in one job for long. Clifton would also keep his distance from his brother, who was about to be born. The Carnageys lived in Harmony Church, a small town ten miles northeast of Maryville, Missouri, and on November 24, 1888 their second son, Dale Breckenridge Carnagey, was born. The Carnagey family lived in extreme poverty on a modest farm, ten miles from the railroad tracks. In 1893, when Dale was five, they moved to Bedison; when he turned twelve, they relocated again to the Ira Moor farm, one mile south from Harmony Creek[32.] They were trying to pay off debts through hard work that started at four in the morning but never seemed to end. The problems were terrible: the One Hundred and Two River, a great flow of dark brown water, flooded almost every year, destroying the corn fields. Even if the corn field somehow managed to escape destruction, at this time US agricultural commodity prices were extremely low. Two classes of people were not participating in America's economic success: farmers and the working class.[33] One year cholera killed that year's pigs[34], but the next year, when the piglets survived, pigs sold for practically nothing. Jim bought a mule, a real cause for celebration on the farm; when the animal got into the barn, it stepped onto a loose board and was stabbed in the stomach by a nail. The animal died on the spot.[35] On farms, parents and children worked together to earn their daily bread.

Dale was no exception and from an early age pitched in to help support the family.

Working on a farm has its charms, but there is also a high price. The landscape is an Eden: the air is fresh, the night is silent, birds sing at sunrise, and the colors are vibrant and relaxing. Joys like horseback riding await... The fascination with the prairie and the wild can be traced back to our ancestors, our oldest predecessors. The writer Jack London spoke about the conflict he felt upon dreaming about nature he had never seen before: abundant forests, new varieties or trees, unfamiliar wild fruits and creatures. He attributed this to our ancient ancestors having lived another, very different type of existence long before humans as we know them appeared[36]. In the country, not everything is easy, especially when your only sustenance comes from the earth. Eliot[37], a friend of mine, decided to step out of his routine and accepted an invitation to work a full day at Alfonso's[38] farm. At dawn, Eliot began his duties by lifting a heavy saddle onto his horse, driving cattle to the corral, and riding a few more hours in the hot sun. But that was only the start; the rest of his day was spent vaccinating, branding and tending to the livestock. It was no exceptional task, but when Eliot got home at 9 that night, he was so exhausted that before taking a shower he lay down on the floor for just a moment... and, because of his exhaustion, slept with his clothes and boots on until the next day. Every single muscle in his body ached. But he didn't do a fraction of the hard work that many country folk confront daily. That is mostly why people that work in the country go to sleep so early, at about seven or eight at night. Waking up at sunrise is beautiful, but clearing the land (and risking snakebite at any time), chopping wood, milking the cow, mucking out the barn, caring for the animals, planting the pasture, hauling water out of the well... And let's not forget praying for the rain to stop, or praying for the rain to fall and break a long dry spell, or hoping that no windstorms or hail will destroy the year's crop: any of these problems easily could destroy a full year's blood, sweat and tears. The best case would be to stroll around without commitment, not having to take care of the animals and plants on the farm. But if you were a child like Dale, you got used to helping at a tender age. He pulled his weight on the farm and also worked temporary jobs like picking strawberries and catching shellfish for five cents an hour[39]. Until he was twelve, he did not have even fifty cents a year to spend on himself. When his father gave him ten cents for him to spend as he wished, he felt like he held all the riches of India.[40] One of the most exciting days of Dale's life was when he visited a big city, Saint Joseph, for the first time. His father had sold a few pigs that needed to be shipped by train. As James had received three tickets to accompany the shipment, Dale came along. Saint Joe, as it was known, at that time had about sixty thousand inhabitants. Dale looked at the city buildings in awe, having never seen anything like them before. When they returned home on the Ravenwood train, it was two in the morning and they still faced a four mile walk to the farm. Dale was so tired that he fell asleep and dreamed while walking.[41]

Despite a decade of hard work, the farm became mortgaged and debts threatened not just the family's livelihood, but the property itself. For children, country life also presented real and almost countless dangers: they could get lost in the woods, accidentally hit a beehive, strike their own foot with an ax, get caught in quicksand, get kicked by a horse or gored by a bull... well, Dale also learned from trial and error; luckily for him, the errors were not as deadly as they could have been. One day, Dale was playing in an abandoned house, and decided to jump from the attic. When he jumped, the ring he was wearing got caught on a nail, and he lost part of his left index finger. His reaction: *I screamed. I was terrified. I was positive I was going to die. But after the hand healed, I never worried about it for one split second. What would have been the use?... I accepted the inevitable.*[42] This was a very noticeable characteristic in Dale: taking lessons from life. It became more and more evident over the course of his works. And yet, for him, learning was very difficult, or in other words, he had to overcome his own insecurity. His self-knowledge developed only along with scars and battles. A hero is not born ready. We can get an idea of how Dale later viewed his feelings during this hard period of his life: *...one day while helping my mother pit cherries, I began to cry. My mother said, 'Dale, what in the world are you crying about?' I blubbered: 'I'm afraid I'm going to be buried alive!' I was full of worries in those days. When thunderstorms came, I worried for fear I would be killed by lightning. When hard times came, I worried for fear we wouldn't have enough to eat. I worried for fear I would go to hell when I died. I was terrified for fear an older boy, Sam White, would cut off my big ears-- as he threatened to do. I worried for fear girls would laugh at me if I tipped my hat to them. I worried for fear no girl would ever be willing to marry me. I worried about what I would say to my wife immediately after we were married. I imagined that we would be married in some country church, and then get in a surrey with fringe on the top and ride back to the farm... But how would I be able to keep the conversation going on that ride back to the farm? How? How? I pondered over that earth-shaking problem for many an hour as I walked behind the plow.*[43] It is interesting how some great figures of humanity faced such immense challenges in childhood.

May Evans was his sweetheart. She lived on a neighboring farm and went to school with Dale and his brother. She said that Dale liked to play pranks. Once he showed up at school with a dead rabbit in a bucket, which he stealthily set on top of the pot-bellied stove that heated the schoolroom; the smell soon became unbearable. May clearly remembered her teacher's reaction on that occasion.[44] When Dale was twelve, his grades were already quite good: in 1900, he earned a 99 in reading from his teacher, Miss Rose. In that same year Dale did something that was relatively common, but had long lasting impacts on his abilities: he made his first public presentation at Sunday school. His topic was *"The Saloon, offspring of Hell"*.[45] What person present that day, could have guessed that this boy would develop a new and more efficient model for the art of public speaking? Four decades later, Harold Abbott would say that this phase was very important to Dale, a time that he would never forget: *Simple things in life interested Mr. Carnegie. He liked to fish, he loved the country. Several times while we were visiting in Nodaway County, we walked from one of the farms where he grew up, across country to the Rose Hill School which he had attended.*[46]

Unable to face losing yet another crop to floods, and unable to pay the dollar a week for his children to live in the town where they could study (despite the fact that the Warrensburg School, today a university, gave scholarships to students in need), Jim Carnagey sold his property in 1904 and bought a farm near the State Teacher's College in Warrensburg, Missouri.[47] Besides his studies, Dale's responsibilities on the farm were also growing along with his strength: he now cut wood, and woke up during the night to take care of the Duroc-Jersey piglets, keeping them fed and warm by the wood stove to make sure they would live long enough to help sustain the family. As Lowell Thomas said: "Faithful to nature, the little pigs demanded a meal at three in the morning. So, when the alarm clock rang, Dale Carnegie would put on his slippers and quickly would get the basket and take it to the little pigs' mother where it waited. After that he would again bring them back to get warm near the fire."[48]

No one's personality is free from influence, and Carnegie was no exception. He received enormous influence in leadership and strength from his mother, Amanda. She encouraged him to seek solutions to the challenges he faced.. In college, only with great difficulty was he able to travel the three miles between the farm and the campus. Carnegie only had one change of clothes to go to school in, and even those were not very presentable. Under-dressed, noticeably poor, clumsy, and living separately from his classmates, he was the object of derision and scorn. The year he died, Carnegie told an interviewer about a conversation he had with his mother about the clothes he wore: *When I went to college, I wore my Sunday suit. It had been bought long ago, several sizes too large, so that when I grew bigger it would not be too small. But as time went on, I kept growing* *but not the suit. The first week in college I was terribly ashamed of that suit. One evening, I couldn't help saying to my mother, 'I'm ashamed to stand up in class in these clothes. I am afraid other students will laugh at me'. Mother broke down and cried: 'Dale,' she said, 'If we could afford it we would get you better clothes. But we can't'. I was sorry I had complained to Mother. My sainted mother tried so hard to make my life better. If anyone had an angel for a mother, I had one. But she couldn't ask my father to buy me better clothes. He was toiling in the fields and praying that the cholera wouldn't strike too hard.*[49]*

Dale tried to shake off his outsider status and become more involved by trying out for the football team, but he didn't make the cut. Football would have been the easiest way to stand out at his college (now known as Central Missouri State University), but he was skinny and not good at sports. But his mother was there to support him again, and encouraged him to participate in activities connected to speech, which changed the trajectory of his life. Dale also had the good fortune to hear a speaker from the Chautauqua Institution. Chautauqua was a concept named after the city in New York where the movement began in the late nineteenth century; its premise was based on a Methodist bishop's idea that religious study was also a great opportunity to present secular education to people. Speakers from this movement would travel, especially to poor rural regions such as Maryville and Warrensburg. In their speeches, Chautauqua speakers showed the son of a humble farmer that he could dream of and attain more than just drudgery in his life. This experience, along with support and encouragement from his mother and a teacher, Nicholas M. Souder[50], led Dale to join the school debate team. Dale started to prepare in earnest by speaking to the trees and the cows. At home, the barn became his debate room, and he spoke to the pigeons and the horses (which were more scared than persuaded).[51] He practiced nonstop, but even so, he lost the first contests. Not just his first contests, but at least his first dozen contests. He became so disappointed that he even thought about suicide.[52] However, he decided to keep going. He kept studying and learning speeches by Abraham Lincoln and Richard Harding Davis.[53] One day there was a contest that judged competitors on their ability to memorize and recite a classic work of literature. He read both Lincoln's and Davis' speeches, but ended up presenting Lincoln's Gettysburg Address. Persistence brought him his first victory, and from there victories came one after another; he won contest after contest in school. He was the first boy to win against the girls. He started being sought after by his classmates. Finally attaining the prestige and recognition he had sought, he was elected class president in 1907.[54] Perhaps it was his initial success with Lincoln's speech that motivated Dale to later write his fabulous biography of Lincoln.

In his last year attending school in Warrensburg, Dale won the debate contest, the boy he tutored won a public speaking contest, and the girl he tutored won the declamation contest. He had acquired the social status he had craved, no doubt quite an achievement for him.

Dale dropped out of university in his junior year after failing Latin. Yet in this same year a chance encounter marked a turning point in Carnegie's life. A school friend named Frank Self convinced him to follow his example and sell correspondence courses. In 1908, Carnegie wrote to the International Correspondence School in Denver. He got the job, although later he learned he was only hired because the school directors believed that any product would be an easy sell for a speech champion.[55] Carnegie went to Denver, the first truly big city he was to visit. He carried twenty-eight dollars hidden under his shirt in a special bag his mother had made for him. On his first night in Denver, fear dominated his thoughts; murderous gangsters and swindlers terrified him. As a precaution, he left his light on and, without realizing it, fell asleep. He was awakened by banging on the door in the middle of the night. Was the end near? The sinister truth: the night guard wanted him to turn off the light! Phew! His fear dissipated, but was replaced with shame so strong that he hid his head under the pillow.[56] Some time afterward, Carnegie evaluated his bleak mission and realized that not even the best salesperson could succeed. At that time, selling instructional courses to farmers in West Nebraska's sand hills seemed an impossibility. Carnegie spoke about the experience with good humor: *My desperation reached such a point that I would stop farmers on the street and ask them if they weren't interested in studying electrical engineering by correspondence. Remembering those times now, it seems like something out of the movies of 'Laurel and Hardy'.*[57] While passing years allowed him to look back and laugh, these days were truly painful. Carnegie worked hard, sometimes walking six miles to meet a farmhand who might be interested in the course. But when he arrived there, he didn't make the sale. He would go back to his hotel, lay down and cry because he did not want to go back home without finishing his mission, although he did not even really know what that mission was. The fruit of all this effort and travel was one single sale, to a line employee for the telegraph company.[58] The man was so high on the pole that he couldn't hear what Carnegie was saying. He came down and listened to the sales pitch. He decided to think about it, and invited Carnegie to meet his family. The boy's parents approved of the correspondence course and the benefits an electrical engineering course could bring their son. And with a payment of eighty-eight dollars, Carnegie closed his only deal on the job.[59]

Lowell Thomas describes this outstanding passage in Carnegie's life: *The discouragement got to him in such a way that he went to a hotel room in Alliance, Nebraska: at noon, he threw himself on the bed and cried desperately. He wished fervently to remove himself from this struggle in life; but he could not. He decided then to move on to South Omaha and look for another job. He did not have enough money for a ticket, so he traveled in a freight train, serving water and food in two horse cars, in exchange for his passage.*[60] The idea to seek a new job was inspired by an experienced salesman Carnegie met one night in a grocery store. This salesman advised him to sell things that people would always need, for example food,[61] that clients would return to buy again and again.[62] A simple idea, but one that shows Carnegie's ability to listen to more experienced people who could effectively add to his own quality of life. But his own situation was so bad that he did not even have money to buy train tickets. Still, without realizing it, he was already adding to his routine another quality that grew to dominate his life: determination.

Carnegie learned that if a farmer sold his animals and shipped them by train, he would receive two free tickets to travel along with them. So Dale looked for a rancher and offered to feed, water and care for his animals during their trip  He disembarked in Omaha to try his luck with Armour and Company, which was in the business of selling necessities like meat and soap. The area he was assigned to was the worst possible;  he traveled on horseback, by freight train or on foot, and suffered through the worst accommodations one could imagine. This period shaped his personality greatly.  He read about everything from salesmanship to horse training, and experimented with bartering, accepting shoes as payment and later reselling them to railway workers.[63] He would get off the train, run to get new orders, and then jump back on the train to travel again. Although he worked one of the most unproductive regions in the business (his area, South Omaha, was known as the 'badlands'), he climbed from the fifty-second ranked salesman to the first. The secret of Carnegie's new-found success was likely the familiarity he developed with country people.  After all, he grew up on a farm and knew very well how to walk into a store or a restaurant and talk about agriculture and husbandry with potential clients. It is critical for a salesperson to know his or her clients well: their needs, their desires and their difficulties. One of the best ways to be accepted in a community is to speak the same language, and he was a perfect fit. I also believe that another force that drove him to work furiously was the fear of having to return to the same painful  life he had had on the family farm.

Carnegie soon wrote to his mother that he was 'lucky' because he had saved five hundred dollars. One might have expected him to cling to such a job, but he was more daring and changed his course yet again. He credited this new direction in his life to a conversation on a train he had had with a reverend by the name of Russell, a man who taught drama classes and produced plays. Carnegie told the clergyman that he was thinking about going to Boston to study speech and drama. But Russell had taught in New York, and advised Carnegie to go try his luck at New York's great American Academy of Dramatic Arts.[64] The idea became akin to an obsession to Carnegie. The sales company he worked for offered him a managerial position, but he declined and quit. He had a bigger ambition, which was to make his fortune in the East as an actor!

In order to attain this dream, Carnegie needed to be accepted at the prestigious Academy, whose famous alumni include Robert Redford, Lauren Bacall, and Kirk Douglas; its graduates have won more than seventy Oscars and two hundred Emmys. What tools did he carry to help him gain admission? As we have seen, his mother's influence was very important in his younger years, as were the motivational and instructional messages from the Methodist Chautauqua School. There was also his immense effort to study important public speakers and try at Warrensburg State Teacher's College until he was able to be recognized as a respectable junior public speaker; this certainly helped his chances of gaining entrance to the drama academy. Add to it all his magnificent experience with the correspondence courses (a failure) and the sales of meat and soap (a success). Ups and downs are part of life; a life without bumps does not offer the necessary foundation needed to confront the biggest challenges. Yes, Carnegie was ready to face the selection process. He started his life in a humble rural region; he had his hands full starting out as a timid young man from the country, with no experience and no qualifications for the most competitive job in twentieth century American society. But Carnegie was able to change that stereotypical profile, and in fact changed it so much that he was accepted to the Academy. I imagine today how much hope must have shone in his eyes, how much optimism for a better life. Carnegie saved a considerable amount of money from his job at Armour, and had just been accepted by the American Academy of Dramatic Arts. Attaining his dream of being an actor seemed sure. He knew the secrets of public speaking and had experience in sales; how could such plan fail?

Classes started and he was excited. The Academy's method of making the artist interpret a character was so convincing that the public believed the actor  really was the character.[65] It was a new phase in theater, a new type of dramatic interpretation that preceded technical and intellectual smoke and mirrors, and enabled  the cult of imagination and sensation, the nature of things that were only discovered by an actor acting with his or her very soul.[66] How much this influenced Carnegie's future, the reader can decide.

Beyond the superlative classes, Carnegie believed he had invented a method to make him a great actor. He found it incredible that no one had thought of it before. His plan was as follows: he would study the best theatrical effects of the successful actors of the day. In this way, he would apply each one's best method, creating a synthesis! About this decision, which later even Carnegie thought a mistake, he commented: "How silly! How absurd! I had to waste years of my life imitating other people before it penetrated through my thick Missouri skull that I had to be myself, and that I couldn't possibly be anyone else."[67]

After graduating from the Academy of Dramatic Arts, and an almost endless series of auditions, Carnegie landed a role in a traveling musical production about circus life. Molly Mayo's *Polly of the Circus*[68] follows Polly, a bareback rider who is injured during her performance and then nursed back to health by the kind Dr. Hartley (played by Carnegie). Carnegie treated the main character's physical wounds, not knowing that years later he similarly care for the spirituality of interpersonal relationships. In the meantime, however, he also worked as a clown and a barker in the same production.  Since the pay was shamefully low, he arrived early to help carry trunks and set up scenery; after the curtain went down, he would stay to break down and carry out again. In this way he was able to earn some extra money, the same way any other artist would to make ends meet. And Carnegie also sold suitcases and ties.

Of course bigger stars had more comfortable lives. *Polly of the Circus*[69] was the best Carnegie ever got though, traveling in bad conditions (nothing new for him), sleeping in even worse places, probably having to do all sorts of odd jobs behind the scenes... he learned first-hand that life as an actor was not easy.[70] If all those sacrifices resulted in a brilliant acting career, it would have all been worth it. But when the play was over, Carnegie couldn't find another role, not even the smallest  bit part on Broadway. The rejections were countless. The life of an artist was hard indeed. I can imagine how many talented people lived through this very situation, some finding their place in the spotlight, but others who were just as good or even better succumbed and gave up. I remember reading a biography of Buffalo Bill; he explained his incredible adventures by stating that people equal to or better than him succumbed to tiny details, just as he himself could have, but in the end, he prevailed in the prairies. All those people, whether they became successful or not, deserve the same respect. Some people do not understand why things went wrong; sometimes they do not realize that the universe's designs are complex. At this moment, Carnegie will move on, frustrated after two years of desperate attempts with no positive results. But later, he will jump for joy when things turn around. Even so, it is hard to imagine the suffering Carnegie endured, and the consequences of this time for his life.  Many years later in 1947, in a different context and with no intention of becoming a movie star, he would appear in a movie called *Jiggs and Maggie in Society*[71], depicting himself! But this was almost four decades later, when Carnegie lived a much different life. For now, things were not going well.

The money he had saved from his successful sales with Armour was long gone and he lived from hand to mouth. He had poured all his savings and energy into his dream of being an actor in the big city, but it just didn't happen.   It was time to go back to work, to find anything that would enable him to support himself. What else could he do? He found a job in another sales department, this time at the Packard Motor Car Company's New York showroom.

# CHAPTER 2

## TRIUMPH IN NEW YORK

*Who would have thought that*
*from that humble start today*
*we would be changing the lives of*
*people in a world scale.*
(Donna Carnegie)[72]

Many people dream about going to live in the big city; the entire dream involves going to the city and becoming successful. Someone born in the city can't really understand what moving to the city means to someone who comes from the countryside. So many have dreamt of New York, a city with a history of conquest through hard work.

In 1911, before attaining success, a person had to focus on getting by one moment at a time. To be able to survive in New York, Carnegie's task was to sell Packard automobiles and trucks. But he did not like the job, did not understand anything about cars, and, despite the growth of the American automotive industry, he made very few sales. The car business was booming: the number of automobiles jumped from eight thousand in 1900 to thirty-two million in 1941.[73] But it is painful to imagine Carnegie standing, waiting for clients to walk into the showroom, putting aside his recent theater and public speaking experience, neglecting his reading, and letting his latent creativity sit untapped.

Curiously, this work with cars may have traumatized him for life; Carnegie always preferred train travel to driving. Years later he told his second wife, Dorothy, that he hated anything mechanical, that he did not understand machines and never would. It is understandable that someone who had never come in contact with an automobile would be unable to answer simple questions asked by clients. It was easier to talk in general terms about the integrity of the owners, J. W. and William Packard. Carnegie led a miserable life, doing something he hated and collecting an equally miserable salary. He tried to sell during the day and write at night. Writing was something that sustained him and kept his hope alive.[74] He wrote a text, but when he finished it he came to one conclusion: it was horrible. He thought he would never be able to finish this project. But somehow he found the strength to keep going and find something to keep him motivated.[75] At twenty-four, Carnegie was in bad shape. His work was going badly, and it made him feel even worse. He wore the same suit of clothes, ironed so as to be barely passable. His social life was nonexistent; he had no friends. He lived in a tiny room in 244 West 56th Street, in Hell's Kitchen, a neighborhood as dirty as it was dangerous. When he came home after work, his dinner was either chicken or sausage sold from a street vendor. The neighborhood was dominated by gangs, whom even the police feared; the streets were lined with trashcan fires that warmed the many homeless people who lived there. If he decided to spend the four dollars he earned that day on a restaurant meal, any establishment he could afford would certainly be dirty and full of roaches. In the morning, when he grabbed a tie from a nail on the wall, cockroaches ran everywhere.

I visited Carnegie's old address in July of 2008; today, this gracious building houses a hotel and a pub. I talked with employees there but nobody had any idea who had lived there over a century before, unsurprisingly. What used to be Hell's Kitchen was now part of a more gentrified Manhattan, with astronomical property values. However, a century ago, Carnegie struggled to pay his monthly rent on an apartment that was only the tiniest step above sleeping on the street. Things got worse and worse for him; living miserably, suffering alone, working at a dismal job. Yet again, he hit bottom, and yet again he thought of suicide. It was time to rethink, reevaluate and make a decision. Carnegie wanted to write; he wanted to write the great American novel, describe American life, maybe write about the life out west that he knew so well. One of the successful books of the era was *The Call of the Wild* by Jack London, which narrates a dog's transformation from a soft-living house-pet to a fighter, living by its instincts in the cold and snowy wild.[76] Carnegie's own life resembles the tale: a forced change of plans. For him to change the trajectory of his life, it was necessary to find time to write. Working at Packard gave him a headache, his feet hurt, he couldn't sleep and he was depressed.[77] When he got home, he was too exhausted to work on his book.[78] It was time to establish a new plan: find a night job so he could have time to write. He thought about what he could do best. He had achieved the most by teaching people how to speak in public, so that was his first idea. He went to Columbia University and proposed a nightly public speaking course. After all, with his resume, it would be easy. But it wasn't. Columbia University refused his offer. The next step was to try New York University, but NYU wasn't interested either. In his excellent Wayne State University thesis, Stephen Kirkland posits that these universities did not accept Carnegie because he lacked teaching experience and because his resume was far too humble.[79] More than three decades later, Carnegie would remember his rejections: *"I applied for a position teaching public speaking in the night extension courses both at Columbia University and New York University, but these universities decided they could struggle along somehow without my help."*[80]

It's interesting how people imagine the path they will take to reach their objectives, thinking that they know all the different details and detours to come. Truly, often we think that things that happen to us are "bad" when they are actually a blessing in disguise. This was the case with Carnegie's rejections from the universities in New York. Today, we can speculate on the reasons he wasn't hired: his country accent, his unfinished degree, the fact that he was a salesman and not a teacher.... All in all, we can say that he wasn't the type one would expect to find in academia. At a dead end with the universities, Carnegie went next to the 125th Street YMCA. During his interview, he tried something different and recited a popular poem of the day by James Whitcomb Riley: *Knee-deep in June*.[81] He made a great impression.[82] He and his course were accepted on the spot, but with a condition. Some time earlier, the YMCA had tried a course in public speaking for businessmen, but it was a disaster, and they didn't intend to lose any more money. The Y was unwilling to pay the two dollars a night Carnegie asked, so they were at an impasse until Carnegie offered to work on commission if the course turned a profit.[83] He would shoulder all the risk, since he depended on the classes' success to support himself, and the YMCA would lose nothing if the course was a failure. Despite the low risk to the YMCA, Carnegie needed all his salesmanship to convince the director, and even made the solution sound as if it had been the director's own idea. Finally, Carnegie was getting his big chance. Would the students come?

On October 22, 1912, Carnegie noticed something interesting about the six students sitting in his classroom at the YMCA. These people who had enrolled were not the scholars he had been expecting. They were professionals who had to work hard to provide for themselves: receptionists, salespeople, storekeepers, all people who were expected the course to help them keep their jobs.[84] Yet again, the situation was not what he had expected. Not only was he not teaching at a university, but he wasn't going to be paid until his students finished the course – if at all. And now, the students weren't what he had been expecting. Traditional methods of oratory are extremely precise in their gestures and moves, just like the disciplined society Foucault criticized. They also are based on memorizing extensive classical speeches and poems for later recitation.[85] Carnegie realized that he could not teach the traditional principles of public speaking. Pompous, lengthy, theoretical speaking would be tedious, inadequate and a waste of time for all involved. These students needed practical and immediate instruction in order to succeed in their work, and without this knowledge they would be lost. How many classrooms today exhibit this same potential disconnect between teacher and student? A teacher's complex speech can impress some people, but will not help him towards his main objective: imparting knowledge through interaction with his students. Teaching is more than just displaying one's erudition; teaching is talking, touching a student's heart, persuading her of the necessity of thought and research, persuading her to participate in the learning process in a balanced manner, not only to read but also to take action.

Carnegie knew better than to vainly attempt to pass himself off as an intellectual or to try to create a respectful distance between the student and the teacher. Although he was young, Carnegie knew enough about the world to avoid vanity. He was a quick thinker yet wise, and brought a lifetime of experience with him. Longgood referred to Carnegie as a man with little patience for theory and abstraction; later, he described Carnegie as practical, ordinary, functional and with an incredible pragmatism "… the ability to learn from everything in life."[86] Kirkland stated that Carnegie continued with his concepts developed over the years, but he could change some of them when necessary.[87] I don't doubt these observations, but believe that what stands out about Carnegie is his ability to reflect on what he already knew without ceasing to ask if he could continue to improve. To Carnegie, theories needed to be proven in practice to earn their usefulness. Another central point is his ability to notice the people around him, to listen attentively and empathize with others' points of view and feelings. Carnegie thought of people as truly *visible*, important, not only in a speech but in reality. What made Carnegie stand out so much was his ability to truly see the other, to really sympathize with people's wants and needs, to respect them as he respected himself.[88]

He quickly realized that he had to help his students meet their specific needs, not teach what he wanted to teach. After all, the class was for the students, not for him.

So the class started with six participants. Carnegie might have been nervous, but he could never have imagined what would happen that night. Carnegie talked about the principles of public speaking for a while and then suddenly realized that he had gone through all of his notes. Only thirty minutes had passed, and there was still an hour and a half to go. The students waited for him to continue, but he had nothing left to say. In the awkward silence, students and teacher looked at each other and... Carnegie gestured to a student in the back of the classroom and asked him to come forward and speak. One can only imagine the response. "Me? Say something? What? What do you mean?" "Talk about yourself, your life, your job". In doing this, he brought out something original and unexpected: directly facing the great fear of speaking in public. One thing anyone can do is talk about himself or herself; we are all experts on at least this one subject. After talking about something that needed no memorization or research, the students found that they had already taken the first step, and had survived something they had thought impossible: speaking in front of an audience. The students liked, even loved the idea. I can imagine their feelings, the goosebumps they must have gotten when they realized they could speak in public, conquering their fear with action. This was just as interesting to Carnegie: he learned from his students' experiences, knowledge and opinions. He was able to expand his course to fantastic proportions when he paid attention to his students' needs, their fears, their desires and those things that all people share: struggle, sacrifice, defeats and victories, sadness and happiness, difficulties in relationships and the stress that comes from leading an agitated and worrisome life. Of course he evaluated everything and started to help those people, to really help them, and in the process, Carnegie himself was being greatly helped. He encouraged his students to avoid of the snare of talking about what they didn't like or didn't know; he counseled them to make their speech come from the heart, advice from a sure speaker who knew what he was talking about. I believe various factors contributed to Carnegie's ingenious new approach to public speaking: a) his own knowledge of public speaking; b) his work tutoring his classmates during college; c) his having been under-prepared for his first class; d) the value Carnegie placed on his students as people and e) the low number of students in class), which favored the use of dialogues.

This last factor would be the one responsible for Dale Carnegie's distinctive brand: group work and practical speaking beginning in the very first class. Years later, when Carnegie was already considered the master of public speaking in the United States, he explained the nature of his method to an interviewer, saying that it was no good to teach a boy fifty hours of theory about swimming. The boy needed to get into the water and learn for himself. Public speaking is no different; the best teacher is practice, and the biggest obstacle is fear.[89] This was when the technique of "baptism by fire" began to be used, where the class confronts the speaker, who must dominate his fear in order to ride out the storm. Only then can the fear of speaking in public be beaten.[90] Carnegie created a safe environment where his students could develop their abilities without fearing humiliation or ridicule. They could talk bravely, freely. Carnegie explained his formula and accompanying techniques this way, describing student participation during the classes: "Without knowing what I was doing, I stumbled on the best method to conquer fear".[91] William Longgood, who wrote an excellent book on the Dale Carnegie Course, explained that it wasn't just about simply confronting fear with rational arguments, or showing the foolishness of being afraid, because that approach does not solve the problem.[92] Carnegie's solution went to the root of the problem: *Do the thing you fear to do and the death of fear is certain.*[93] Fear destroys one's self-confidence, said Carnegie. And as he foresaw a new way of life, a new concept of finding one's path, where it was necessary to banish fear and free the individual. Once that is accomplished, people can even be freed from illnesses caused by fear and anxiety, and consequently can have a better life.[94]

Another tactic was to the accentuate the positive instead of criticizing the negative. Carnegie focused on the good things his students did. Carnegie's critics went crazy because they couldn't understand how someone could teach anything without criticism. But that was the secret, knowing how to build students up without tearing them apart. Carnegie didn't say "no" and point out "mistakes"- he simply showed ways to improve. Specialists and college professors started attending the Course and, understanding its revolutionary nature, began to adopt Carnegie's methods. One example cited by Longgood is Dr. L. Gray Burdin, a teacher of public speaking at Butler University in Indianapolis. Burdin stated that the foundation of Carnegie's teaching philosophy was to never criticize, but instead to show how things could be done better, while focusing on the person as a whole. In his words: "We want no one to sit down with the feeling that he failed. For that reason we use praise and inspiration as our teaching tools".[95] Of course implementing such innovations required Carnegie to commit to them intensively, for society at that time was not used to this attitude. Teachers were supposed to correct others and point out their faults. Teachers are not the ones who desire to 'fix' other people's faults, as Carnegie knew. So while the path was complex, he accepted it and was able to lay the foundation for his course that today is used the world over. I do not know which is more impressive, creating the method, or the fact that instructors adopted it. But Carnegie succeeded. We will talk about these and other techniques later on, when we analyze his books, but it is worth focusing now on one important point of Carnegie's work, the concept of "act as if..." in order to overcome fear. For example, overcome sadness by smiling in front of the mirror, then going out and acting happy, greeting people energetically. See what kind of change occurs if you try this for yourself. If you are in pain (after seeking medical advice, of course), try to ignore it, pretending that pain does not matter and all that is important is what you like to do. Facing fear requires confidence, and confident behavior brings confidence itself. Likewise, if a speaker does not show confidence and enthusiasm, how can an audience find him convincing? Enthusiasm was so important to

Carnegie. In one of his classes in Philadelphia, a young insurance salesman named Frank Bettger did an improvisation exercise and spoke with no enthusiasm. Bettger had been a baseball player for the Saint Louis Cardinals at the beginning of the twentieth century, but injury soon put an end to his career. Things declined from this point, until he spent three years cycling around the city, working as a bill collector. After realizing that job was going nowhere, he decided to try his luck at selling insurance. He tried hard, but what impressed his colleagues was only the fact that someone could make so many calls and still get no sales. Not surprisingly, he was fired. He still had a family to support, so he tried to negotiate a lower salary with the insurance company, but it was to no avail. Unemployed and desperate, Bettger went to the Philadelphia YMCA, where the receptionist gave him a tip that would change his life: there was a very good course going on that would solve all his problems. The receptionist introduced Bettger to Carnegie, who informed him that the course was already underway, but another would be beginning soon. Bettger was so panicked by his situation that he asked Carnegie if he could start immediately. Carnegie took him by the arm and brought him into the classroom, saying that he would be the next to speak, and urged Bettger to tell his story.[96] Later on, in a session on enthusiasm, Carnegie interrupted Bettger, saying: *Mr. Bettger, hold on a moment... just a moment. Are you interested in what you are talking about?* The student, shocked, replied: *Yes... of course I am...* Carnegie continued: *Well, then why don't you speak with some enthusiasm? How do you hope to keep your audience interested if you do not put life and imagination to what you talk about?* Then, Carnegie gave the students a real-live demonstration of enthusiastic speaking, getting so riled up that he threw a chair against the wall and broke one of its legs. This impressed Bettger greatly, and that evening after class he contemplated the reason for his only past success with baseball before he got hurt. Why had he been successful? Bettger had been the most enthusiastic player in the league. A journalist claimed he had a "barrel of enthusiasm". The team had been so impressed that his salary shot from twenty-five dollars to one hundred and eighty-five dollars a week. It wasn't his game, but his enthusiasm that made him different from the others. His earnings continued to increase until he was injured. At that moment, Bettger understood that what made him so good at baseball was what he lacked in his job selling insurance; he would have to put the same amount of enthusiasm into selling insurance that he used to put into baseball. He went back to his old bosses and asked for another chance, with such conviction that he was accepted for a thirty-day probation period. Three years later, Bettger was the company's top salesman, a position he maintained until he was able to retire on his profits at age forty-two.[97] Frank Bettger overcame his personal barriers so well that he spoke about noticing over the years that enthusiastic salesmen were successful, while salesmen that were not thrilled about their product failed terribly. Bettger professed that enthusiasm was, by far, the best indicator of success in sales; he also believed that people weren't born with enthusiasm-- they acquired it. How? Bettger answers: by forcing yourself to act with enthusiasm.[98] He is phrase was adopted for use in the course: "Act enthusiastic and you'll be enthusiastic"![99] Besides Bettger, a multitude of Carnegie's followers adopted the 'enthusiasm principle'. Where did Carnegie's interest in enthusiasm spring from? On his first trip to London a few years later, around 1919, Carnegie visited the Speaker's Corner in Hyde Park, and noticed that the speakers who showed the most enthusiasm drew the biggest crowds. On a later trip to London in 1948, Carnegie noted that his finding still held true: the most successful speakers were those who talked most enthusiastically.[100] According to Longgood, Carnegie's method made people face the world with a different perspective.[101]

Carnegie also democratized the art of public speaking. What had before been a topic restricted to those few with access to old-fashioned courses, and was unsuited for modern expression, was now accessible to anyone who wished to express himself or herself publicly. Another of Carnegie's visions extends far beyond his era into the future. The method with which educators worked with adults needed to be rethought in order to give adults better access to speaking in public and relating with other people. First Carnegie listened to his students, then he brought out solutions to be discussed in class; in this way, he was able to improve the content of his classes. His students' progress was noticeable and impressive. Some people trembled or froze up just hearing that they might possibly have to say a few words in public. After the completing the course, their lives changed: they became top-flight salespeople, they got promoted, they gained public accolades and became recognized as amazing public speakers. It was not rare for people to become emotional upon observing their progress and personal achievements that they never thought they would make. Some participants had spectacular results in just three weeks. As people came to know that Carnegie was performing 'miracles' with his students, his course was sought out by people from all over. New students arrived with trepidation, scared people who stood to gain professional or social standing if only they could present themselves better in public, nervous about attaining what they had considered impossible A few days later, those people not only presented themselves well in public, but became known as brilliant speakers; they appeared in the newspapers, and nobody could imagine what they had been like before they had participated in the course.[102]

According to Giles Kemp and Edward Claflin, Carnegie measured the validity of new topics and experimental techniques for use in his course by asking two questions: first, did the method work with the students? Second, did the students keep coming back?[103] If Carnegie worried about student response to new topics and techniques, we can consider it a great step forward compared to the extreme severity that was typical of other teachers of the era; many of them reinforced their lessons with physical punishments. In those times, the relationship between teacher and student could be represented with the teacher being at the top of a mountain, and the student at the bottom of a well. Reducing this distance in any way represents a significant victory for education. We see again that the universities' rejections and Carnegie's freedom to develop his own curriculum at the YMCA came together to precipitate the development of the new, personalized style of public speaking that Carnegie taught. The result? In 1938, the National Association of Teachers of Speech acknowledged the Dale Carnegie Course as the best course in public speaking available.[104] And from this point, the techniques developed by Carnegie start to appear in textbooks...[105]

As a direct consequence of serious and efficient work, the course grew, and Carnegie was able to see what he had gained by listening to his students. Classes were full. And since he was not paid by the hour, but instead on commission, what before had been a risk had now become a wonderful source of income.[106] Despite this success, he did not let success go to his head, and established a limit to his ambition, namely that quality must come before any notion of profit. As he incorporated other instructors into the course, he was known to refuse or even fire any who could not meet the exacting standards he had established based on his own experiences. Another constant concern was ongoing improvement in the areas of enthusiasm, ease and organization.[107]

Carnegie also applied various techniques to help his students communicate, as was the case of the use of an object to maximize their abilities. One of these was a rolled-up newspaper, which he used to tap on students' heads, symbolizing the beginning of a new attitude. That occurred in the confrontation session mentioned earlier, in which classmates the instructor would challenge the speaker; this was a masterful technique in developing a speaker's ability to keep her poise even when facing a tough crowd.

Three years after starting his course, Carnegie was making thirty dollars a night. He rented an office in Times Square, made pamphlets, and hired more instructors. His income hit four hundred dollars a week. He was invited to give courses in Philadelphia, Baltimore, London, Paris... At this time he met Lowell Thomas, about whom we will talk more deeply later, who opened new horizons for Carnegie. Thomas was a well-known broadcast personality at the time, known for his travels across the US and abroad. Lowell asked Carnegie to write a speech for him, and ended up hiring Carnegie as his official spokesperson. Carnegie accompanied Thomas on a trip to Europe, where Thomas was shooting a scene. On this trip, Carnegie visited many countries; on his return, he noticed that although his students could overcome their fears of expressing themselves in public, not everyone necessarily wanted to be a speaker. The natural extension of his course then moved to human relations. Carnegie also compiled the principles of his course, which would be more useful for him than he could have ever imagined.

With the widespread acceptance of the course, his life improved; not only could he now afford a better place to live, he also made friends with the people he had met through his classes. Along with his intense work, Carnegie began to enjoy the highlights of the big city in which he lived, which became lifelong enjoyments. He attended plays and visited museums, walked around the markets and went to restaurants that had previously been beyond his means. Over time, he learned to ski, and never stopped his childhood pleasure of horseback riding. He now had a secret desire to learn to play the accordion,[108] and began to photograph landscapes, with his camera perched on his shoulders in a leather bag. He loved to travel and visited such diverse places as China and Alaska. When he married his second wife, Dorothy, they habitually took long, spur-of-the-moment trips.[109] As one could imagine, he was an avid reader who thirsted for information, be it classic texts, statistics or even trivia, like the fact that over a billion seconds had passed since Christ's birth.[110] Generally, he used this data to reinforce and illustrate his thoughts. He dressed impeccably for work and special occasions – normally a suit in somber colors, black shoes and eventually a scarf – but his overall mien was very elegant, carefully pressed. His glasses were elegant, nothing too flashy. We can extrapolate his care in dressing (dressing carefully, yet not extravagantly or in a flashy manner) from his need to value every encounter; it is as if Carnegie were saying: *Hey, this moment with you is very important to me, this is my way of saying I respect the occasion.* Deeper down, his elegance could be a response to his past, when his mother wept to hear how embarrassed he was to wear the same set of rags every day for years. Who knows if, when comparing old times with his new success, Carnegie savored the new day with a new feeling of freedom? He had finally managed to free himself from the misery he had suffered. Other battles would come, to be certain, but he would never again have to face ridicule about his clothing. Yet he never lost his ingrained simplicity; everyone who knew him described his behavior as humble, although everyone would express it in his or her own way. Collie Small described him in an interview when Carnegie was already in his sixties: *When he is not working on a new lecture tour, he putters around his garden, takes long, meditative walks in a nearby park, constantly exclaiming over the wonders of nature, and regularly inspects a set of dinosaur footprints he purchased last year from Yale University.* [111] In an old newspaper clipping I found but could not identify (though it was likely from a Missouri newspaper), the journalist said: *Certainly Mr. Carnegie is not one of those so-called 'personality boys' although his business is to teach others how to develop a personality.* This best encapsulates my perception of how he behaved in public. That is to say, as he became more famous, people expected him to be an eccentric character like the stars of the day, and yet found him to be a simple human being, authentic and respectful in his interactions with others. This simplicity shocked some and left others perplexed.

Regarding his other habits, Carnegie rarely smoked or drank.[112] Wherever he was, he would pick up oranges, bananas, apples and grapes; he enjoyed going to a restaurant for some good pancakes. After lunch, he would take a nap; when his work was intense, he would cover his eyes with a dark cloth and take a catnap, unaffected by surrounding noise or activity. He liked old things, but only if they were still useful[113], which shows his pragmatic view of life. He was also interested in archeology and dinosaurs, keeping a dinosaur footprint in his backyard.[114] Above all, Carnegie loved nature, and admired the birds and squirrels in his garden as much as his pampered plants. He especially enjoyed watching a certain squirrel that would come into his office and eat off his desk. Nature helped him relax and meditate, as did his cocker spaniel Birdie. Another companion on his walks was a Boston bulldog named Rex.[115] His favorite garden plant was the white mallow, because it reminded him of the plants back on the farm. When he worked in the garden and found insects on the roots of his plants, he would toss them in the pond for his fish to snap up; the fish would follow him around the pool, waiting for treats. He replenished his energy and inspiration by admiring nature and working with his plants. Later he would relate his enjoyable moments to his wife Dorothy and his daughter Donna. He did not frequent a church on a regular basis, but he was respectful of the ministers, and gave lectures for free when requested.[116] Change had come for Carnegie; at this point, he had already started to conquer New York.

# CHAPTER 3

## A SOLDIER READY FOR WAR

*"During the depression", said the cowboy to me, "I used to hop freights at least once a month. In those days you'd see hundreds of men riding a flatcar or in a boxcar, and they weren't just bums, there were all kinds of men out of work and going from one place to another and some of them just wandering. It was like that all over the West. Brakemen never bothered you in those days."*

(Jack Kerouac)[117]

On the second day of March, 1916, Mrs. Amanda Carnagey, Carnegie's mother, wrote a long poem for her hometown newspaper, *The Belton Herald*. In this poem, she paid homage to her whole family, her parents, husband and sons. Concerning Carnegie, she summarized his life in that year:

*My baby boy Dale is alone in New York,*
*Single just now, but to marriage some day may resort.*
*Just now he is teaching in the Y.M.C.A*
*Of Brooklyn, New York, Trenton and Philadelphia*
*Spare moments, writes for the American magazine,*
*And sometimes for others, it will be seen.*
*He's happy and contented, with his busy life, [...]*

His courses were prospering and Carnegie started to rent the beautiful auditorium at Carnegie Hall to give lectures that invited the audience to enroll in his course. At these events, Carnegie asked graduates of the course to speak about their progress. This was a stroke of genius, because his students had made really remarkable progress; their brief accounts ranged from the emotional to the comical. Some people attended these sessions with the intention of heckling the course but ended up enrolling. "They came to laugh and stayed to pray," witnesses said. Some people were pushed by friends to sign up, themselves doubting anything would come of it. Yet their lives changed. A participant in Minnesota, for example (we'll call him John), was distressed at the thought of sitting in a classroom. He thought he already knew it all and there was nothing left to learn. John decided to try the 'golden rules' emphasized in session after session, just to disprove their efficacy... but they did work, and every application brought more and more impressive results. As a result, John became one of the course's strongest boosters, after winning more prizes than any other student.[118] Carnegie invited outstanding students to become instructors, and these instructors became passionate proponents of the course's principles and their results not only in the classroom, but in their own lives. Longgood tells of instructors who had auto accidents and abandoned the scene, flagging down a ride to make it to class on time.[119] The instructors stepped into Carnegie's role as a support for people who needed and wanted to make progress, support for those who conquered passivity and dove wholeheartedly into the course.

It is at this time that Carnegie changed his last name from 'Carnagey' to 'Carnegie'. One speculation is that he was motivated to associate his name with the name of the ballroom where his lectures were now taking place, Carnegie Hall[120.] Even today, associating himself with this glamorous place makes good marketing sense. Similarly, others consider that he changed his name to link his name with that of the magnate Andrew Carnegie (the original Carnegie of Carnegie Hall).[121] But taking advantage of Andrew Carnegie's fame doesn't make much sense in light of the fact that by 1916 Dale Carnegie's courses were receiving accolades based on their own merits, not because of false advertising. Quite to the contrary, conversations with those who knew Carnegie led me to consider another motivation. Apparently, Carnegie felt that having to spell out his name hindered communication; his friends out East spelled his name wrong, and Carnegie said he wanted to spare them any embarrassment.[122] Changing his name was just a simplification, and as such makes sense. We should also remember that Carnegie was a performing arts graduate, and artists commonly change their names in order to advance their careers. After Carnegie's intense involvement in theater, despite its short duration, he may also have considered a more adequate name a necessity.

In June of 1917 Carnegie was drafted to serve in the military, just shy of twenty-nine years old. He was sent to Camp Upton, in Yaphank, Long Island. Equipment was scarce (there were neither weapons nor even uniforms for all). Sergeant Carnegie was responsible for answering telephone calls and chauffeuring a major, who was so strict that Carnegie was not allowed to read the paper during his downtime. A year and a half later, at the end of the war, Carnegie returned to the safe haven of his life, the Course. He was starting over, but this time he had some advantages and disadvantages to take into consideration. On the one hand, the course was already well-received, and maintained the support and trust of the YMCA; on the other hand, most people had no money, because the entire American economy had been plunged entirely into war efforts, and people first needed to return to their civilian lives in order to generate money to spend.[123] But Carnegie already had the magic formula for success and was able to get himself back up in the saddle again, reviving his course. Success seemed a sure thing, for him and for the course. What else could possibly happen?

## ECONOMIC CRISIS: BEATING THE DEPRESSION

When the depression arrived in 1929, Carnegie was better equipped than anyone to give lectures about how to individually and collectively face and overcome economic disaster. He himself had survived the worst problems, and felt he needed to tell people that that the darkness was temporary, that it would end and that everything depended on individual efforts. Carnegie's "fake it until you make it" formula again became an alternative to lying awake at night worrying. Another piece of advice he gave was to exercise and maintain physical activity: the body and mind influence each other. When nature prepares someone for a mission, the person is called at the right moment to act for all and to come to the aid of all. Carnegie faced and overcame so many challenges that, suddenly, he was the guide who would tell those willing to listen how to get through the crisis. How could he ever have imagined that this could happen? Which one of his schoolmates who teased him, mocking his mannerisms, his clothes, his poverty and shyness, which of them would have thought that Carnegie would be the person to bring hope to those troubled by the depression, by fear of hunger, misery and desperation? Carnegie took up the grand mission of teaching the anxious, showing them how to react, how to overcome their problems and how to win. What a triumph of nature, which we can never underestimate.

Carnegie himself had also lost a significant sum in the stock market, and it was a dark time. He had doubts about the survival of the course. From 1929 to 1932 he was able to rebuild some of his savings, and during the October break period between courses, he decided to go to China, a trip he considered to be one of the biggest adventures of his life. When his steamship arrived in Shanghai, he saw things that made him realize that Americans knew absolutely nothing about economic depression. In China, he saw the lowest of the low: people clamored to catch some of the water used to swab the galley's deck in case some food had been picked up with the mop; a child immediately picked up and ate watermelon seeds a man had spit on the floor. And this was nothing new, it had been happening in China for thousands of years. Two million Chinese people fell victim to floods, disease and starvation every year; those who were lucky enough to get a job there worked fourteen hours a day for a paltry seven cents. Yet what most impressed Carnegie was the people's happiness in spite of it all. He talked to a missionary, who confirmed the revelation that the people there had more fun than Americans did.

This despite economic "depression" conditions in China for three thousand years! Carnegie reminded Americans that the Chinese "... don't moan around and say '– Uncle Chin Fung is about to be fired. Oh! Whatever will become of us?'"[124]

He learned from everything he saw. He considered that if his courses didn't pick up due to the slow economy, he could always wash dishes somewhere; after all, helping his mother in the kitchen had given him first-hand experience. He could even go back to the farm and plant corn and milk the cows. When his ship docked in San Francisco, he said he wanted to dance in the streets, because even if he lost every penny in the recession, his suffering would be nothing compared to the lives of most of the Chinese he had seen. If he lost his house, he could always live in a furnished apartment; if he did not have a place to live, he could eat and drink water without the fear of cholera, which was wreaking havoc on the Chinese population at the time. After this trip, everything that had worried him before seemed foolish.[125]

Realizing that people were emotionally beaten down by unemployment, the precariousness of the few remaining jobs, hunger, the cold, the lack of housing and maybe worst of all, the seemingly boundless repercussions of the stock market crash, Carnegie wrote an article in 1938 that was a perfect summary of the way he tried to help his country and the world through this miserable, discouraging situation. True to his clear, didactic and exemplifying style, he started with a simple example and wrote about the dread he felt about having to have a tooth extracted under anesthesia. After describing all his fears, he presented his prescription to thwart anxiety and avoid worrying about remote possibilities: – *I resolved to relax because I knew that being all wrought up inside never cured anything and would make matters worse. So I got my mind off things by reciting Lincoln's Gettysburg Address* ...[126] Suddenly he woke up and the surgery was successfully done; the doctor said he was one of the most relaxed patients he had ever worked on. Carnegie asked himself about what was different between an earlier dentist visit (where he was restless and fidgety) and this more recent extraction, when he was able to sit calmly and focus on Lincoln's speech. *Not very much,* he answered himself. *Nothing but a changed mental attitude.*[127] What he goes on to say later in the article seems so simple, but was critical to help his readers clear their minds of the foggy, uncertain future: he talks about China. Carnegie contemplates the Chinese people he met, people who still felt they had a right to have fun and make the best of what they had, even if they were out on the street and hungry. Americans would be wise to be thankful for what they had, and to be lucky that though hunger loomed, things could be much worse. He cites Solomon: "As a man thinketh in his heart, so he is." He continues "And what we think, we sooner or later act upon. If we think fear, we act fearful; if we act brave, we are courageous. It is as simple as that."[128] Our challenges are determined by our attitudes. People can face enormous difficulties and eventually win, but some give up the struggle because they believe the end is near; belief is the most important factor for success. And even the great sometimes suffer setbacks, like General Grant or Napoleon: "Every winner loses a battle," said Carnegie. He also cited Ralph Waldo Emerson: "Do the thing you fear, and death of fear is certain". The African explorer Martin Johnson explained that the key to safety around wild animals involves not displaying any fear; if they sense your fear, you become prey, but if you do not show fear, you can deal with them safely. If you lose your job, Carnegie suggests, you needn't be scared, just have a healthy attitude and look for another job. Carnegie backs up his statements with true stories about everyday people to prove that those who have courage and determination cannot be defeated. According to Robert Ingersoll, "The biggest test of courage on earth is to bear defeat without losing heart."[129] Writer and dog expert Albert Payson Terhune defined courage as "hanging on one minute longer".[130] Will the Americans hold on, or will they mourn together alongside those who say that nothing can be done, asked Carnegie. His answer: "Of course we can do it!"[131]

What an effect this article, and others like it written during the recession, must have had on America and the world alike.

In the 1930s, Carnegie held on in the face of the economic crisis and came out on top. Now his theories about success were well proven, for he made continuous progress, despite the depression surrounding him. Carnegie now began to host a Sunday radio show on WABC (CBS's first affiliate in New York, later to be known as WCBS), which regularly featured a five-minute biography. The show was transmitted from the Paramount building, and presented new music alongside portraits of the great names of the day, from scientists and writers to artists and other celebrities.[132] Nowadays, TV shows that present biographies are very successful. Decades earlier, Carnegie held up the lives of the successful as an example. He wrote three biographical books, hosted a radio show, wrote articles, and gave interviews; his writings were full of anecdotes about the human experience. He was interested in both great names and anonymous lives. Based on the belief that every person has great potential, Carnegie realized that, through the course, his contribution was enabling people to write their own great life story.

According to Giles Kemp and Edward Claflin, Carnegie didn't see people as winners and losers. Everyone was a winner, and winners were made by good public speaking, and that is why communication is the strongest point of the course. Speaking in public is a way for people to be themselves, but Carnegie's training teaches more than just public speaking: it teaches how to reach one's objectives. For Carnegie, there were more important things than money. Although Henry David Thoreau said that people can only reach what they desire, it comes as a shock to see many people that enrolled in Carnegie's course attaining goals they had never imagined, never mind planned.[133] There are, still, those that discover many methods to drastically change the lives of those who adopt them, for the better. This is what we will talk about next.

# CHAPTER 4

## THE COURSE TO PREPARE A PERSON FOR FULFILLMENT

> "All that I am, I owe to my mother
> and to Dale Carnegie". [134]

On a beautiful day in August 2008, I arrived at the hotel where I would have my first contact with the Dale Carnegie Course. The hotel is near a shopping mall, across a plaza from Curitiba's City Council building. Although it is a well-known area of the capital city, I did not often go there, which together with the novelty of the course piqued my expectations. And these expectations were immense, for I had read and reread all of Carnegie's books (some more than ten times) and many times I had seen the contact information at the end of the books that described how to participate. For twenty-six years I had thought about enrolling in this course that had now been passed down from generation to generation since 1912. It was like its own culture that had been passed down from teacher to teacher, guided by study manuals, and survived as customs. The course gives the practice necessary to transform knowledge into action. Can you imagine studying culinary theory for years without ever setting foot in a kitchen? Well, I spent years reading Carnegie's principles and trying to apply them to my daily life, but I was about to realize that the course has its own energy to upgrade the learner: it teaches through practice.

The elevator door opened, and as I passed through the hallway I saw the sign: *'Dale Carnegie Course'*. I felt like I was moments away from re-establishing contact with a long-lost friend. I was surrounded by people busily and efficiently preparing for class. The instructors, Edson Barbosa and Giuliano Alcântara, switched off rapidly during the sessions, maintaining the class's attention and keeping the mood dynamic. They were assisted by course graduates who were preparing themselves to eventually become instructors. William Longgood noted the excellence of Carnegie Course instructors, and their excellent performance over the decades. In the 1960's, Longgood described the facilitator who is modestly called an 'instructor' but had to, according to Longgood, *...be a combination of teacher, psychologist, actor, stage manager, master salesman, raconteur, cheerleader and counselor. He is also expected to dress neatly and conservatively, always look well groomed... do much reading, studying and thinking... have a keen sense of timing and tempo... do a superb job of communicating his ideas and feelings to the class...*[135] Longgood added more qualities and requirements: put the students' interests before the instructor's own experiences. Be enthusiastic without being noisy. Pay close, helpful attention to the students at all times. Think about how to solve their problems, and know how to reward their progress. Find out the students' abilities and turn them important tools they can use. Be modest, but have contagious enthusiasm. Have a sense of dignity and call the students by their first names without being too intimate.[136] He describes signs that the instructor is ready to teach the course: they spend hours without sleep, before and after the course, dedicating their time to meditation, reading and filling out profiles about each student. Some devote themselves exclusively to the course, while others have other jobs; when these instructors teach the course, their coworkers at their day job notice that they are agitated, they walk differently and they greet others with their minds on something else (the course).[137] Enthusiasm, emphasized so often by Carnegie, is foremost in the instructor, because he is so completely absorbed in the course, so focused, dedicated and thoughtful about each step and then later analytic about how these steps can be improved. It seems like the perfect formula for professional behavior: believing in what one does and dedicating oneself to it absolutely. Anyone can become a Carnegie course instructor, but they must be dedicated to becoming a true professional: their purpose is to give their all to their students.

It is very rewarding; far beyond any stipend they earn, nothing can compare to the testimonials and letters of thanks that students send their instructors. But instructors must remember Carnegie's foremost requirement: to be and remain a Dale Carnegie Course instructor, they must, above all, have "...a desire to help others".[138]

Countless students have passed through the course and left pages and pages of accounts describing their struggle. The best promotion of the course is done by the students themselves, many of whom become real missionaries, perhaps as a way of showing their gratitude, consciously or unconsciously. As soon as they realize the magnitude of the course, many students make noteworthy sacrifices to be able to guarantee their attendance. Longgood describes students traveling great distances to attend the course. Some would take the course at night and then board a train home, going directly to work in the morning when they arrived. Some of these cases are truly impressive. In Longgood's words: *In 1947, Robert Driver, then over 70, traveled by train each week from Brockville to Toronto, Canada, a distance of 434 miles. Sam Rosenberg came from Australia to the United States just to take the course, before it had spread to that continent.*[139] Countless other examples of student dedication can be related: in Jamaica, a student traveled a hundred and thirty miles over horrible roads to attend each class. He showed his instructor, Arthur S. Brueckmann, the bullet holes in his car that bore witness to the danger he confronted to get to class, but the student said he felt more than compensated by taking the course. World travelers like pilots, for example, took the course in many different cities, since students were allowed to take classes over again. Visually impaired students arrived with their guide dogs, and bedridden people sought out ways to attend classes despite their infirmities. People suffering from speech impediments became more confident speakers, some losing their impediments entirely. A housewife started to moonlight as a cook, and saved the money she earned for four years in order to take the course. A Mrs. Stitts, who attended classes in Rochester, Minnesota, gave birth the day after the tenth session but was back in class a week later for the eleventh. More examples of students' heroic efforts to improve themselves can be related by modern day instructors and participants. Longgood also related the participants' positive outcomes, from promotions and pay increases, improvements in studies and new companies to freedom from stuttering and headaches or even gaining a beloved's hand in marriage.[140] How can one quantify the value of a self-confident, serene, more capable, more efficient, more productive, friendlier, or, well, a better person?

My class started promptly at eight in the morning. From this point, the scheduled activities introduced the thirty or so participants to a different, organized, positive and evolved world. Quick, objective instructions were followed by activities that slowly warmed up the body and soul. This was the first course I attended that truly allowed the participants to participate equally in all activities. From the beginning, conversation exercises were practiced in pairs, then in groups of three, then in a larger group; little by little, students gain the self-confidence needed to feel more relaxed and speak to the group as a whole. The evolution was noticeable. One of the students in my class, Jean,[141] was tense and trembling, and it seemed he would never be able to talk in public or even express himself in a reasonable way in front of someone, never mind organize his ideas or discuss business. By the fourth week, he was voted the student who had made the most improvement. He shone in each week's sessions, touching the class with his clear communication. There are many examples, but each person's personal evolution is impressive, regardless of which activity in which they participate. The instructors demonstrate an appropriate yet natural posture, they show how to avoid harmful mannerisms, and teach how to correct flaws in speech and gesture. Of course this is possible because the class can mirror the instructors' correct example. They dress impeccably, are respectful, resolute but polite, and their behavior models ideal professional behavior. Their sincere compliments work as effective incentives; indeed, how many teachers, parents, friends, employers, counselors and governors would see improvement in their interactions if only they recognized virtues instead of criticizing? What a transformation that would be. And yet Carnegie had already applied that a century ago.

I surprised myself with each Saturday morning meeting. Edson Barbosa and Giuliano Alcântara would give assignments, check the week's work, call an assistant to speak on a topic; the whole class began to visibly improve, myself included. Actually, a whole new world was opening up in front of me. I started to focus more on my job, on my studies, on leisure time, on the people I loved and on those I was yet to meet and love. I didn't know how it was happening, but I went through a splendid transformation. The criminal law classes I taught became more appealing to my students. I knew some lecture techniques, but only after the Course did I start to apply them; others were new to me and their discovery changed my relationship with teaching. In a class about firearms legislation, for example, I taught the theory, but also brought live ammunition and a model gun to liven up my presentation. I also invited a guest speaker, and brought my class to a shooting range. I brought the theory to life, and my students were amazed. I selected a scene from the movie *The Untouchables* where a criminal takes a hostage and a sharp-shooting police officer saves the victim. We reenacted the scene at the shooting range, to see if the Hollywood stunt could be reenacted in real life... The following day, I invited the students out into the streets with me to simulate "crime scenes"; we checked tire tracks, looked at dents in cars, tire marks, glass shards collected off the street, footprints on walls, the positions of people and objects. Next we entered a park in Goiânia, where my classes were being held. Once in the park, we entered the woods and I asked my students to collect objects that could have any bearing on investigation of a homicide and the discovery of a hypothetical hidden body. At the end of the activity, the students were visibly impressed, and they came to tell me that not only had they never seen anything similar, but that they wished all their classes could be conducted in the same way. We concluded by having lunch in a restaurant, time well spent celebrating good teamwork. Something better in me started to show, something more human, more deserving, more constructive and more productive as well. Everything from my studies to my professional interactions started to improve as a result of the techniques I learned and, most importantly, these techniques were not empty showmanship, there was a philosophy and a natural truth behind them. I then understood Longgood's statement from almost fifty years before: *Whatever reason people give or have for taking the course, one thing is certain: they recognize that life has more to offer than they are getting, whether their goal is tangible or intangible.*[142]

I received an email from my classmate Mary[143], a lively and enthusiastic twenty-year-old: *I missed Saturday's class because I overslept and decided it would be better not to walk in late. I think I regret it. What was the assignment for next Saturday?* Coincidentally, I had also overslept and almost missed this session myself. I decided that it would be better to arrive a minute or two late than miss the whole session. Being on time is one virtue that the students learn; punctuality shows personal organization, dignity and commitment. I was habitually punctual; my friend at Sussex University, Dr. Richard Vogler, joked that my punctuality was "more than British". And yet I found myself arriving a minute or two late to each session! What was happening? Perhaps psychoanalysis could best explain why I was doing something so out of character, especially in a course that emphasized organization and punctuality. But after the sixth class, I was back to my old self and began arriving on time again. Over the years, Carnegie carefully organized the times of the conversations and speeches in the course, creating a structured beginning and end, using a rigidity that facilitated the learning process. But a good enough speaker could cause even Dale Carnegie to bend his timetable. It happened in January of 1950, when Carnegie was observing Harold Abbot leading a course for inmates at the federal prison in

Leavenworth, Kansas. During the session, a gangster began speaking about the gunfight that had landed him in prison. He found himself in an alley, face to face with his arch-nemesis, each with his gun trained on the other. Just then, the bell rang, and the instructor started walking up and down the aisles to give feedback. Carnegie jumped up and said: "I have to hear the rest of the story, even if you need another five minutes!" The session went an hour and a half over schedule; the other participants got excited and wanted to share their own stories as well. The instructors had to adapt the next two sessions for it all to get back to normal.[144] We can observe that it was not inconsistency that caused Carnegie to abandon his rigid schedule that day: instead, Carnegie himself affirmed that some speeches can be so interesting, and so absorbing, especially when the speaker is so close to the topic, that one must listen to the end.

Maybe I had begun the course at a time in my life when I most needed it, a time when even my concept of punctuality was becoming muddled in my mind. I feel the need to mention that this was a very serious concern to me. At times I had thought I was even too punctual, until my travels took me to places where I saw that I was not the only one, that there are many of us who are not only punctual, but who mean what we say, whose word is our bond. This encouraged me, and helped me to establish friendships and trust with people I met around the world. Of course, "correct" people exist everywhere, but in some places it seems there are waves of bad habits. I found that better awareness of commitment in terms of time presented an opportunity for those who fulfill simpler obligations, such as punctuality, to be considered for other, more diverse opportunities. Doing the right thing brings one closer to other more serious, more respectful and friendlier people. I learned this from Carnegie's books and in his course. Because of the practicality of the training, in every class we approached the participants' real-life challenges, and the whole group ended up contributing to the solution, because everyone visualized themselves in the shoes of the individual with the challenge. And there is more.

When we realize that our problems are no different from other people's problems, we can no longer claim that our problems have no solution, or that we are powerless to improve our lives. Carnegie realized this a long time ago, and is considered to be one of the pioneers in organizing group solidarity among people naturally expressing their own difficulties and, in turn, making common progress. Many consider Carnegie to be the founder of support groups, another tool that has helped millions find strength in numbers. These groups have evolved as groups of people needing support have grown in number: groups for those addicted to alcohol, drugs, tobacco, gambling; groups for people with special needs, with cancer or HIV, ex-convicts... The list goes on and on. These people overcome their physical challenges and natural limitations, as well as the stigma that may be the biggest challenge of all. To understand that our troubles are more common than we thought, that other people suffer from the same problems we thought were our unique cross to bear, to be able to learn from each one's experiences; one person's experience can be another person's key to survival. These small tips can be the key to surviving our own pain, our own grief, a way to abandon addiction or compulsive behavior for once and for all. Life only makes sense when we share our findings and experiences with others. This doesn't just apply to people we already know and love, like the weekly family meal, but even to a homeless person who shares a meal or even a cup of coffee by chance. One can see why even one of Carnegie's biggest critics stated that it was 'easy to explain the success of support groups' that Carnegie had developed. Gail Thain Parker, who wrote a pessimistic article meant only to discredit Carnegie, admitted that "Carnegie had discovered the power of the support group"[145], though she neglected to mention the difficulty in creating these groups, and the special fraternity that came about as a result of them. Regarding the question of whether

Carnegie was the "inventor" of support groups, my own opinion is that nobody starts from scratch in science or history. We are always building on foundations built by our predecessors. But if new, relevant additions that are significant enough to become widely accepted as helpful are applied to existing ideas, then we can give the person who made the additions well-deserved credit. The final result is that in only one year, 80,000 people enrolled in the Dale Carnegie Course, and even then, the company was able to maintain its own high standards, earning its *ISO 9001* certification.

After enrolling in the course, I was now able to consider and establish the differences between just reading Carnegie's books and actually taking the course: I) By reading the books, we reflect alone and do our growing in silence; II) By taking the course, we benefit from the warmth and security of the group environment, soaking up the strength to make progress. Both mechanisms complement each other. Who would Lincoln have been without his solitary studies? Without the interaction he had with his subordinates? The strength of the group becomes clearer. I started to better understand the great generals of history, and how they interacted with the soldiers under their command. Now I could see that successful business partnerships benefited from the synthesis between partners; underdog sports teams overcame difficulties and achieved the victory they wanted so badly. Bernardinho, the respected coach of the Brazilian men's volleyball team, stresses the importance of heavy individual practice, but also points out the importance of team work. On a volleyball team, the only individual action is serving. The rest is group interaction.[146] But shouldn't life be the same way? Can we really live self-sufficiently? From reading a book to attending a class or buying bread at the grocery store, we are interacting with people; we need to learn the potential of human relations and participate in a harmonious way. Carnegie noticed this, saw it as an echo of the law of cause and effect in individual and social spheres. At the moment I am writing, a bird is drinking from a puddle of water on my windowsill.

Seeing this show of life is like receiving new energy. It is also necessary to learn how to interact with the plants, creatures and all other things in the universe; in this way we can reach our potential.. Many poems are written about the great thing that is the Universe; Dale Carnegie wrote a manual on how to enjoy it kindly, continuing to perpetuate this magnificent force that is Nature.

The course's class sessions are exciting in the same way. The only regret would be to miss a class, although it was always possible to make up any missed classes, thankfully.

When my classmate Mary contacted me, even though I had been in the session I wanted to be certain I passed on the right assignment. Since the course assistants are responsible for orienting the participants and answering their questions, I called up John. John told me we had to prepare a one-minute speech about a personal ability. We had already been provided with a blank poster board on which to draw any images that would help to express that ability. I drew the components of my Italian coffee pot, and then I drew the whole coffee pot with the burner turned on. After I had given the speech, I asked for the e-mail addresses of all my classmates, so I could pass on my own special coffee recipe. The other activity for that session consisted of preparing a two-minute lecture about something that had happened in my life that had made me angry. In this last assignment, we explored the consequences of anger. This was perhaps best described by the Brazilian Rui Barbosa, who referred to "righteous anger", saying that good wrath is not about exploding pride, but rather an indignation that illuminates. When we arrived to the next Saturday's session to talk about our indignations, we were surprised. We were supposed to start off by saying: "I know people of action. People who will always act. Want to know why? I'll tell you why. Because they always finish what they start". The activity went very well, and we spoke enthusiastically on the topic until our energy was spent. At this point, I could see how much of Elbert Hubbard was applied in that session; Hubbard wrote a well-known text called *A*

*Message to Garcia*. Hubbard was a nineteenth century journalist who decided to write an article based on an argument he had had with his son Bert over breakfast, whether Rowan had been the true hero of the Spanish-American War. Rowan had been assigned a very difficult mission by the president: to deliver a message to a certain Garcia, the troops' leader in Cuba. Despite difficulties and risks, he fulfilled his mission. From this, Hubbard talked about the immense number of people that receive a simple task and are stymied by doubts: is it really that urgent? Is it my problem? Where do I start? Can't someone else do it? Why bother? Etc. This mission might have been assigned by a boss, teacher, parent, or friend. All of these doubts can be (and often are) proffered as explanations to why the mission wasn't or couldn't be carried out. Hubbard suggests thinking about the messengers that fulfill their tasks and deliver the message, no matter how difficult the task. There is a certain attraction, no doubt, for who wouldn't like to exchange twenty lazy and unmotivated people for just one efficient messenger like Rowan? One time I was teaching on the topic of human rights in Brasilia and I gave my students the text by Hubbard for discussion. James, a clever participant, questioned the validity of *A Message to Garcia*, saying that many orders are unethical and cannot be fulfilled, and in any case can and perhaps ought to be challenged by one ideology or another. We are not robots, of course, but I assume Hubbard referred in his text to our need to "do what needs to be done", whether it is our professional duty, some need to help others, or simply because we made the commitment for work, friendship, passion, or just because we feel we ought to. Any excuses or roadblocks that we perceive can turn the task into an annoyance for all involved, creating negative energy. Carnegie noticed this and transformed *A Message to Garcia* into a practical enunciation: 1) for those who decide to take up a task; 2) for those who are assigned a task for which they are capable; 3) for us to simply be helpful to others; 4) for us to carry out a project of personal importance. In this way, those people who want to move forward, to be recognized professionally and personally, find means to progress in the course and ways to create positive habits. Inactive people can be turned into people of action, as long as they are invested in the process. But when someone wants to prosper, they now have not only the right to do so, but the means. Some people believe that they are already efficient, but when they come across the course, they realize they have room for improvement, and begin to effectively make that improvement.

When looking for a serious course of study, one naturally first looks to serious and established institutions, such as the Carnegie Course. At this point, we can start to consider who would be the target client for the course? We would get a better answer by changing the question: who would not benefit? Our group consisted of students of marketing, engineering and law, an intern, someone applying for internships, a salesman, a job hunter, a director of human resources, an accountant, the owner of a print shop, the manager of an international business, a delivery person, a teacher and so many others. Who would not take interest in the course? Probably only someone well satisfied with his or her life who thinks there is no need to learn or evolve any more. If someone considers their professional and personal profile to be incapable of improvement, then maybe they do not need the course. But such diverse people take the course, improving their lives and seeing results with their very own eyes, that the superiority of the course's methods is evident. I remember the words of Peter Handall, one of the US directors of the course: "What Dale Carnegie began, we are continuing, with pride from our past and trust in the future."[147]

On October 17th, 2008, I woke up tired. It was cold and gray in Curitiba; I was almost overcome by laziness, but it was impossible to deliberately miss a class. In this day's session we would complete a task that would touch us all. We formed groups of five and we had to compliment each person, and the compliments had to be real, based on evidence. When I looked at my classmate's qualities and started talking, I realized how this exercise made us recognize each others' virtues, something that we wouldn't have looked for on our own initiative. The full task was to recognize the dignity of others, to see that everyone has virtues and qualities that deserve recognition, and that true and deserved compliments allow us to see others in a fuller light, without the risk of being egocentric and ignorant of the people surrounding us. It is a fantastic discovery, an illuminating new way to look at the world and others. How can we have any success at work, with studies or in a relationship without noticing the real qualities of those whom we meet? Each person starts from birth to develop abilities unique to himself or herself, special abilities and gifts that often they themselves cannot identify. These gifts could include knowing how to use one's voice well, being good with one's hands, solving problems skillfully, being helpful to others, having some unusual physical strength, charisma, athletic ability, being a good driver, agility with a bicycle or motorcycle, the ability to pilot a ship, to fish, to be a good painter (whether painting a landscape or just a fence), being quick with a smile, forgiveness, helping, teaching, protecting, investigating, loving...

Another task we were assigned for the next session was to present an inspiring example of someone who overcame personal obstacles: I had no doubts about choosing Helen Keller, whose story was one of the most impressive I've ever heard. Helen was born in Tuscumbia, Alabama, on June 27th, 1880. When she was nineteen months old, she lost her hearing and sight to a strong fever. She faced a difficult situation; a deaf child can use her vision to communicate with signs, or a blind person can still speak, but Helen didn't have these alternatives. How could a little child with only a handful of words, now suddenly plunged into darkness and silence, still learn to communicate with the world? As Helen grew, the lack of any type of special methods for teaching her made her life a nightmare. She was bitter but could only suffer in silent darkness, unable to express herself. It is hard to even imagine how she felt. We can learn from Helen, for if anyone really had reason to complain, she did: she struggled with being unable to show what she wanted, to ask for the things that all children do, to explain her feelings and needs. Her frustration was so great that she broke dishes and her own toys. Her mother, in desperation, sought far and wide for someone who could help her little girl. She finally found a light of hope at the Perkins Institute, where a child with similar challenges, Laura Bridgman, had learned to read and write through the efforts of one Dr. Samuel Gridley Howe. Unfortunately, Dr. Howe had since passed away, but the Institute suggested Mrs. Keller contact a recent graduate named Anne Sullivan.[148]

Helen's father Captain Keller offered Anne a position as Helen's tutor. Although she lived far from the Keller family, Anne needed the job and accepted. With her own very limited vision, Anne read Dr. Howe's reports about Laura Bridgeman, and arrived to begin her work on March 3rd, 1887, when Helen was almost seven years old. The first days were difficult; Helen ate with her hands and was aggressive, threw objects, etc. It is said that Anne left their first meeting in tears. In a letter she wrote to a friend, Anne said: *That is, my good friend, why we study and graduate. When it is the moment to apply the theories, everything fails. We have to trust in those innate capacities that we discover in us only when it is time to act.*[149] Anne had to specially plan every interaction with Helen. She started with a radical idea, asking the parents to leave her and Helen alone for the first days. Anne's approach was not received easily by Helen; on one occasion Helen punched Anne in the face, breaking two of her teeth.[150] I couldn't help but be touched when I read about Helen's progress, for example when she learned that objects had names, and in her excitement swatted her teacher's hand, asking for more and more names before hugging Anne in thanks. For the first time, she kissed her teacher![151] Anne helped Helen to understand that beans and watermelons grew from seeds first sown in the ground by making Helen plant seeds and follow the whole process.[152] Now, how did Anne teach Helen all the colors, and that her hair was brown and beautiful? And how did Anne answer Helen's questions about 'the color of thoughts', mountains, the ocean, the sky, night and day, time, etc.? Anne taught Helen Braille.[153] As a result Helen began her own diary: *I got up, washed my face, brushed my hair, picked three violets for my teacher and had breakfast...*[154] She continued on, writing about her day, about a book she had read about wild animals, about the letter she wrote her uncle James, a doctor, about how much she liked ice cream and about Robert and his wife Mrs. Newsun, about Jumbo and Pearl, about Natalie, about Mr. Maio and Mr. Farris, and other people and events... all this in just one page. Some details I would never notice during my day, but Helen let nothing escape unnoticed until she finished with *Now I am going to bed.* She signed her work: *Helen Keller.*[155] This passage I have quoted here was written in March of 1888, when she was almost eight. But how would she learn how to talk? That was not all. She also wanted to learn about love and god, why the sun was hot, where she was before she was born and before and before, and how was Earth so heavy and wandering in space?[156] She moved ahead, she read the best books, she learned to understand what people were talking about, training for years to be able to "hear" what people were saying through her fingers, carefully placed on the speaker's face. In this way, she talked to Mark Twain, Enrico Caruso, Feodor Chaliapine and Jascha Heifetz. At thirteen she started to study Latin, German and French, again with her hands over her language teacher's lips.[157] She studied geography, physics and mathematics, and wanted to go to college. At this time, people began to criticize her, to call her a fraud; she was either a parrot, repeating mindlessly, or the recipient of some divine miracle, because of her astounding intelligence. Both teacher and student started to suffer as a result of this criticism. Here, I remember Carnegie's lesson on unfounded critics. In 1900, Helen applied to college and was accepted. Her challenges at university were so numerous that they are difficult to summarize briefly. But she read Schiller, the life of Frederic the Great, and Goethe, among others. She listened to music,

feeling the vibrations throughout her body. She graduated in 1904.[158]
I learned these details about Helen Keller from Gabriel Chalita's book
*Mulheres que Venceram Preconceitos: Mulheres Célebres que
Trouxeram e Trazem Benefícios à Sociedade (Women Who Beat
Prejudice: famous women who benefited and continue to benefit
society)*[159], and from the author's recommended further reading,
Helen's books: *The Story of my Life, Optimism, Out of the Dark*, and
others. But the story is even more fantastic, because Helen decided
to learn how to talk! In 1913, she made her first public speaking
appearance, the first of many lectures she and her teacher Anne
would give. She always finished her speeches by saying "I am no
longer a mute".[160] Her speeches presented ideas that were
revolutionary for the time about how people with special needs could
work and participate in society. By the beginning of World War I, she
had traveled to many countries, charming the world and continuing to
share her ideas, which had already been translated into many
languages.[161] When they returned to the United States, Helen and
Anne gave a series of lectures around New York, right around the
same time that Carnegie's course was growing. Gabriel Chalita
described Helen's thought process, stating: *A person who has a
physical impairment only gets to know her own strength when she is
treated as a normal human being, and encouraged to build her own
life with hard work.*[162] And this, of course, was how Anne had treated
Helen since childhood, as an equal, and she never allowed people to
treat her Helen differently. In this way Helen was able to develop her
character fully. An older Helen Keller said: *I am blind, may I give a
suggestion to those who see, advice to those who should use their gift
of sight fully: use your eyes as if tomorrow you would go blind. The
same principle applies to all the senses. Listen to the music of voices,
the song of a bird, the powerful chords of an orchestra, as if tomorrow
you would stop hearing. Touch everything you wish to touch as if
tomorrow you would be deprived of the feeling of tact. Breathe the
perfume of flowers and savor your meals, as if tomorrow you would*

*lose the sense of smell and taste.*"[163] While Anne Sullivan is a renowned teacher who inspired masters, the name Helen Keller is synonymous with struggle and victory, a real-life example of how no personal hardship – none – can be a barrier to struggle and progress. A lot of people complain about the difficulties they have with studies, work, or personal interactions. Helen Keller had a serious disadvantage, but she triumphed, leaving a message to all humanity: it does not matter what the problem or who the critic, it is always possible to overcome our challenges. That is why I admire Helen and Anne so much. The experience of these women did not go unnoticed by Carnegie, who admired them both, comparing Helen Keller's life to that of Napoleon; Carnegie noted that, according to his own admission, Napoleon did not even have six days of happiness in his life, while Helen Keller considered life to be 'so beautiful'.[164]

It is astonishing how Dale Carnegie's courses continue, to this day, to influence the lives of millions. William Longgood quoted some phrases that students always use to describe the course: *"I understand people more". "I learned to control myself better". "People became more interesting to me". "I became a better father". "I learned to accept life as it is and enjoy it". "The course saved my marriage". "I'm a happier and more complete person". "I found myself". "I discovered that the men and women that came to my store were not clients or prospective sales, they are people".*[165] And, of course, people improved their health, their incomes, their personal discoveries, their love lives, and their personal projects. All because the course is about more than just public speaking or human relations, it gives the participant a different perspective on life. Carnegie saw all this personal progress as natural, because he believed that dedicated participants would naturally improve their productivity, they would naturally become happier, they would naturally speak more efficiently, sell more products, persuade others to see their point of view, etc.[166] One of the most accurate descriptions of the course may be that written by Harold Abbot in 1957:

*It has been my privilege to visit Dale Carnegie classes in Tokyo, Manila, Hong Kong, Zurich and I had the privilege of instructing the first class in Copenhagen, Denmark in 1957. Since that time every Christmas, I get at least one or more letters from graduates of that class, telling me how the training benefited their lives.*

*"Now about two million people have taken Dale Carnegie's training. More than eight million have read the book* How to Win Friends. *Another million have read his book* How to Stop Worrying and Start Living. *Dale Carnegie is a Missouri farm boy who dared to do and he reached the heights.*

*One hundred years from now, Dale Carnegie will be even more quoted than he is today because his simple truths of human relations will not change – because human nature will not change.*[167]

# CHAPTER 5

## STILL TIME FOR LOVE AND FOR FRIENDS

> *As soon as people take the risk of saying what they think,*
> *do not punish them for being sincere.*
> *Do not do anything – anything at all – to discourage them*
> *from taking the risk of communicating again.*
> (Stuart R. Levine and Michael A. Crom)[168]

### THE UNFORGETTABLE MOTHER AND FATHER

Carnegie's strongest, most unshakable support undoubtedly came from his mother, Amanda Elizabeth Carnagey. From his upbringing to encouraging him to fight and advance, Mrs. Carnagey was always a strong influence. Carnegie never forgot that. Among his writings I found one of the many letters he wrote to his mother. In this letter, I noticed how he needed to pay his respects and keep in touch with her no matter where his travels took him. I leave the reader to make his or her own conclusions, only pointing out the growing popularity of that new invention, the telephone. What seems most important to me is the way he expresses himself to someone both so familiar and so worthy of his admiration:

*Dear Mother,*

*Since writing you last week, I have decided not to start West with those travelogues until the latter part of August or the first September. My first stop will probably be Duluth and then on through Winnipeg and Edmonton out to Seattle and Portland. Naturally it will not be convenient for me to come to Kansas City and I don't know whether I can arrange to meet you at Aunt Beck's or not. The matter is still up in the air and I can't be very definitive at present.*

*The New York Telephone company had an invention on display during the victory loan drive here, by which a wireless telephone or a person could play a Victrola record down in Washington, DC., and you could hear it without the aid of any wire. They tried to get me on the long distance telephone one day when I was in Philadelphia and when I came back to New York they wanted me to go up and inspect the invention and give them suggestions for improving it. Really, I couldn't keep from smiling at that. They said they wanted to have the best known public speaking instructor in the country to investigate it and to tell them how to talk through it most advantageously and also to say something about the subject of public speaking in connection with it. They were going to have these interviews printed in the newspapers all over the United States, but owing to the fact that it rained the last two days, I was unable to go up and investigate it.*

*I have told you this because it is the only news that I have, otherwise things are drifting along about the same as usual. With love, Dale.*

Carnegie always worshiped his parents, recognizing the sacrifices they made to support him and provide him with an education during times of poverty, something he always appreciated. Harold Abbott gives us an idea about the love he had for his parents:

"I have heard Carnegie lecture from Miami, Florida to Portland, Oregon, and I don't believe I ever heard a time when he did not mention his boyhood in Missouri, the farms in Nodaway County where he grew up and his parent's farm at the edge of Belton. Dale Carnegie revered his parents as few people do. He was constantly referring to something he had learned from his mother or father".[169]

## THE RELATIVES

Carnegie was not known to have been very close to his brother Clifton; but his relationship with his other relatives, even distant ones, was warm according to Abbott:

> *He liked people. One of the most enjoyable evenings I ever spent with him was spent in Belton at a family reunion dinner of cousins and their families. He invited me to go along with him. There were 20 to 25 people there and most of the evening was spent reminiscing, reliving the experiences of their childhood. There were few times I ever heard Dale Carnegie laugh as much as he did that evening.*[170]

## A FRIEND FROM MARYVILLE AND OTHER GOOD FELLOWS

People hold the places where they were born and raised in high regard. It is one of the means people use to differentiate themselves from others.

Maryville is still a small town in Missouri. When Carnegie and Homer Croy lived there, it was even smaller; and although Carnegie had not yet gotten to know his fellow countryman Croy, they later had many good conversations remembering the hardships they overcame there. Carnegie remembered being a barefoot child watching well-dressed musicians in the Linville hotel as they sat there smoking their cigars. Carnegie's dream was that one day he would stay at that hotel himself. Little did he know that staying in the world's best hotels would become routine; yet staying at the Linville was much more of an emotional accomplishment. And later he was there, reliving the past with his friend Homer Croy. While Carnegie talked about passing through Wilcox, a village some seven miles northwest of Maryville, Croy talked about a city six miles east, Bedison, and its narrow roads. It was a memorable day for both of them.

They had actually met when they were in college and found some things in common. One of them was that Croy also dropped out of college after failing English, while Carnegie had failed Latin. But Croy was also accomplished and became a pioneer in journalism, attending the first course that existed at the University of Missouri.[171] Another common factor was the fact that both were successful and well-established in New York. These coincidences, though, did not extend to their personalities. Croy was more opinionated and introduced Carnegie to friends in his own circle, people with radical opinions and tendencies, anarchists, atheists, liberals, etc. I imagine meetings with such interesting characters with such conflicting opinions must have been interesting. Carnegie's friendship with Croy lasted a lifetime, and Carnegie spent almost every Sunday in the company of Croy, often traveling together with him.[172]

Another good friend was Frank Bettger, the former baseball player that took the Carnegie Course in Philadelphia, who from then on became Carnegie's disciple. After abandoning athletics, Bettger incorporated Carnegie's principles so successfully into selling insurance that, encouraged by Carnegie, he published a book called *How I Raised Myself From Failure to Success in Selling.* In many ways Bettger's story resembles Carnegie's. He was very poor and left school at fourteen to work assembling steam engines, helping his widowed mother to support the family. During his childhood and youth, Bettger and his brothers often suffered from cold and hunger.[173] Bettger, who followed Carnegie's lecture tour to promote the course, stated that he would never forget what the Dale Carnegie Course had done for him, in business and in life, and he would take every opportunity to show that gratitude.[174] Frank Bettger was part of a long list of people grateful for Dale Carnegie's Course and books.

Lowell Thomas was another prominent friend, a studious man with a master's degree in law. He was known for his lectures about Alaska, and was eventually invited to speak to congressmen and senators on the subject. He used to get lost in his speeches and ramble, and he did not want it to happen in such an important venue. Being a perfectionist, he looked for the best preparation he could get and found Carnegie. He meticulously prepared his lecture, and Thomas received a standing ovation. This was the beginning of a fabulous partnership. When World War I began, Thomas was asked by Secretary of State Franklin Lane to observe and record the battles, and so he went to Europe, around the North Sea, and then to Saudi Arabia. Thomas then arrived in Egypt accompanying the British, and followed behind T. E. Lawrence, who he introduced as the famous 'Lawrence of Arabia'.[175] Lowell Thomas had documented the actions of Lawrence and the British general Edmund H. Allenby during the war, and wanted to give lectures on what he had seen. He scheduled a presentation at Covent Garden Opera House in London two weeks later. He knew he could count on Carnegie, who was living in a rented house on Fire Island at the time.[176] Carnegie once again was an invaluable adviser to Thomas and the lecture was full of prayers, movies and other scenes together with Thomas' carefully prepared presentation. As a result, the opera had to be postponed six weeks because of the popularity of the lectures; people stood in line for hours to get tickets. The mission accomplished, Carnegie returned to New York, but Thomas soon called him again for help with a new task that would not be as successful. Thomas now wanted Carnegie himself to give the lectures, which would now be divided in half, because Thomas wanted to travel to Australia with his wife. Despite evidence that shows Carnegie did all he could, the project was doomed to failure from the start because the public had identified with Lowell Thomas and they did not want to see anyone replace him, no matter how good a speaker. This episode angered and deeply upset Carnegie because he did not live up to his friend's expectations. Thomas understood the situation, and when he was later called to direct a radio show in the United States, he again contacted his friend Carnegie for help. Thomas was considered to be one of the biggest names in radio, and always honored Carnegie, especially when he published his best-seller *How to Win Friends and Influence People.*[177]

## FIRST MARRIAGE

In 1921, Carnegie met Lolita Baucaire, a woman who hailed from the border region between Germany and France and claimed to be a countess- at least she acted like one. During their first years of marriage they lived in Europe. They moved to a residence near Versailles, where Carnegie started an audacious project, a novel he titled *The Blizzard.* The work was a burden to him. He wrote and rewrote passages up to forty times, but he refused to give up. Even his agent said the book was horrible and that he was no good at writing novels. The publishers that rejected the novel, though, had no way of knowing that in a few years he would write a book that could have made them all rich. But he was so discouraged that he decided to return to the United States and restart his work with the course. Years later, Carnegie spoke about this difficult work: *The title was a natural, for the reception it got among publishers was as cold as any blizzard that ever howled across the plains of the Dakotas. When my literary agent told me it was worthless, that I had no gift, no talent, for fiction, my heart almost stopped. I left his office in a daze. I couldn't have been more stunned if he had hit me across the head with a club. I was stupefied. I realized that I was standing at the crossroads of life, and had to make a tremendous decision. What should I do? Which way should I turn? Weeks passed before I came out of the daze....* Carnegie continued: *Am I glad now that I made that decision? Glad? Every time I think about it now I feel like dancing in the street for sheer joy! I can honestly say that I have never spent a day or an hour since, lamenting the fact that I am not another Thomas Hardy.*[178] Ten years and forty days after their wedding, he finally separated from Lolita Baucaire. It was such a painful union that it took a long time for Carnegie to be able to talk about it.

## SECOND MARRIAGE AND THE BELOVED DAUGHTER

In 1942, Carnegie went to give a lecture in Tulsa, Oklahoma. It seemed like it would be like any other presentation, but it wasn't. He met and later had lunch with a young woman named Dorothy Vanderpool, her mother, and H. Everett Pope, an eventual booster of the Carnegie Course who would represent it at the Oklahoma School of Business, Accounting, Law and Finance (now known as the Oklahoma Junior College). Dorothy was a little over five feet five inches tall and had red hair and green eyes. In one of fate's twists, Dorothy's mother had known Carnegie's parents back when he was still a child on the farm in Missouri. Ten months later, Dorothy moved to New York to work as Carnegie's secretary. On November 5th, 1944, they were married in the Methodist Church in Tulsa. Carnegie was overwhelmed by emotions and told a friend that only now, eight years after publishing *How to Win Friends and Influence People*, had he finally been able to influence a woman to marry him. The wedding was like simple, like the newlyweds, with some select friends and Dorothy's family present.[179] They played Oklahoma music and Carnegie said that if they played *People will say we're in love* he would cry. The song was played, but he was so excited about the wedding that he did not cry. Harry Hamm noted that even Carnegie got nervous in front of such special company.[180]

Dorothy was a very dynamic person who enjoyed fencing and ballet, and she began to develop activities related to her husband's business. This strong involvement with the business became evident on a trip to the mountains in Canada. Longgood says that Carnegie woke up at sunrise to hike, climb and admire the landscape during the day; when night came, Dorothy wanted to go out to dance, but Carnegie was so tired from his activity that he needed to go to bed. Dorothy got bored, so Carnegie suggested she write a course for women.[181] From this point on, she focused on women's issues and how she could use Carnegie's methods to clarify matters that were especially pertinent to women. She promoted the courses aimed at the female public, and in 1953 she wrote *How to Help Your Husband Get Ahead in His Business and Social Life*; she followed this in 1958 with *Don't Grow Old, Grow Up.* Dorothy was fundamental to the maintenance of the Dale Carnegie Course. According to Harold Abbott: *His widow, Dorothy Carnegie, together with executive vice president John Cooper, who works closely with her[182], have done a masterful job in guiding the Dale Carnegie organization into an educational course of world wide fame. Mr. Cooper got his start in the Carnegie work as an instructor in Kansas City in January 1951.*[183]

Dorothy learned a lot by going through the course herself, living with Carnegie and then running the Institute. She was a focused person with a strong personality, who always stated her opinions with resolve. She wrote about the essence of the course's methods:

> *We're concerned with helping people take off the layers of inhibition and repression, in removing all the barriers that lock the personality inside so it can't be free to express itself. We're interested in helping the individual to express himself to one or one million people, his boss or his wife; and to operate on the highest level of his own capabilities. We are fundamentally concerned with enabling people to communicate with each other, not only on a business level of speaking to groups, selling and presenting ideas clearly and forcefully, but on a personal and individual level also. The pace at which most of us live today, the competition and struggle, the mechanization of life – these seem to result in blunting our sense of individuality. We tend to think of ourselves as mere units in a large group rather than as free-speaking, free-thinking, strong and individual personalities. One reason for the tremendous success of our Dale Carnegie Course is our insistence on the importance of the individual. We work entirely on this fundamental principle –*

*that all of us are all different from each other, and that difference must be recognized and respected. Everyone has this vital core of individuality; it is up to us to help remove the wraps that swathe it so that it can shine out and be free to operate. When that happens, a person is communicating his thoughts, feelings, and ideas to others in his own highly personal and distinctive style. It is a great release of energy, strength and resources of personality which may have lain dormant and untapped.*[184]

Dorothy dedicated herself to the Dale Carnegie Course; she kept it active and alive even after Carnegie's death. In doing so, she allowed people to continue to benefit from the course, but she also perpetuated Carnegie's image. When speaking about her purpose in life, she shows how much she herself had evolved and matured through Carnegie's principles: *If you're going to get the most out of life and yourself, you must be a spiritual being; along with all the other things, you need to believe in yourself and other people. We try to help women have a definite aim about what they want out of life, to sharpen their goals, to pin themselves down. In the end, to stand and say, 'This is what I want out of life, and this is what I am doing to achieve my goal'.*[185]

When I think about Dorothy, I remember one of her most significant moments with Carnegie. He was already in his sixties and was agitated and bad-tempered from a visit that had not gone well. He paced throughout the house, becoming sadder with each lap. Dorothy raised an eyebrow and said: "Here comes the man that wrote The Book".[186] We will better understand why she said that later.

In 1951 Carnegie's only daughter, Donna Dale Carnegie, was born. Initially, Dorothy wanted to keep the pregnancy quiet and was upset when Carnegie, at the time traveling in Italy, couldn't contain himself and ended up announcing to the press that he would be a father for the first time.[187] He loved to take the baby out for walks. She remembered many of those walks, even though she lost her father when she was only three. She remembers visits to the farm in Missouri, where Carnegie went almost every month. She remembers eating ham while sitting in her father's lap, weeding with him in the garden, catching turtles to release in their garden, and a trip to Bermuda, where they stayed in a house with a beautiful porch and had picnics on the beach. In all the photos in which she appears with her father, Donna is smiling.[188] Years later, when her father was already gone, her features turned more serious. Dorothy passed away in 1988 and Donna took over as the President of the Board of the business. The course had been conducted in seventy countries, and more than two hundred permanent offices had been established. By this time, over six million people had passed through the Dale Carnegie Institute.

Appearing in a promotional CD-ROM for the Dale Carnegie Training, Donna Carnegie stated that the Course is still the foundation of the organization, and that Dale Carnegie's philosophy is considered to have had great impact on the twentieth century. She thanked the clients that left their 'comfort zone' to take the Course, and also those who work at the organization and fight daily to maintain the Course's excellence. As Head of the Board, she showed commitment to maintaining the spirit of the company created by her parents: *My father constantly looked to the future and was quick to adapt to new demands. We are continuing this work. As we move forward, I see a future with many possibilities and opportunities that allow us to grow together, keeping our traditions, but always open to new ideas.*[189]

## HOW TO ENTERTAIN STRANGERS

Relating to one's friends and family is one thing, dealing with strangers is another. But history shows that Carnegie talked freely with people he had just met, regardless of who they were. This habit made a lifelong impression on these people. When Harold Abbott met him for the first time he was very anxious, as Carnegie was already quite famous. Abbott describes the meeting, which took place on August 15th, 1941:

> He opened the door from his suite at the Stevens Hotel; stretched out his hand with a big smile and said: 'Come in, Harold. I am happy to see you, you look just like your photograph.' Instantly I was completely at ease and at home with him. Mr. Carnegie had the ability to make people at ease. Two weeks later, I went to work for him and started what turned out to be the most pleasant and exciting job a man could have had.
>
> Many people have asked me 'What kind of man was he? What was his personality like? How did he treat his employees?' In this aspect, I would have to say that he practiced what he preached. He was a very humane individual. He had his flaws. But courtesy and comprehension were only two of his many virtues. [190]

Carnegie made a huge number of acquaintances who considered themselves friends, and in a sense still do years after his death. People who read his books were grateful for what they learned; many who took the course expressed this in different ways. William Longgood, who dedicated himself to researching the course in the 1960's, says that every type of person took the course and, in the end, gave thrilled reports, from an ambassador who desperately needed to improve his speaking ability to students, teachers, employees and so many others who came to feel close to Carnegie as a person. Longgood himself attended the course and stated: *Some said they had gained tremendously from the training, others were more reserved; some said they had gained materially, others spiritually, some said they got both. Everyone said they had benefited in some way. Everyone agreed that it had been an enjoyable experience and they were sorry to see it end.*[191] The point is that of the thousands and even millions of people who benefited from Carnegie's work, certainly some of them realized the true dimensions of Carnegie's ideas. It is impossible to measure the true extent of how they benefited from the master's lessons, and the boundless results they reaped, but some of these fruits were recorded by Longgood, who related the emotions at the end of a course: *After the presentation of diplomas, Hugh Bigelow, the instructor, made a touching speech, recalling a scene from Thornton Wilder's* Our Town *when Emily, after dying, begged to be returned to life. Given her choice of when she wanted to live again, she picked her twelfth birthday, recalling how good it was just to be alive, to be aware of life and the little things which make up life.*

> "'Do any human beings ever realize life while they live it? – every, every minute?' Emily asked the stage manager. 'No,' he replied, and pausing, added, 'the saints and poets, maybe – they do some.'"

*Bigelow said that was what he had hoped the course had given to those who had just completed it – a sense of being alive. 'My hope is that you will go out of this course and realize your life,' he said. 'God bless you.'* [192]

# CHAPTER 6

## THE COINCIDENCES BETWEEN CARNEGIE AND LINCOLN; CARNEGIE'S RECIPE FOR WRITING A BIOGRAPHY

*Einstein had two rules of conduct.*
*The first: have no rules.*
*The second: be independent*
*of others' opinions.*
(Dale Carnegie)[193]

What do we gain by reading a biography? Well, if we consider the fact that biographies portray people who strongly impacted society, from military leaders (Julius Caesar), artists (Michelle Pfeiffer), and scientists (Isaac Newton) to politicians (Margaret Thatcher), then we should become familiar with their histories, and learn from their successes as well as their mistakes in order to apply these lessons to our own lives. For example: John D. Rockefeller was considered to be the richest man in the world. He had accumulated such a large fortune that he could have heated his home with furnaces burning dollar bills and would not have made a dent in his bank account. Yet he became so sick that even soup was too upsetting for his stomach. But why? Because of the worries he accumulated along with his fortune, while he was living only to make money. When he neared his fiftieth birthday and disease was threatening his life, his doctors prescribed three rules that he had to follow for the rest of his life if he wanted to stay alive: 1) Stress about nothing, no matter what happens; 2) Take light exercise outdoors and then rest; and 3) End a meal while still a bit hungry.[194] It is said that these three rules saved his life. So what can we learn from Rockefeller's life? We certainly can learn many lessons on how to make money, but we also can learn just as much from the missteps that brought him to such poor health, so poor that at one point he was only able to digest human breast milk and crackers. This is a good example of the impact biographies can have. By reading them, we can discover great recipes for success in the most varied areas of life such as work, sports, religion, philosophy, family, and ecology. But we must also study mistakes that were made. In Rockefeller's case, we see that his gravest mistake was neglecting his own well-being, abandoning simple joys like leisure, playing sports with friends, visiting loved ones, meeting interesting people, doing favors without expecting anything in return, etc. It is as important to learn about methods of success as it is to learn about how and why people failed. It is always important to keep in mind that we can find gems of wisdom to respect. When I read biographies, I think about how a conversation with this person might be if we got to know each other; this imaginary exercise helps me to see the person's life even more clearly.

It was one spring morning, while staying at the Dysart Hotel in London, that Carnegie looked for news of the United States in the *Morning Post* and had an epiphany about a piece he could write. T. P. O'Connor, the 'Father of the House of Commons', in that morning's paper had written an article titled *Men and Recollection* in which he wrote about some more interesting and less well-known aspects of Abraham Lincoln, such as his worries, his poverty, his successive political failures and his love for Ann Rutledge, as well as his dramatic marriage to Mary Todd.[195] This coincidental article pointed Carnegie toward a different path; he realized that Lincoln's fascinating personal details and political context had never been researched and explored at length. That was how Carnegie described the excitement he felt as he realized the possibilities: *I read the series with profound interest – and surprise. I had spent the first twenty years of my life in the Middle West, not far from the Lincoln country; and, in addition to that, I had always been keenly interested in United States history. I should have said that of course I knew Lincoln's life-story;*

*but I soon discovered that I didn't. The fact is that I, an American, had had to come to London and read a series of articles written by an Irishman, in an English newspaper, before I realized that the story of Lincoln's career was one of the most fascinating tales in all the annals of mankind.*[196]

When he realized how little he really knew about Lincoln, Carnegie decided to write a biography. He went to the library of the British Museum and began reading what he could find about Lincoln. So, what would Carnegie's biography of Lincoln be like? Carnegie knew that he was not the kind of author who would write a lengthy discourse, and in any case there were plenty of those already.[197] He aimed at those readers who did not want to become experts on Lincoln, but who wanted to be well informed in an objective way, learning the most important and profound details about the great statesman.[198] In Carnegie's words we can notice his preoccupation with the 'other' (in this case, the reader) and his or her needs: *... after reading many Lincoln volumes, I did feel that there was a genuine need for a short biography that would tell the most interesting facts about his career briefly and tersely for the average busy and hurried citizen of to-day. I have tried to write such a book.*[199] Carnegie's treatment of Lincoln is simple, clear, objective and interesting. When reading *Lincoln, the Unknown,* one gets the impression that Lincoln is an old acquaintance. The proximity to the great man that Carnegie creates is impressive. Besides just historical information about Lincoln, Carnegie also explained how he came to write the biography. I tried to explain his process because it is a priceless guide for anyone who intends to write a book, layman or expert, in a serious and original manner. On the other hand, what matters most is the effort and tenacity needed to carry out any mission or achieve any goal. It does not matter that Carnegie's biography of Lincoln did not have attain same success his other books did. What counts is the way the author faces his project: as a man clutching a rope preventing him from falling into the abyss. That brings profundity. If one isn't interested in doing things in depth, then why even bother? With that said, I will try to outline Carnegie's process for approaching this Everest of a biography:

## 1) READ VORACIOUSLY ON THE TOPIC

For a full year, Carnegie researched Lincoln in Europe, then researched two more years in the United States. He said that after three years of musty library air, he threw away all he had written and went to Illinois. But before we move any farther, let's think a little. Even though Carnegie thought he had wasted his time, it evidently was not a waste at all. At times, it seems that in-depth study does not bear any fruit, but this is just superficial, because in reality those who study and read eventually see results. A reader may not notice daily evolution and growth, just as we do not notice the air that we ceaselessly breathe. Einstein said that he would think about something ninety-nine times and not find an answer. He would stop thinking, go into a deep silence, and the answer would appear. Carnegie loaded his mind with valuable information so he could understand things better and leave the rest to his intuition. His own intuition led him to go deeper into the details of Lincoln's life.

## 2) KNOW THE SCENE: GET INVOLVED WITH THE TOPIC

Studying in depth and writing about another's ideas and principles naturally leads us to investigate milestones of the author's life, traumas suffered, and victories gained; the context in which he or she lived, and the influence this environment had upon him or her.

In my opinion, Carnegie fell in love with the topic. He saw that reading alone would not be enough to write a compelling account of Lincoln's life. So Carnegie spent months with people whose parents and grandparents had known Lincoln personally. He got to know them and got access to documents that added depth to these personal accounts.[200]

## 3) LET THE INFORMATION FLOW, AND LET INTUITION BRING THE ANSWERS

Every human being can take something positive away from Einstein's process of intuition. After reading, interviewing people, and exploring documents, Carnegie went even farther by spending time in places where Lincoln lived. He passed a whole summer in Petersburg, a town about a mile away from New Salem, a city that was fundamental in Lincoln's life; there, Lincoln worked as a blacksmith, studied law, met the only love of his life, and chose to follow a course that would place him among the great names of history.[201] The fact is that, through this process of investigation and trial and error, suddenly a harmony of words occurs and the text flows. Carnegie describes how he felt while writing, poetic words for those who wish to follow in his footsteps as authors:

*The same white oaks under which Lincoln studied and wrestled and made love are still standing. Every morning I used to take my typewriter and motor up there from Petersburg, and half of the chapters of this book were written under those trees. What a lovely spot in which to work! In front of me flowed the winding Sangamon, and all about me the woods and the hay-fields were musical with the call of the bob-white; and through the trees flashed the color of the blue jay, the yellowhammer, and the redbird. I felt Lincoln there.*

*I often used to go there alone on summer nights when the whip-poor-wills were crying in the woods along the banks of the Sangamon, when the moonlight outlined Rutledge's tavern against the sky; and it stirred me to realize that on just such nights, about a hundred years ago, young Abe Lincoln and Ann Rutledge had walked over this same ground arm in arm in the moonlight, listening to night-birds and dreaming ecstatic dreams that were destined never to come true. Yet, I am convinced that Lincoln found here at New Salem the only supreme happiness that he ever knew.*

*When I came to write the chapter dealing with the death of Lincoln's sweetheart, I put a little folding table and a typewriter in a car and drove out over country roads and through a hog lot and a cow pasture until I reached the quiet, secluded spot where Ann Rutledge lies buried. It is utterly abandoned now, and overgrown. To get near her grave, it was necessary to mow down the weeds and brush and vines. And there, where Lincoln came to weep, was set down the story of his grief.*

*Many of the chapters were written in Springfield. Some in the sitting-room of the old home where Lincoln lived sixteen unhappy years, some at the desk where he composed his first inaugural address, and others above the spot where he came to court and quarrel with Mary Todd.*[202]

## WHAT CARNEGIE AND LINCOLN HAD IN COMMON

It is necessary to talk about the incredible coincidences between Lincoln and Carnegie, especially at the time when Carnegie wrote Lincoln's biography. Looking at both their lives, I wonder if Carnegie felt moved to write about Lincoln in order to reevaluate his own existence. The first coincidence was clearly Lincoln's unhappy marriage to Mary Todd. The real love of his life, however, was Ann Rutledge, whom he met when he was a young man in New Salem. Lincoln waited for Ann to break a tormenting engagement to a swindler so that he could gain her hand in marriage. Carnegie masterfully described the lovers' encounter in the following way:

*For both of them, now, life had taken on a sacred tenderness, a new and strangely beautiful meaning. When*

*Lincoln but stood and looked down into Ann's blue eyes her heart sang within her; and at the mere touch of her hands he caught his breath and was amazed to discover that there was so much felicity in all the world...*[203]

So did Carnegie yearn for this happiness as well? While Carnegie was writing these romantic words, he was suffering through his own disastrous first marriage. After this bliss Carnegie describes, Lincoln decided to become a lawyer and planned to marry Ann Rutledge just as soon as he could establish himself as an attorney.[204] But both struggled with financial problems, with Ann taking a job in a farm kitchen, and Lincoln working as a plowman on the same farm. Carnegie described Lincoln: *In the evening he stood in the kitchen wiping the dishes which Ann washed. He was filled with a vast happiness at the very thought of being near her. Never again was he to experience such rapture and such content. Shortly before his death he confessed to a friend that he had been happier as a barefoot farm laborer back in Illinois than he had ever been in the White House.*[205] But storm clouds were gathering; Ann began to feel tired and queasy, and then fell ill. She had typhoid fever, and to make matters worse, she was treated according to the treatment of the day, exactly contrary to today's standard of care.[206] Ann Rutledge passed away shortly after becoming engaged to Lincoln, and she desperately called his name during her agony. Lincoln was almost out of his mind with grief, nearly giving up on life, but somehow managed to survive. His survival came at a high price, however, as he became a mournful, melancholic and truly somber person until the end of his life. Even the poetry he memorized was tormented.[207] However, Lincoln moved on, getting his degree in law and beginning his career as an attorney in Springfield in March, 1837. In 1839, Lincoln had the great misfortune of meeting Mary Todd, and according to Carnegie, the resulting suffering would continue to the end of his days. They became engaged, and were to be married on January 1, 1914, but Lincoln did not appear at the ceremony[208]; two years later, he married Mary Todd. On the way to the church, someone asked Lincoln where he was going. Lincoln replied: *To hell, I suppose.* And it seems that he was right, according to Carnegie's portrait. It appears that she was a woman who suffered immensely, and did not have the supports she needed to help her deal with her own mental and emotional issues. While I don't believe Mary can be held entirely responsible for Lincoln's unhappiness, many said that the biggest tragedy in Lincoln's life (after Ann's death) wasn't the great war, but his own wedding, after which both partners probably pushed each other closer to the edge of insanity. Eventually, Mary Todd's mental health decayed, most intensely in her widowhood, until her last years were spent in misery and abandonment. At her own son Robert's request, she was judged insane and committed to an institution; a year later she was released, but continued to struggle with mental illness until her death.[209]

As mentioned earlier, Lincoln's extreme unhappiness with Mary Todd seemed to have encouraged Carnegie's research; as we remember, Carnegie also had an unsuccessful marriage to Lolita Baucaire, whom he met during one of his trips to Europe. The ten years between his marriage in 1921 and his divorce are not well documented, but Carnegie's second wife Dorothy reported him saying that there was no happiness in the ten years he was married to Lolita Baucaire. Coincidentally, by the end of his marriage to Lolita, Carnegie was writing Lincoln's biography, highlighting Lincoln's unhappy married life. In 1937, Carnegie was interviewed on this subject, and he mentioned that the book about Lincoln could be seen as autobiographical.[210] I wonder if Carnegie's research about Lincoln's long-suffering marriage did not bring him to re-evaluate his own unsuccessful relationship.

Another common point in both men's lives was extreme poverty. Misery makes the distant past seem closer, and the need to fight for survival carries easily from one generation to the next. Hardship and violent need, when handled well, turn human beings into demigods. Victor Hugo describes Rabelais, the courageous

Parisian street urchin, fearful of nothing, who ... *scorns superstition, deflates exaggeration, laughs at mystery, sticks out his tongue at ghosts, brings pretension down to earth, caricatures the over-blown epic.*[211] The young Rabelais is so courageous that his exclamation, upon seeing a great monster before him, would be a smiling *Well, hello, boogeyman!*[212] But if asked from whence Rabelais came, the great city Paris would claim him as its very own.[213]

Poverty can make a human being stronger, if he can conquer it and accept it as a companion. But this process is almost as hard as faking madness: there can be no ceasing when trying to deceive pain, whether bodily pain or the pain of the soul. But poverty has its way. Those who can find in poverty an indescribable state of freedom, because destiny is free. Those who live or have lived with this awareness can more deeply comprehend this than others who lack the experience. Lincoln lived a life of extreme poverty and instability very similar to Carnegie's own; his first fourteen years of life were spent in the deep woods, where one could not walk a yard without tripping over vines, or being scratched to shreds by branches and thorns. According to Carnegie, Lincoln was able to handle poverty like no other, not even the slaves he would one day free.[214] In his childhood home, there was no milk, eggs or bread: Lincoln's meals in Indiana were hunted game and gathered walnuts. Perhaps the wild and ruthless nature of Lincoln's country home was the same cruel nature that Jack London saw in his nightmares.

Another characteristic common to both Lincoln and Carnegie was a tireless individual search for answers that went far beyond standard education. Lincoln did not finish his education for a long time, but taught himself from borrowed books. His step-mother gave him five books that he read avidly: the Holy Bible, *Aesop's Fables, Robinson Crusoe, The Pilgrim's Progress* and *Sindbad the Sailor.*[215] He soon became a fanatic reader, devouring everything from the Indiana Civil Code to the United States Declaration of Independence and Constitution; he also read Washington's life (written by Parson Weems). Lincoln became known for the poetry and speeches he made and for his unique oratory style: any similarity to Carnegie? Carnegie highlighted Lincoln's interest in speeches and public speakers: *But in all his book-borrowing expeditions, he never made a richer find than Scott's Lessons. This book gave him instruction in public speaking, and introduced him to the renowned speeches of Cicero and Demosthenes and those of Shakespeare's characters.*[216]

Lincoln worked in the fields early in his life; when his horses stopped to rest, he read, diving into a world of imagination and dreams. He walked over twelve miles to listen to lawyers' debates and Baptist preachers; when he returned to his work, he repeated the speeches to the field hands[217] and the animals, just as Carnegie would himself do. Another interesting fact: just as Carnegie felt compelled to study and describe Lincoln's life, Lincoln too admired self-educated authors who did not attend school: Robert Burns and Shakespeare.[218] When he describes Lincoln's struggles to learn and advance intellectually, Carnegie seems to be describing his own life:

> *On his way home he carried an open book in one hand, studying as he walked. When he struck a knotty passage, he shuffled to a standstill, and concentrated on it until he had mastered the sense. He kept on studying, until he had conquered twenty or thirty pages, kept on until dusk fell and he could no longer see to read.... The stars came out, he was hungry, he hastened his pace. He pored over his books now incessantly, having heart for little else.*"[219]

Lincoln was constantly caught reading in the most unusual places: at the top of a stack of firewood, during walks through the woods. He would read out loud, check that he had understood, and continue to attack the topic until he understood it well. When a teacher by the name of Graham told him that he would need to learn grammar in order to progress towards his goal of studying law, Lincoln traveled miles to borrow a grammar book from Kirkham. He studied long hours to learn the best way to turn a phrase. Like Carnegie, Lincoln studied the biographies of Jefferson, Clay, Webster and characters of ancient history and the Roman Empire.[220] After all, who could describe their lives better than those who had lived through similar hardships? As you can see, both Carnegie and Lincoln showed that personal achievement came only through a strong will to learn and a strong desire to win, even despite their not traveling a traditional path, and especially in the face of enormous personal or circumstantial obstacles. At this moment, I think of the stutterer Demosthenes... Thomas Edison, Isaac Newton... in Brazil, Garrincha, one of the greatest soccer players, whose doctor told his mother that her son would never walk...

Carnegie also expressed his opinion about the exaggerations and hostility that provoked the Civil War, demonstrating that his teachings about individual moderation could also be applied to international relations:

> And what was the result of this well-meant but fanatical campaign of overstatement waged by the Abolitionists of the North? Did it convince the Southerners that they were wrong? Far from it. The effect was such as might have been expected. The hatred stirred up by the Abolitionists did what hatred always does: it bred hatred in return. It made the South wish to part company with its insolent, meddle-some critics. Truth seldom flourishes in an atmosphere of politics or of emotion, and on both sides of the Mason and Dixon's Line tragic error had grown to its bloody blossom time.[221]

By analyzing Lincoln's countless defeats, for example, in successive elections that he lost and then later during the war, Carnegie seemed to use a reflection of himself to describe the President of the United States:

> Failure and defeat were not new experiences to Lincoln. He had known them all his life; they did not crush him; his faith in the ultimate triumph of his cause remained firm, his confidence

*unshaken. He went among the disheartened soldiers, shaking hands with them, and saying over and over: "God bless you. God bless you." He cheered them, sat down and ate beans with them, revived their drooping spirits, and talked of brighter tomorrows.*[222]

Another observation that Carnegie made about Lincoln was that we all make impressive mistakes while evaluating ourselves; we usually underestimate our own value, or we believe we didn't do as well as we could have, when in reality we lose sight of how big an impact we can have on tasks and situations. It is not rare for people to be surprised by recognition they never thought they could deserve, let alone receive. Let us look at an example of the real repercussions and value of our actions, and our constant feelings of limitations imposed by non-ideal working conditions; who doesn't frequently complain about lack of time for study, or a lack of this or that. Does anyone, anywhere, have a life in which everything happens just the way it should? It seems as if nature is more intelligent than we are considering things that should be done. We trip over a rock and think that things are going badly, but that fall enables us to see a pot of gold we would have missed had we not fallen. In this spirit, one of the best-known and most stirring speeches ever given was considered by Lincoln to be his worst, as we will see.

In the spring of 1863, the Confederate army led by General Lee was winning battle after battle and, feeling confident enough to expand outward, moved seventy-five thousand men across the Potomac River into Pennsylvania.[223] When the artillery moved forward to Harrisburg, the Union army attacked the Confederate lines of communication, causing Lee to fall back and the army to regroup in the small village of Gettysburg. Here in Gettysburg, the most important battle in the United States took place. Twenty thousand Union troops perished on the first day, victims of General Lee's new plan: attack and crush the Union troops in an open field. General Longstreet did not agree with the plan, which to him went counter to Lee's expectations. They would have to go forward through fences, over hills and other obstacles for a mile until they reached Union lines.[224] After saying that in his Army, a soldier would never fall back and would follow any order given, Lee assigned General George Pickett to take over the mission.[225] Carnegie's perfect narrative of the battle deserves to be fully reproduced here:

> Pickett's troops swept forward at an easy trot, through an orchard and corn-field, across a meadow, and over a ravine. All the time, the enemy's cannon were tearing ghastly holes in their ranks. But on they pressed, grim, irresistible.
>
> Suddenly the Union infantry rose from behind the stone wall on Cemetery Ridge where they had been hiding, and fired volley after volley into Pickett's defenseless troops. The crest of the hill was a sheet of flame, a slaughter-house, a blazing volcano. In a few minutes, all of Pickett's brigade commanders, except one, were down, and four fifths of his five thousand men had fallen.[226]

The next fall, local government decided to pay homage to the dead at the new cemetery where the war dead were buried, and invited the most famous speaker of the day, Edward Everett, to deliver a speech. Invitations were sent to many other important personalities, but response was weak. The President had been invited but was not expected to attend. But Lincoln decided to go. One of the motives mentioned by Carnegie was that he wanted to dispel current newspaper reports that he made jokes while fallen soldiers were being buried. Carnegie explained the incident very well, demonstrating that lighthearted dialogues between Ward Hill Lamon and Lincoln were not related to the war in any way.[227] Lincoln saw the ceremony as the perfect opportunity to confront criticism while paying homage to the dead. However, Lincoln had very little time to prepare his speech, which he intended to project sentimental value. I will again cite Carnegie's narration of the event, specifically noting Carnegie's attention to the two speeches, a natural point of interest for such a master of public speaking:

*Edward Everett, the selected orator of the occasion, made two mistakes at Gettysburg. Both bad—and both uncalled for. First, he arrived an hour late; and, secondly, he spoke for two hours.*

*Lincoln had read Everett's Oration and when he saw that the speaker was nearing his close, he knew his time was coming, and he honestly felt that he wasn't adequately prepared; so he grew nervous, twisted in his chair, drew his manuscript from the pocket of his Prince Albert coat, put on his old-fashioned glasses, and quickly refreshed his memory.*

*Presently he stepped forward, manuscript in hand, and delivered his little address in two minutes.*

*Did his audience realize, that soft November afternoon, that they were listening to the greatest speech that had ever fallen from human lips up to that time? No, most of his hearers were merely curious: they had never seen nor heard a President of the United States, they strained their necks to look at Lincoln, and were surprised to discover that such a tall man had such a high, thin voice, and that he spoke with a Southern accent. They had forgotten that he was born a Kentuckian and that he had retained the intonation of his native State; and about the time they felt he was getting through with his introduction and ready to launch into his speech—he sat down.*

*What! Had he forgotten? Or was it really all he had to say? People were too surprised and disappointed to applaud.*

*Many a spring, back in Indiana, Lincoln had tried to break ground with a rusty plow; but the soil had stuck to its mold-board, and made a mess. It wouldn't "scour." That was the term people used. Throughout his life, when Lincoln wanted to indicate that a thing had failed, he frequently resorted to the phraseology of the corn-field. Turning now to Ward Lamon, Lincoln said: "That speech is a flat failure, Lamon. It won't scour. The people are disappointed." He was right. Every one was disappointed, including Edward Everett and Secretary Seward, who were sitting on the platform with the President. They both believed he had failed woefully; and both felt sorry for him.*

*Lincoln was so distressed that he worried himself into a severe headache; and on the way back to Washington, he had to lie down in the drawing-room of the train and have his head bathed with cold water.*

*Lincoln went to his grave believing that he had failed utterly at Gettysburg. And he had, as far as the immediate effect of his speech was concerned. With characteristic modesty, he sincerely felt that the world would "little note nor long remember" what he said there, but that it would never forget what the brave men who died had done there. How surprised he would be if he should come back to life now and realize that the speech of his that most people remember is the one that didn't "scour" at Gettysburg! How amazed he would be to discover that the ten immortal sentences he spoke there will probably be cherished as one of the literary glories and treasures of earth centuries hence, long after the Civil War is all but forgotten.*

*Lincoln's Gettysburg address is more than a speech. It is the divine expression of a rare soul exalted and made great by suffering. It is an unconscious prose poem, and has all the majestic beauty and profound roll of epic lines.*[228]

At this point, I can't help but include Abraham Lincoln's original speech, as perfect as Carnegie's comments are, one master text that brought about another:

*Four score and seven years ago our fathers brought forth on this continent a new nation, conceived in liberty, and dedicated to the proposition that all men are created equal.*

*Now we are engaged in a great civil war, testing whether that nation, or any nation, so conceived and so dedicated, can long endure. We are met on a great battle-field of that war. We have come to dedicate a portion of that field, as a final resting place for those who here gave their lives that that nation might live. It is altogether fitting and proper that we should do this.*

But, in a larger sense, we can not dedicate, we can not consecrate, we can not hallow this ground. The brave men, living and dead, who struggled here, have consecrated it, far above our poor power to add or detract. The world will little note, nor long remember what we say here, but it can never forget what they did here. It is for us the living, rather, to be dedicated here to the unfinished work which they who fought here have thus far so nobly advanced. It is rather for us to be here dedicated to the great task remaining before us—that from these honored dead we take increased devotion to that cause for which they gave the last full measure of devotion—that we here highly resolve that these dead shall not have died in vain—that this nation, under God, shall have a new birth of freedom—and that government of the people, by the people, for the people, shall not perish from the earth.

# CHAPTER 7

## WHAT CAN BE EXPECTED FROM A GREAT PUBLIC SPEAKER?

*One day George S. Foster, who was a student and instructor*
*of the Course, asked Carnegie what was most important to effective*
*speaking and he responded with no hesitation:*
*"The subject, because without the right subject, no amount of oratory will*
*save it, but with the right subject, the talk makes itself."*
(Rosemary Crom)[229]

In 1984 I lived in Curitiba, a city in southern Brazil, and anxiety had its claws well into me. I was sixteen years old at the time, and had just decided to run for class president at my school, Marista Santa Maria. The school had just moved to its new location, and the imposing building seemed to represent my own imposing challenge: to speak to my class and be chosen as the best candidate. This was when I bought my first copy of Dale Carnegie's *Public Speaking and Influencing Men in Business.* According to *Current Biography,* this book originated from pamphlets summarizing the oratory principles taught in Carnegie's course.[230] In reality, the process of writing the book was more complex; in the book, Carnegie states that he originally began by compiling books on public speaking, but then abandoned the idea and developed his own book.

I cannot remember how I found his book, which was to change my course in life. I do not have my original copy, for through the years I got into the habit of giving books to close friends. After I read *Public Speaking,* I made my stump speech to my classmates; there was a noticeable difference in my mode of expression after reading the text. The feeling was indescribable. The book had the power to completely change the way in which I expressed myself. This new natural way of speaking enabled the first of many victories brought about by good expressive ability: class president, high school valedictorian, winner of the traditional academic "Jury" prize while studying law at The Universidade Federal do Paraná.[231] During my five-year course in law, I saw that a course in public speaking was to be taught by Father Marcelo Motta Carneiro; I enrolled immediately. I had learned one of Carnegie's lessons: the importance of constantly seeking to improve and make personal progress. Professor Motta's course was very good. At the end of the first lesson I went to talk to the Professor about Carnegie's book: his response? "Carnegie's book *Public Speaking* is excellent, and it is also one of the texts I recommend to my students."[232] It is very common to find references to *Public Speaking* in important books or courses on self-expression.[233] Later on, from a field of seven candidates, I was elected class valedictorian, and gave the farewell address at my graduation from the school of law at the Universidade Federal do Paraná in 1991. Two years after receiving my bachelor's degree in law, I saw an advertisement in the newspaper seeking law teachers for a test-preparation school. The next morning, I went to talk to the director of the school. He asked me to prepare myself to give a lecture the following month, when the selection would be held. I replied that there was no need to wait, I could teach the class at that very moment. Surprised, he agreed, and after the my demonstration class, I found myself teaching the night class in my first job as a teacher... These career achievements may be simple, but they were important to me. I assure you that none of these accomplishments could have happened without the contribution of Dale Carnegie. Our lives depend, for the most part, on the masters who teach us. They cast the light that illuminates the path to our personal conquests, benefiting not only us, but our communities as well.

How can we define a visionary? The dictionary defines a visionary as a person with imaginative ideas.[234] Dale Carnegie was, without a doubt, a visionary. Just like the fisherman Santiago, in Hemingway's *The Old Man and the Sea* wants to escape the monotony of life in his fishing village[235], Dale Carnegie always tried to go beyond the boring routine of school work. While Albert Einstein revolutionized physics by going beyond Newton's formulas, Carnegie revolutionized the way we find solutions in our boring lives, in relationships with people, in making adequate communication with others possible. Carnegie made unparalleled contributions to the art of communication. One could say that he democratized the ability to speak in public; indeed, by following his principles, one is confident speaking anywhere, on the phone, in a job interview, in a quick conversation with a future love, while proposing a business deal. To Carnegie, *good public speakers are good at almost everything.*[236] By learning to speak in public, we develop our personalities. *Public speaking,* to Carnegie, was *the high road to self-confidence, which in turn is the key to making friends and influencing people.*[237] While he spread his ideas, he came to be known for putting them into immediate practice. A Turkish man visiting America in order to purchase locomotives enrolled in the course, became infatuated with it, and decided to bring it to Turkey. Many other foreigners did the same. The phrase that seemed to be the motto of many course presentations – 'people come to scoff and stay to pray'- was constantly confirmed. The journalist Collie Small, who conducted a long interview with Carnegie, stated that some of the biggest industries in the United States, including Hollywood, would send their executives to visit and get opinions from Carnegie. According to Small, a *... former mayor of Baltimore, the president of a large shoe company, and the manager of one of the world's greatest hotels have taken the Carnegie course. The Coast Guard currently has several high-ranking officers enrolled; there is a United States Army general taking the course...*[238] Small went on to cite people from the four corners of the earth who benefited from the course, everyone from missionaries from Africa to a diplomat who wanted to become an ambassador. People arrived with all kinds of fears and blocks, some who fainted in front of a small audience, but Carnegie energetically assured them that they would improve, and they did.

From his youth, Carnegie exhibited interest and success in teaching his classmates techniques for improved public speaking. Carnegie's career as a public speaking teacher started at the 125th Street YMCA in New York, in 1912. He began his writing career in 1915, when he and J. Berg Esenwein published *The Art of Public Speaking,* which corresponded with the course and the needs of its participants. After gaining more practical knowledge and experience, Carnegie alone published *Public Speaking: a Practical Course for Business Men* in 1926; this book also was meant as an accompaniment to the course. As Dorothy Carnegie explained, the course was directed not towards "the giant of the pulpit", but instead towards the salesperson or average professional *... who merely desires to express themselves more easily and self-confidence in his own medium, could not afford to waste time or money studying the mechanics of words, diction, oratory rules and the art of gesticulation. The Dale Carnegie courses about how to speak efficiently had instant success because they gave these men the results they desired.*[239] In this book, recommended even to those who have no intention of becoming public speakers, what we find is the basis of all efficient communications, simple and solid rules that we cannot break, without risk of misunderstanding. Beyond this, Carnegie was always innovating and bringing forward new resources that really favored the spoken word. I will cite an example to better explain. Nowadays there are many great books on personal motivation that are based on focus and guided visualization of goals. This type of literature shows that positive thinking help us make favorable changes in our lives.[240] Carnegie uses the same technique in a passage from *Public Speaking*, in which he basically hypnotizes the reader to be successful in public presentations: *Now, reader, start to imagine yourself in front of an audience to which you were called to speak. See yourself going forward confidently, notice the silence when you start to talk, feel the* *alert absorption of the audience as you get closer to your goal, relish on the warmth of the applause when you come down from the stage and listen to the words of appreciation the individual members of the audience greets you when the lecture ends. Believe me, there is a true magic in all this, an excitement that will never be forgotten.*

One of Carnegie's main secrets to efficient communication is: talk about a subject you know well, from personal experience. By doing so, we can talk with propriety and conviction. In one of the courses, a student of chemical engineering spoke unsuccessfully on the topic of Bolshevism. Carnegie commented that the student's mistake was that he was as afraid of Bolshevism as he was afraid of the boogeyman. Carnegie then advised the student to talk about something he knew well. The student then proceeded to give a great presentation on sulfuric acid, showing the audience how chemical compounds are used everyday products like toothbrushes, razor blades, clothes, cars, books, etc.[241] This sounds simple and obvious, but it is not. Many people seize up when talking in public and have difficulty choosing a subject. To demonstrate the precision with which Carnegie treats the topic, I selected a few snippets from an article he wrote for *Coronet* magazine in 1941. I ask the reader to observe the precision of the words he uses to explain the principle, and the clarity of his ideas. The simplicity of his writing style should be a model for all writers. At the time of writing, Carnegie was over sixty years of age and his intellectual vigor is impressive:

> *Don't spend ten minutes or ten hours preparing a talk. Spend ten years. Don't attempt to speak about anything until you have earned the right to talk about it through long study or experience. Talk about something that you know, and you know that you know. Talk about something that has aroused your interest. Talk about something that you have a deep desire to communicate to your listeners ...*

*You are prepared right now to make at least a dozen good talks – talks that no one else on earth could make except you, because no one else has ever had precisely the same experiences. What are these subjects? I don't know. But you do. So carry a sheet of paper with you for a few weeks and write down, as you think of them, all the subjects that you are now prepared to talk about through experience – topics such as 'The Biggest Regret of My Life', 'My Biggest Ambition' and, 'Why I Liked (or Disliked) School'. You will be surprised how quickly this list will grow.*

*Talking about your own experiences is obviously the quickest way to develop courage and self-confidence...*

*Take something simple, something that came from an idea that got to you, instead of you getting the idea. Once you begin looking for topics for talks, you will find them everywhere – in the home, the office, the street.*[242]

But what if we have to give a talk on a subject we don't really know much about? Carnegie discussed this with Ida Tarbell, one of the most distinguished American biographers – another confirmation of the value Carnegie placed on biographies. While Ida lived in London, she took on an assignment from McClure's Magazine to write a two-page article about the transatlantic cable. She then interviewed the manager of Atlantic Telegraph, who had already given her permission to write on the topic. But Carnegie saw that she did not stop there; she researched any and all articles or books she could find at the British Museum Library on the topic of marine telegraphy. She also read the biography of Cyrus West Field, who had been responsible for placing telegraph cables in the Atlantic. She also observed exhibits related to the subject at the British Museum. Finally, she visited a factory in the London metropolitan area to see how the telegraph wires were made. Ida Tarbell described her process in Carnegie's words: *I had enough material to write a small book. But that vast amount of material which I had and did not use enabled me to write what I did write with confidence and clarity and interest. It gave me reserve power*[243]. Imagine that, to do all that just to be able to feel honestly confident enough to write two pages about an unfamiliar subject. Carnegie concluded: *Ida Tarbell had learned through years of experience that she had to earn the right to write even 500 words. The same principle goes for speaking. Make yourself something of an authority on your subject. Develop that priceless asset known as reserve power.*[244] It is interesting to see how Carnegie worked with the inductive method, which is to say that from some cases he would extract general principles, enough to prepare a text or even talk in public. It is worthwhile to see one more usage of this fantastic technique to prepare lectures or debates. The biography we look at now is that of Will Rogers, who was the star of a famous Sunday night radio show in an era before television and computers, when the radio was the most wide-reaching and important means of communication. Will Rogers' preparation for a show aimed at such a wide audience was done over an entire week, and he practiced his discourses in his daily life with friends or acquaintances. He was able to test his jokes and debate themes and see if his audience enjoyed them or took interest. To Will Rogers, this was a good way to select his topics and rehearse. Going against the traditional oratory of measured gestures, Carnegie concludes: "That is an infinitely better way to rehearse a speech than trying it out with gestures in front of the bathroom mirror."[245]

Some of the precepts of *Public Speaking* show that Carnegie had an exceptional ability to  see the other. When we reject or fail to understand someone, it could be said that the "sensor" that enables us to see the other is not functioning. But if we want to see beyond our own nose, we need to see the other. A whole philosophy utilizes this perspective, this recognition of the other. Christ was a pioneer of this philosophy, through his teaching that we should do unto others what we would have done to us. John Rawls developed a theory of justice quite similar to the Christian principle: basically, a position is predetermined for each member of society, from poorest to richest, without any foreknowledge of what they will get. In this way, minimal freedoms, opportunities, rights, belongings are provided for, but all must be compatible with the rights of the other, and only in this way can inequality be balanced and opportunity created for all.[246] In Charriere's work *Papillon,* when the main character arrived at the penal settlement's leper colony on Pigeon Island, he showed what a respectful dialogue can be like, an example of seeing another as if seeing oneself. Allow me to transcribe a passage from one of my works about this fascinating interplay:

> *There can clearly be seen a dialog between the stigmatized: Papillon – publicly despised, a convict, outsider and outlaw – who seeks shelter with his friends Clousiot (wounded) and Maturette (completely effeminate[247]) at the leper colony. The lepers live on an isolated island, visited by almost no one,[248] which keeps them isolated from the rest of the world just as stigmatized people live in general. They are outsiders of all races and creeds who suffered received commonplace aggressions. At this point, there are two groups of stigmatized people, the ones led by Papillon on one side, and on the other side, those who follow Toussaint.[249] In a situation like this one, which could easily represent many situations predominant in the world[250] and the possibility of anyone being stigmatized, a conflict is to be expected.  At least according to what usually happens, it is to be expected, but that is not what happens on Pigeon Island. It is because Papillon refuses to arrive armed for a talk with the  island's inhabitants, his close physical approximation on meeting them, and because of his responses when questioned about his opinion on the crimes – marks/stigmas – committed by the lepers, that Papillon creates a trusting relationship.  Instead of censuring them, he sympathizes with them, taking advantage of his own comprehensive attitude.*

*But the closeness increases still when they share coffee and cigars, and Papillon has the courage to live with the stigmatized, treating them equally and seeing himself their place, as someone who wished others would act with respect in such a situation. "It looks as if they were the ones who would run from us."[251] "..." "And the lepers of Pigeon Island! Those wretched convicts struck with such a terrible illness, who still found the nobility in their hearts to help us!"[252]*

*The result of this dialog and unusual social event could not be more illustrative: Papillon received from the lepers ('the others') all the resources he needed to continue his journey.[253] "It was odd, but not one of us mentioned the lepers' terrible deformities. We talked only of their kindness, their generosity and honesty, and our luck in meeting the Masked Breton."[254][255]*

One of the demonstrations of Carnegie's capacity to 'see the other' is noticed at the beginning of the public speaking book: *... we would like speakers to talk with us and not speak to us.*[256] Throughout the book, respect for the audience is taught, and the means for arriving at respect for the audience: only by putting oneself in the audience's place: *If you, with your speech,* says Carnegie, *add too many details, your audience will eliminate your observations, refusing to give their complete attention. And, for the one who is speaking, there is nothing graver than lack of attention.*[257] Another of Carnegie's conclusions reveals his belief in the authenticity of discourse, belief in what the speaker is talking about: *If the person that is talking believes in something with enough sincerity and refers to it with enough sincerity, there will be support to his cause, even if he states he can produce grass out of walnut ashes. Our convictions would be more compulsive if they were put beside common sense and the truth.*[258] Seeing the other is sharing all the contents of the speech with the other, because *... successful communication depends on how much the speaker can do for his words to be a part of his listeners, and them* *a part of his words.*[259] Carnegie's precepts on public speaking are full of references to interaction with the other: *have an honest and sincere appreciation*"[260], *identify yourself with the audience*[261], *make the audience participate in your lecture*[262], *be humble*[263], *cite the advantage the audience can expect*[264], *use visual aids*[265], *earn trust, making yourself deserving of it*[266], *talk with contagious enthusiasm*[267], *show respect and affection to your audience*[268], *start out friendly*[269], *don't try to imitate others, be yourself*[270], *talk to the audience*[271], *put your heart into what you say*[272], *be warmly sincere*[273], *prepare your presentation with care*[274], *express your sincere feelings*[275], etc. As you can see, Carnegie's humanistic sentiment is natural, persistent, and symptomatic in his thoughts. When you dedicate your valuable time and attention to listening to someone, you give them credit, and this provokes a necessary question: how would you like the speaker to act? Wouldn't it be the same way Carnegie proposes? So, in truth, *Public Speaking* is not only a book for public speakers, but especially for listeners! It is a book that can aid all types of listeners, teaching speakers to respect their audiences.

Carnegie's secret to showing his thoughts well seems to be in the passion with which he writes and his close involvement with the reader. He really seems to be seeing himself in the reader's shoes and, even more, his text feels like a sincere conversation with himself which he started from the reader's point of view, giving a sensation of closeness and sincerity. As a side note, the word 'sincerity' comes from a curious Roman context. According to legend, the towers of tall roman buildings often showed small imperfections, which were covered with thin layers of wax. Accordingly, when one was asked to not cover one's faults, or to show work as it really was, one was asked to show it *sine cera* or without wax, which evolved to the modern words 'sincere' and 'sincerity'.[276] Carnegie expressed himself *sine cera*, directly and, in open dialog; he avoided any of the superiority often seen by writers, some of whom would appear to see themselves as coming down from on high to enlighten poor mortals. Carnegie avoids this trap, knowing that nobody likes to be patronized, but as his *sine cera* goal is learning, developing, and progress (of people in general and also himself, of course due to his ability to place himself in the same location as the reader) he leaves the wax off of his writing and speech, which is one of the reasons why his style is so involving, persuasive and frank. Of course, this attitude permeates his lessons; we can see it, for example, in the passage of *Public Speaking* where Carnegie recommends against memorizing speeches. *If we memorize word by word what we are going to say, we will probably forget when we stand in front of our listeners...*[277], he said. But if we really think about it, preparing a memorized speech stops us from feeling the moment, from opening our hearts to the opportunity as well as the people to whom we speak. Of course, it goes without saying that the subject must be well prepared and ideas well organized; good preparation is a prerequisite for a good speech. Carnegie said *... only the prepared speaker deserves to be confident. How can someone think about attacking the fortress if they go into combat with obsolete weapons or no ammunition? 'I believe', said Lincoln, 'that I will never be old enough to talk with promptitude, when I have nothing to say.'*[278] But if we again pay close attention, isn't Carnegie saying that speakers cannot lie or be insincere? You are not supposed to lie, be fake, talk about something you don't believe in or try to fool people. Only the truth prevails. This shows Carnegie's public and social commitments; he doesn't want to provide people with the tools to trick or manipulate others. No! He does not intend to prepare a method without worrying about the end results. This responsibility, seen throughout all his writing, shows the stability of his character: *Especially when the goal of our talk is to convince, it is necessary to temper our own ideas with the intimate blaze that emanates from the sincere conviction. We need first to be convinced, before trying to convince others.*[279] Carnegie's warning explains a lot: *Above all, remember this: acting with sincerity, you will feel sincere.*[280]

Good public speaking is a step beyond speaking well face-to-face, but certainly the rules of oratory found in Carnegie's books can also be applied to individual conversation. It just so happens that Carnegie also created a milestone for human relations with another of his works: *How to Win Friends and Influence People*[281]. Yes, we can win friends, as we will see next.

# CHAPTER 8

## HOW CAN WE MAKE FRIENDS? THE SECRET TO SUCCESS!

*There is an ecstasy that marks the summit of life, and beyond which life cannot rise. And such is the paradox of living, this ecstasy comes when one is most alive, and it comes as a complete forgetfulness that one is alive. This ecstasy, this forgetfulness of living, comes to the artist, caught up and out of himself in a sheet of flame; it comes to the soldier, war-mad on a stricken field and refusing quarter; and it came to Buck, leading the pack, sounding the old wolf-cry, straining after the food that was alive and that fled swiftly before him through the moonlight. He was sounding the deeps of his nature, and of the parts of his nature that were deeper than he, going back into the womb of Time.*

*(Jack London)*[282]

Cecilia approaches the counter at a well known New York coffee house. She is surrounded by a circle of admirers, all of whom fight for a place near her; she seems to be a magnet for friends, confidants and suitors. At the other end of the counter we have Francine, who leads a solitary life, no fun and no friends. If we could see them through a magic telescope, we would see that while Cecilia has the habit of smiling at others and sparing them her complaints, she really takes interest in the lives of those who are close to her, listening to what they have to say. On the other hand, Francine is egocentric, thinking that the world revolves around her, that everything in the world happens because of her. Worse, she doesn't yet know the basic root of true friendship: it goes both ways. If we ask friends for favors, we certainly have to help them and be useful to them in return. If you studied in the same class as Francine and Cecilia, either one might ask to borrow your notebook; but only Cecilia would call to thank you and invite you out with her friends, or take you out for a coffee, or wish you a happy birthday. Francine would probably also call you, but the call would likely be a request for another favor...

Situations like these appear in *How to Win Friends and Influence People,* a book that by its very title promises many benefits to the reader. We are naturally suspicious of promises made in books, in stores, or even personally. *How to Win Friends* makes some promises at the beginning, but its promises are modest, taking individual potential into consideration:

"EIGHT THINGS THIS BOOK WILL HELP YOU ACHIEVE
1. Get out of a mental rut, think new thoughts, acquire new visions, discover new ambitions;
2. Make friends quickly and easily;
3. Increase your popularity;
4. Win people to your way of thinking;
5. Increase your influence, your prestige, your ability to get things done;
6. Handle complaints, avoid arguments, keep your human contacts smooth and pleasant;
7. Become a better speaker, a more entertaining conversationalist;
8. Arouse enthusiasm among your associates.

This book has done all these things for more than ten million readers in thirty-six languages."

Let's admit it: if we knew that one book could bring all these benefits, we would read it, wouldn't we? So I can say that this is an indispensable book. Reading it won't necessarily give you immediate and automatic perfection in the art of dealing with people, but if you can follow its precepts, you can certainly acquire more human behavior, and why not, a better public image. At the very least, you will know when your observations are mistaken, which is already an improvement, since recognizing mistakes is the first step to correcting them.

After fervently (and unsuccessfully) pursuing an acting career, Carnegie threw his efforts into writing, at which he also failed, at least on his first tries. In 1926 he published *Public Speaking: a Practical Course for Business Men*. The book was embraced along with the course by the YMCA, and the book was used specifically as an accompaniment to the public speaking courses. The book was updated in 1931 as the course evolved and improved every year.[283] But writing a book aimed at students of a specific course is not uncommon, and doesn't necessarily imply editorial success; teachers commonly prepare books for preparatory courses. In 1932, despite the author's best efforts, Lincoln's biography did not yield any results. The better-known publishing houses in New York took no interest in it, and although a small publisher named Greenberg eventually published the book, sales were very modest.[284] In 1934, the same publishing house released *Little Known Facts about Well Known People*[285], based on research and interviews that Carnegie conducted with everyone from the famous names of the day to his relatives and acquaintances. The book is very interesting and discusses famous personalities of the present and past such as Albert Einstein, Cleopatra, Greta Garbo, Marconi, Catherine the Great of Russia, Walt Disney, Mahatma Gandhi, Alexander Dumas, Lenin, Christopher Columbus, Mozart, Thomas Edison and many others. Carnegie's idea was genius, because through tireless research he was able to uncover interesting yet little-known facts about great icons. Many narratives illustrate a particular theory I support: the great names of history, the great biographies, the great winners all had to endure enormous personal hardship in order to triumph later in life, which made them famous for generations to come. The book starts with one of these profiles, describing the young Albert Einstein, a boy who looked as if he would never achieve anything important, or even the slightest success. As a child, Einstein was slow, scared, a late bloomer. He had difficulty even in speaking. His teachers considered him developmentally delayed, and his own parents feared he was abnormal. Carnegie emphasizes the fact that years later, Einstein was astonished to learn that he was considered one of the most famous people on the planet[286] (coincidentally, three years later it would be Carnegie's turn to be astonished by the success of a book he was writing: *How to Win Friends and Influence People*). But could it be that the tendency to belittle people has changed? A few years ago I was at a cigar bar with some friends. At the next table I saw an well known cinema personality, a legendary figure, also smoking a Cuban cigar. I remembered how this person's career began: he was disregarded and completely underestimated. During the filming of the movie that launched him to fame, the producers kept a back-up director on hand so that they could replace him at any moment. As if that were not enough, the actor he was banking on was ridiculed by the other artists involved in the shoot; they laughed at him behind his back and he was generally considered by everyone involved in the film to be a tasteless actor. Who was the actor? Al Pacino. The movie? *The Godfather.* Who was the director smoking a cigar next to me? Francis Ford Coppola. Carnegie's history was similar, he was ridiculed during his youth. But does anyone remember the names of the people who mocked him or underestimated his potential? The bottom line is this: believe in your dreams, no matter what others say about you. If you believe in your dreams, you will achieve your goals. Carnegie would call this being a 'person of action'.

So we can see that Carnegie had a profound concept of great personalities. But he also had the profound idea to write about them. Seventy-plus years later, we have successful books like *The 100 Most Influential Books Ever Written*[287], which includes Einstein's *Relativity* in its top one hundred monumental books.[288] In writing, Carnegie had a vision of the topic (personal struggle and success), a vision of the book (interesting topic) and vision of himself (he himself as an exponent).

The courses were going well, but in the beginning, Dale Carnegie did not succeed with the public as a writer. There were several frustrated attempts, including a Western-type short story that never saw publication. As a result, he basically abandoned his dream of becoming an important author- or at least he thought he had abandoned it, since fate tends to play tricks. Larchmont is a prosperous village twenty miles from New York where Carnegie was giving a lecture one night. It would have been like any other talk promoting the Carnegie Course if not for the presence of Leon Shimkin, who worked for Simon & Schuster. Shimkin sat through the night's program, saw the excited testimonies of people who had made immense progress, lawyers, executives, managers and so many other professionals who enthusiastically showed how they overcame their inhibitions in order to move up in the world. Shimkin decided to enroll in the course. In the eleventh session, Shimkin was impressed with how Carnegie proposed a solution to resolve conflicts, seek reconciliation and even create cooperation with former adversaries.[289] Leon Shimkin must have thought to himself... "Carnegie's voice is limited to the lecture room, but if he wrote a book on the art of dealing with people, his voice could be heard throughout the country".[290] Shimkin thought about approaching Carnegie on behalf of Simon & Schuster so that he could write such a book. One of the factors that most motivated Shimkin was the active involvement of Carnegie's students, who were willing to apply the principles, propel the course forward and continue learning. Shimkin knew the idea was excellent, but the response was incredible. When Carnegie heard that the publishing house was Simon & Schuster, his response was: "I can't submit yet another book to Simon & Schuster; besides, I am too busy."[291] Carnegie did not want to write the book! The rejections of both *Lincoln the Unknown* as well as his book on famous people had left him resentful. Tom Sant commented about this historical moment, saying that Shimkin had already learned Carnegie's principles of persuasion, and applied them to Carnegie himself to persuade him write the book![292] Shimkin's strategy paid off. Carnegie started work on the book in 1934. His secretary, Vera Stiles, took notes in his classes. Carnegie also wrote early in the mornings, after his walk and breakfast. he was living in a house at 27 Wendover Road, in the Forest Hills section of Queens, New York. He bought this house in 1931, and stayed there for the rest of his life; he was so grateful to live in a middle class home that over the next two decades he often stopped to contemplate his house, saying: *It is incredible to me that I could live in a comfortable house like this. I just wish I could have known in the days when I was so poor that I would have a garden, be able to travel, and own antiques.*[293] Carnegie could often be found in his office on the third floor of the house that was so dear to him. He would sit in a comfortable lounge chair, ruminating over every passage of the book until he found the perfect phrase. Today I understand why Carnegie's books were so well written: he was very demanding with himself. He would write a single paragraph dozens of times, and on some occasions would have to abandon it, going for a walk or a turn in the garden until he was relaxed enough to return to work.[294]

The title Carnegie initially suggested for the book was 'The Manual of Human Relations', but it was suggested that he provide a more adequate title. Two years later in 1936, the first edition of *How to Win Friends and Influence People* was published. Leon Shimkin went beyond arranging a publishing deal; he began promotional activities, presenting hundreds of course students with a complimentary copy and suggesting that not only would it be useful for review, but that it would also be ideal for giving to friends. A full page report in the *New York Times* citing Andrew Carnegie and John D. Rockefeller aided in promotion, and Shimkin released photos and snippets of Lowell Thomas' introduction in an advertising campaign. At the same time, a newspaper article appeared, trying to scheme against the two friends. Margaret Case Harriman stated that Thomas had done the course with Carnegie in 1916 and had written the introduction of the book, but had been unprepared to see his commentary in advertisements plastered across the country.[295] I find it hard to believe that Thomas made such a comment, for obvious reasons. We have already seen that Lowell Thomas and Carnegie shared close ties and great friendship in the United States and England; their good relationship was very well known. Why would Thomas write a preface for the book and then feel betrayed that his words were used to promote his friend's book? As every article written by Harriman was slanted against Carnegie, it seems that she must have taken Thomas' words out of context. This brings Thomas away from how Harriman's article portrays him, as a spoiled brat, back to what he was publicly known to be: fearless. Even more, the preface was not written for some unknown student who was trying to use Thomas' name as a selling point. It was written for a great friend who was associated with him on numerous occasions. Harriman's bitter article profiled the book as soon as it soared to success. Her words are interesting in that they reflect her attitude about people; she concluded that Dale Carnegie claimed that every single reader has the potential to be as successful as any other person. Thus, according to Harriman, Carnegie peddles what people most need: hope.[296]

The important question here is why did she believe that not everyone can be successful? Are there people that are born better off than others, or are do they build their own stories? At the time that Harriman wrote, women suffered from more stigma than they do today. People took the stigmas with which they were labeled and lived accordingly. It seemed natural to be labeled as 'inferior'. But in Carnegie's vision, each of us builds our own destiny, freeing people from the feeling of inferiority that results from stigmatization. Harriman stated that Carnegie sells 'hope'. In saying this, she implied that people are resigned to living with stigmas and the roles we are assigned by people who do not even know us. It is a depressing thought, assuming that one should walk about with one's head lowered, downtrodden, resigning oneself to the criticism of others, no matter how prejudiced or idiotic these criticisms are. No, Ms.

Harriman, Carnegie did not 'sell hope' to his students. He pointed them to freedom.

What came next was a surprise to all. Simon & Schuster printed five thousand copies and, according to records, did not expect to sell many more, but the book became immediately successful. Dorothy Carnegie wrote: *To their amazement, the book became an overnight sensation and edition after edition rolled off the presses to keep up with the increasing public demand. 'How to Win Friends and Influence People' took its place in publishing history as one of the all-time international best-sellers.*[297] In five months, Carnegie received $150,000 in royalties. It is difficult to imagine the value of this sum in 1937, only eight years after the beginning of the Great Depression. I believe this sum corresponds to millions of today's dollars. It was reported in 1955 that the book had been translated into twenty-nine languages, and was the second most-read nonfiction book in the world, second only to the Holy Bible.[298] The forty-eighth edition, released in 2000, states that over thirty million copies had been sold as of that publication.[299] It is worth repeating the fact that the book was published only eight years after the great Wall Street crash of 1929 and the beginning of the most catastrophic recession to shake the United States and the world. But even so, Carnegie's book sold more and more each day. The author was impressed; after having written some well-planned books that were not popular, the irony is that his best-seller was a book he had not wanted to write![300] In a lecture given in Los Angeles, in the spring of 1946, he said that the book was written on a trial and error basis. The same was true for his famous course.[301]

But Carnegie was still himself, remaining humble although by now he was a millionaire. He continued to live in the same house with the same attitudes, keeping his regular way of life. How many people can stay grounded when achieving success or power? I know of very few. This may have been my main motivation for beginning work on this biography. I watched a bit of the show 'Biography' and it portrayed someone special, not someone who turned into a fool when he attained material success, someone who was really authentic no matter what his experiences. Abigail Connel was responsible for typing up some of his texts; later on, she became the director of the Carnegie Institute. On one occasion Connel found a royalty check for thousands of dollars sitting in Carnegie's drawer, and asked him if she should deposit it. Carnegie responded that he wished his mother were alive to witness his victory. Earning the salary of a first-rate writer, Carnegie said that money in excess was unnecessary: *If I had all the money in the world, I couldn't wear more clothes, and I live exactly where I want to live.*[302] Abigail stated that just two weeks after she began to work for Carnegie, she received a bouquet for her birthday. Later, one of her tasks was to keep a book noting as many birthdays as possible, so that she could remind Carnegie in time to commemorate them, since this act meant so much to the recipient.[303] Carnegie started to receive countless letters, but he tried to respond to all of them personally, asking Abigail to deliver them around town. Abbie, as Abigail was called, started to work for Carnegie in the beginning of the 1930's. At one time, she recalled, she spilled ink on the wallpaper of the newly decorated office. Carnegie reacted with good humor, telling her that if there were little devils hovering around bothering her, she should get rid of them, but in the meantime they should just get a new roll of wallpaper. He knew how to be sympathetic on serious occasions, and when Abbie's mother was about to lose her farm during the recession, Carnegie lent her the money to save the mortgage, and allowed her to pay him over two years, at two dollars a week. When Abbie handed him the last payment, Carnegie told her she must have a special place in Heaven, for she was the only person who had ever paid him back. But the farm was very important to her, and she lived there into her golden years.[304] When Marilyn Burke, his other assistant, got sick, Carnegie paid for her to travel so that she could be looked after by Vickie Price, Dorothy's mother.[305] Another interesting passage is related by Harry Hamm, who one day went to meet Carnegie in his room at the Hollywood Roosevelt Hotel. Hamm was surprised to see Carnegie reading *How to Win Friends and Influence People*. Carnegie told Hamm he read a bit of the book every day. These actions show that Carnegie knew how to deal with people, and lived the principles on which his book was founded. And the book is still successful.

How to explain such success? Well, later we will dedicate a chapter to Carnegie's techniques for success, titled *"Carnegie's Method to Study, Write and Be Successful."* The techniques shown there constitute an amazing lesson for those who intend to evolve and be successful. Curiously, one of his biggest critics (who will later be analyzed in the chapter titled *"Criticism he Received")*, seems to have contributed to this success. This critic is Parker, who claimed that it was 'easy' to explain the success of the support groups created by Carnegie in his course, but found it difficult to explain the success of *How to Win Friends*. However, Parker dared to say that the book simulates a support group situation, replacing the groups with blank spaces to be filled out, stimulating the reader to act and try new techniques, while the rest of the groupmates would be represented by the many testimonies given.[306] I find this conclusion by Parker very interesting. However, as stated before, we will leave the main methods of Carnegie's success for a different chapter and return to analyzing the enormous success of Carnegie's best-seller.

In my opinion, Carnegie did not get caught up in himself because had planned his life for this moment, for a great work. But he did not expect success to happen in the way that it did, for he tried to be an artist and couldn't do it, and tried to write short stories and novels without success. He toiled to write a great biography on Abraham Lincoln, to little positive acclaim. It seemed he was fated to gain success and positive recognition for his courses, but he felt that he had so much more potential, and that things could have gone differently. He did not have the fame and victory he had struggled so hard to gain. But success came when he least expected it; all of a sudden, he was treated like a celebrity, receiving letters from all over the world; unusual requests, everything from helping a woman teach her 'friend' how to get her boyfriend to propose to requests for Carnegie to claim authorship for a third party's book so they could make a fortune. When he arrived anywhere, he was greeted by crowds that had waited to be able to see him, to touch him or to ask for advice (wouldn't it have been easier to just read his books?). In the beginning of 1938, Thomas B. Hollyman, editor-in-chief of *The Student*, a weekly college newspaper in Warrensburg, did an interview that was later fully reproduced in the *Daily Star*, commenting on Carnegie's triumphal arrival in his former hometown. But to Hollyman's surprise, Carnegie did not behave like a 'star'. He stated that Carnegie *"…communicated with people on their level and their language"*. According to Hollyman, Carnegie had realized the power of words and public speaking as related to developing a public persona.[307] It was very common for journalists to comment on Carnegie's simplicity, as if it were out of the ordinary compared to reporting on other famous people of the day. The journalist Collie Small noted the same attitude when Carnegie was expected to arrive by train to cities where he was scheduled to lecture; the welcoming committee usually let him pass unnoticed because, according to Small, they expected a *red-blooded giant to bound from the train, breathe deeply of the good air, and grab in a vise-like grip the hand of the first man who gets close to him. Carnegie is instead a gentle, neat, gray-haired man of sixty with a well-turned sense of humor, a quiet demeanor and a horror of exhibitionists.*[308] But Small continues to remind everyone that he is *a being that talks with an almost hypnotic certainty, and he is one of the most enthusiastic public speakers that exist. Enthusiasm, in fact, is his more lasting quality. It is not unimaginable that Carnegie, the 'pied piper', could take the whole army to the cliff with his enthusiasm. Although there are those in the audience that come to ridicule the man and his ideas, they are truly amazed with what happened.*[309]

I believe that Carnegie did not truly realize the dimensions of what he had created. Either that, or he really carried the traces of the feelings of inferiority that people that knew him talked about, remnants of his hard years in Missouri.[310] I bet on the first hypothesis, though; he hadn't planned to become successful through a book he hadn't even wanted to write. However, could a successful romance have been the cause of such social innovation? If he had reached his boyhood dream of becoming a movie or theater star, would he have revolutionized the realms of social communication? My view is that Carnegie realized his success without noticing the dimensions of his work. Maybe the fierce critics he attracted contributed to his humble view of himself. Another possibility is that his perfectionist tendencies, his enormous will to improve his work led him to never consider his work to be good enough. Despite gaining public recognition, Carnegie complained that when he wrote, he could not express exactly what he wanted to say.[311] The way I see it, the book drew such attention from the public that the critics could not help but take potshots at every given opportunity, and this brought out Carnegie's modesty; as a result, he downplayed any merits to his writing, stating that he had only adopted ideas put forth by various other thinkers. Carnegie's merits lay in taking action based on these ideas, but admitting this would have caused him to shrink back into his shell. The question is whether he knew, deep down, the importance of what he wrote, or if he really thought his contribution was modest. I do not know if it is possible to answer this question for certain. Another point I consider important is Carnegie's humble attitude towards his accomplishments; could it be what made him unable to recognize the magnitude of what he had created? To give an example of how his humility affected his contributions, let me mention an event that took place in June of 1953, in Pasadena, California, where Carnegie was about to give two lectures to a packed auditorium of 3050 graduates. Harry O. Hamm accompanied Carnegie, and was to introduce him once they arrived in the auditorium. He had three introductions prepared: a ten-minute version, a five-minute version, and a two-minute version. When he asked Carnegie which one he should use, Carnegie replied: "Can you do it in ten seconds?" "Yes," replied Hamm. "That is the one I want". So Hamm introduced him by saying: "Ladies and Gentlemen, Dale Carnegie!"[312]

How to Win Friends and Influence People created a life of its own. Maybe what finally awoke Carnegie to his own literary status was being recognized by the public on the street, in restaurants, in theaters. Every time he was recognized he felt surprised. People expected him to play the role of a very pleasant man and demonstrate all the book's principles right before their very eyes, as if they had the right to approach a comedian or an athlete during a family dinner and ask him or her to tell jokes or do stunts on the spot. It is not right, but people do it, and my example is based on a true story. It is certainly the price of fame, but Carnegie was bothered by this new glamorous status that he did hadn't wanted or longed for. I can imagine people telling him their personal problems, whether complex or silly, wanting a free consultation during Carnegie's time off, regardless of what he was doing at the moment, heartlessly violating his right to rest. Harold Abbott described Carnegie at this point in his life:

> He was a very retiring man, not timid, but realized that because he had written a book on human conduct, that people would expect him to be perfect in all of his relationships. He told me one time, 'Before I wrote the book 'How to Win Friends,' strangers did not seek my company. No, I was just Dale Carnegie, Forest Hills, New York, teacher of adult education classes. But once that book was published, I became so well known, people thought I should be perfect in all my relationships with other people. But not one place in that book do I say to do it because I do it, no, no. I studied men like Charles Schwab, Eddie Rickenbacker, Will Rogers and Jesus Christ, men like that who had made a great success of their dealing with people. The book is

*composed of things I have learned from men far more successful in dealing with people than I have ever been. When I get with a group of strangers which I must do sometimes, I begin to realize that I am not measuring up to their preconceived idea of what I should be like – and it is embarrassing'.*[313]

Understanding how Carnegie's book was ahead of its time or, if not that, simply as a part of history (with dimensions approaching that of a work of art), Abbot concluded that "Dale Carnegie is a greater man today than when he passed away 16 years ago."[314]

Effectively, he was able to gain what he had always wanted, success as a writer, by broaching an important topic, the ability to influence people and make friends.

One time a friend approached me and said that in times like these, it was good to have a friend like me, because of my profession. I replied that it was good to have any friends at any time... When do we need a friend? Always. And if Carnegie proposed a method to win friendships, it certainly was an ambitious and motivating work. But the second part of the title of the book is also tempting: *'influence people'.* Such power! This is certainly attractive; who wouldn't like to have the power to influence people? Well, I believe the book's success was partially due to the topic it covered, but the lasting relevance of the book, the fact that sold millions of copies to this day, is dependent on Carnegie's content: easy to understand and memorize, well elaborated, and always keeping in mind respect for others. Persuasion is fine, but deception is never acceptable. The text does not preach a rigorously disciplinarian approach, but quite the opposite, demonstrating the importance of respecting others, good behavior, the ability to listen quietly to others' opinions, and in case of disagreement, the ability to present a kind counterargument; those are the formulas that Carnegie used and that every institution should learn about. Today, many young people and adults who are rude to their parents, hostile to their teachers or people in general, especially those who are stigmatized, could learn a lot from reading and studying *How to Win Friends.* The book teaches a lot about relationships with others, but it also teaches good manners, cordiality, generosity and, above all, intelligence! Yes, intelligence, because even if a person only thinks of himself in his interactions with other people, he can still find a motive to treat others well. For example, if someone greets a street-sweeper with a 'good day', how does he know that moments later he won't suffer some misfortune, such as a robbery or sudden illness, and his life will be in the hands of that one person he greeted cordially?

Treating people well is a sign of intelligence, good personal marketing, and it is synonymous with progress. But it also manifests respect for others by being considerate of them, by seeing the other as we mentioned before, as we would like to be seen, or treat the other as we would like to be treated. While I was still studying law at the Universidade Federal do Paraná, I interned in the office of an attorney who dealt with social security. It was usual for us to work with other sections of the institution, so the law interns frequently came into contact with administrators. When I interacted with these people, I always took the opportunity to apply Carnegie's lessons, and tried not to neglect friendly small talk, like 'Good Morning, how are you?' – 'Excuse me' – 'Thank you' – 'See you soon' – 'Have a nice weekend', etc. One day, Celia, an infamous employee, called me in for a talk. I was a bit startled at first, imagining that perhaps I had done something wrong. To my surprise, Celia said, "Carlos, I would like to tell you that we in the administrative department are very impressed with you. In all the years that we've had an internship program, you are the first intern to treat us well, respect us, to be kind to us, and we want you to know that we all adore you!" Dear reader, this was one of the most touching moments of my life! All that just because I was polite. I would rather not use the words the administrators used to describe the other interns, but suffice to say that they felt mistreated. And I confess that I did nothing unusual, just daily civility. If that were us, or our mother or father, or a friend that worked in the same office, or if we were simply wandering around, wouldn't we also like to be well treated?

Dale Carnegie thought about all of this and tried to masterfully teach the basic rules of cordiality and good manners. His unmistakable and efficient method, rich with examples, metaphors and quotations, slowly brings the reader to comprehension and assimilation of his propositions to make friends and influence people. Let's present now, as an example, some of the main suggestions Carnegie gives in *How to Win Friends and Influence People,* such as fundamental techniques for dealing with people: *Principle 1- Don't criticize, condemn or complain; Principle 2 – Give honest, sincere appreciation; Principle 3 – Arouse in the other person an eager want.*[315] To make people like you: *Principle 1 – Become genuinely interested in other people; Principle 2 – Smile; Principle 3 – Remember that a person's name is to that person the sweetest and most important sound in any language; Principle 4 – Be a good listener. Encourage others to talk about themselves; Principle 5 – Talk in terms of the other person's interests; Principle 6 – Make the other person feel important – and do it sincerely."*[316] To win people to your way of thinking: *Principle 1– The only way to get the best of an argument is to avoid it; Principle 2 – Show respect for the other person's opinions. Never say, 'You're wrong'; Principle 3 – If you are wrong, admit it quickly and emphatically; Principle 4 – Begin in a friendly way; Principle 5 – Get the other person saying 'yes, yes' immediately; Principle 6 – Let the other person do a great deal of the talking; Principle 7 – Let the other person feel the idea is his or hers; Principle 8 – Try honestly to see things from the other person's point of view; Principle 9 – Be sympathetic with the other person's ideas and desires; Principle 10 – Appeal to the nobler motives; Principle 11 – Dramatize your ideas; Principle 12 – Throw down a challenge.*[317] To be a leader and change people without giving offense or arousing resentment: *Principle 1 – Begin with praise and honest appreciation; Principle 2 – Call attention to people's mistakes indirectly; Principle 3*

*– Talk about your own mistakes before criticizing the other person; Principle 4 – Ask questions instead of giving direct orders; Principle 5 – Let the other person save face; Principle 6 – Praise the slightest improvement and praise every improvement. Be 'hearty in your approbation and lavish in your praise'; Principle 7 – Give the other person a fine reputation to live up to; Principle 8 – Use encouragement. Make the fault seem easy to correct; Principle 9 – Make the other person happy about doing the thing you suggest.*[318]

Of course these principles have acquired a life of their own, with the didactic and convincing explanations presented by Dale Carnegie. The interesting thing is that while Carnegie's 'educational' proposal is persuasive and moderated, easily and rationally assimilated, and views the other with respect in a truly contemporary vision, on the other hand a parallel can be made with the model, strongly criticized by Michel Foucault, of rigid and disciplinarian education that came about in the eighteenth century. Foucault interprets the historical moment of change to be the arrival of the 'Century of Light' and Illuminism, a new way to manifest power. Before the arrival of Illuminism, power was manifested through punishments that doubled as spectacle. Foucault demonstrated this in his book *Discipline and Punish*, describing the convict Damiens,[319] who was sentenced on March 2, 1757 to death by an execution that mixed various rites of pain, humiliation and violence: the convicted, clad only in a nightgown, was forced to ask for forgiveness before being mutilated by iron pincers tearing flesh from his chest, arms, thighs, and calves; following this, melted lead and boiling oil was thrown on him, after which he was quartered by horses, etc. This horrifying spectacle showcased sovereign power. At the end of the eighteenth century, a new form of power appeared and spread through society; it targeted the soul rather than the body, disciplining the mind, spreading it in the most efficient ways, in prisons, asylums, convents, factories... schools. Students were rigorously disciplined, from the uniform they had to wear to the minute rules they had to obey in detail, corporal punishment, etc. The power formerly lorded over half a dozen (convicts condemned to brutal and capital punishment) was replaced by power over millions. In a more outstanding way, the transformation was so dramatic that it came to be known as the 'micro-physics of power', since no longer was power concentrated; now it was exercised in small doses that hit most of the population.

Another problem was the enormous vigilance over people[320], the training of body and mind. Foucault made the following commentary on this disciplinary power:

> Not because the disciplinary modality of power has replaced all the others; but because it has infiltrated the others, sometimes undermining them, but serving as an intermediary between them, linking them together, extending them and above all making it possible to bring the effects of power to the most minute and distant elements. It assures an infinitesimal distribution of the power relations.[321]

In Carnegie, there is no 'apprentice control', manipulation of personal development, or marked, adjusted and invented gestures.[322] On the contrary, Carnegie's lessons are democratic, free, encouraging the participant to just "be yourself". It is up to the reader to decide if he or she will act sincerely towards others, recognizing the plenitude of the other and seeking efficient communication and complete understanding through their efforts, exhibiting their evolution by means of legitimate effort. Carnegie opposed fabricated gestures and traps to trick or grab power for oneself. Course instructor Oliver Whiting said: "The Dale Carnegie Course is not a bag of tricks but a Way of Life".[323] No doubt, if it weren't for the stigma attached to him as a 'self-help author', scholars in all fields could benefit from Carnegie's ethic and method as applied to relationships and education. His methods for relating to others meshed perfectly with his course of adult education, which strove towards increasing the apprentice's involvement in such a way that each participant in the course contributed to the group dynamic with his or her own teachings and life experiences.

The most outstanding proof of Carnegie's success came after the publication of *How to Win Friends and Influence People:* the expression became part of the everyday language. However, there were abuses of the phrase, one of the most explicit being Irving Tressler's *How to Lose Friends and Alienate People*, which ran exactly opposite to Carnegie's teachings, and gave easy steps on how to make people hate the reader. After all, according to Tressler, most people were annoying and uninteresting anyway. It seems Tressler did not believe in Carnegie's principles, stating that he only taught people to be tedious when approaching others in a friendly manner. According to William Longgood, biographer of the Dale Carnegie Course, parodies such as Tressler's transformed the image of Carnegie into that of someone with selfish, insincere and manipulative goals, although Longgood admitted that this misleading vision had changed afterward.[324] But the conflict started by Tressler seemed to be his own conflict; that is to say, it seems his not liking others stemmed from not liking himself-- he committed suicide around age thirty-five. This increased the confusion, leading many to believe that Carnegie himself had committed suicide. By establishing a framework for increased misunderstandings between people, Tressler's grand plan came to finality in the greatest misunderstanding of his life, based on hate towards others and towards himself, of course being suicide, which is often linked to a disorderly, selfish and desperate life. Describing both approaches and their real consequences, Longgood compared Carnegie and Tressler: *Carnegie, after a rich life and a successful career, died at his home in Forest Hills, Long Island, in 1955 of natural causes at age 67, optimistic, happy, and vibrant almost to the end. Tressler, when only 35, committed suicide in 1944; his obituary noted ironically that he was best known for his take-off on* How to Win Friends and Influence People.[325] Recently, a book with a cover imitating the cover of *How to Win Friends and Influence People* was taken off the market because it could confuse the reader. Did Carnegie imagine that he would be so imitated, or that he would inspire nearly the entire genre of literature known as 'self-help'? The fact is that when Carnegie received word that the book had sold its first hundred thousand copies, he wrote to Leon Shimkin, the publisher that discovered him: *Every morning I rise and face the east and thank Allah that you came into my life!*[326]

# CHAPTER 9

## THE RECIPE FOR LIVING WELL

*As students work up their talks each week, they must mull over their experiences in life and what they meant to them. For many people this is something new; they have gone through life largely thinking what they were told to think, saying what they were taught to say, never examining their own attitudes and feelings. Some of these people, for the first time, become acutely aware of their real feelings toward various aspects of life; they discover themselves, as it were – what the psychologists call 'coming in contact with the self'.*

(William Longgood)[327]

When Laura picks up the phone, I can hear the noise of the hair salon where she works. She is the main hairdresser there, but the last time I visited her, I thought she was having a hard time. She had broken up with her live-in boyfriend. She had talked about 'self-help' books that she liked to read, so I asked her, "Have you ever read Dale Carnegie?" "No, no, I don't know him." I wrote down his name, what the book looked like, where she could find it... When I left the salon, I thought: What would Dale Carnegie do in this situation? He would certainly go into the bookstore, buy the book and put it in his friend's hands in person. I entered the first bookstore I found and looked for the book; although I didn't find the one I had recommended to Laura, they had Carnegie's other books. I went to the next bookstore, and there it was! I asked the clerk to gift-wrap it for me. I walked anxiously to the salon. Laura asked me: "Did you forget something?" "Yes, I would like you to take off a little more of my hair." "Excuse me?" She looked at me, startled. "I'm just kidding. Here's the book I told you about." "Wow! How nice! Thank you!" Three weeks later, she called me, saying, "It is simply incredible!"

If I had to recommend the first book one should read, not only among Dale Carnegie's books, but as the first to read in life, I would recommend *How to Stop Worrying and Start Living*. This book, which is in its 37<sup>th</sup> edition, is on my table; its cover says that more than fifteen million copies have already been sold. I could present a few of my friends with it, along with various recommendations for where to begin reading. It is not just a book, but a true handbook of personal organization and a compilation of suggestions for a better quality of life. I thought extensively about the reasons for this work's success, a long-lasting and permanent success that reaches generation after generation, breaking barriers of time and geography, reaching people in different countries, with different languages, habits, ages, personally and professionally, individually and collectively. I can talk about this book quite intimately, for I have had the pleasure of reading at it least eight times. Too many? Try it. When Carnegie recommended it as a book to keep on your nightstand to organize your life, he was not joking. The book was written when Carnegie was at his zenith as a writer. *How to Win Friends and Influence People* was a success, so he took up the task of writing a book about daily life, frequent worries, stress and the maladies that worrying too much can cause. Unfortunately, in this area Carnegie had extensive experience, and a good perception of what his content and goals should be. Course instructor Roger Jackson witnessed this when he met Carnegie at the train station in Winnipeg in the late 1940s. On that occasion, Carnegie said that *How to Stop Worrying* was not yet complete, but he created a booklet with the first four chapters because he thought people really needed it. It would be directed towards students in the course when they covered these topics in their respective sessions. "People need help now," said Carnegie, and he couldn't wait until the book was completed.[328] Roger Jackson realized that Carnegie himself felt the need to apply the principles to his own life. But the record shows that in March of 1938 Carnegie had already addressed the most troublesome problem of the day, which of course was the stress and worry that accompanied the recession. Ten years before publishing *How to Stop Worrying,* Carnegie had already written that the ugliest and most evil problem in the world, after war, was worry. "The meanest, ugliest, most trouble-making word in all the world (outside of war) is WORRY. What a sourpuss that is!"[329], he said, following commentaries by dentists who observed that worrying caused teeth to rot and fall out, for example; of course, he followed up with tips to avoid such worries. We could lose a job, or every penny we have, but in the end things wouldn't be so bad, because it would be even worse to lose one's mental health – and consequently one's physical health as well – due to useless worry. Useless indeed, because material possessions can always be recovered, but after a certain point, mental and physical health cannot. More than ten years before he wrote a book about worry, Carnegie was exploring the topic, researching, testing it before the public eye, seeking solutions and improvement in quality of life.

When I learned how to structure a thesis, I was taught that in academic writing, it is not necessary to present solutions to the problems discussed. Often, the solutions simply aren't yet known, or the magnitude of the problem makes it impossible to address both problem and solution in just one article. Just the research that Carnegie conducted on the consequences of worrying would allow us to consider the book as an academic work. However, Carnegie wrote another thesis in a single book, in which he proposed solutions for worry, solutions based on fastidious research. Carnegie brought both theses together into a single book, which covered not only the damages caused by worry, but also ways to eliminate worry and start to live well. It is interesting that among dozens of articles in magazines, newspapers, books that discuss the text, no one ever commented that Carnegie had written two academic theses in *How to Stop Worrying and Start Living.*

So Nuno Cobra was right when he said that emotion should be studied more extensively in college.[330] This great professor of physical and emotional education states the importance of good sleep to increasing quality of life, but relates the difficulty he encountered in talking about such an important subject: *I encountered great opposition in the sixties and seventies, and even in the late 1980s. At that time, when I presented my method and talked about how wrong it was to sleep so little, people looked at me as if I were an alien. And they boasted about themselves, thinking they were really extraordinary, fabulous, because by sleeping less, they did not waste much time. And their goal was to sleep less and less – it was like a competition, especially among entrepreneurs and high-level executives, to see who could sleep less. Terribly, there were those who slept only four hours, and were proud of this health catastrophe.*[331] Imagine how difficult it was for Nuno Cobra to attempt to explain the importance of sleep to his students, despite their desire to evolve and readiness to learn, because of the taboo about this subject at that time.  In Brazil, Nuno Cobra was one of the first who tried to stress the importance of sleep to good health. Dale Carnegie had already talked about sleep and many other ways to increase quality of life and well-being in the 1940s. We could call Carnegie a pioneer on the subject, especially with regards to the way he presented it to the public. He wrote a full chapter on the importance of sleep and the consequences of insomnia. He talked about how people who suffered through grave difficulties with sleep,  including the unprecedented case of Paul Kern, a Hungarian soldier who was never again able to sleep after being injured in World War I. He also mentioned that worrying about insomnia aggravates the problem. He read scientific articles of the day and current research on the topic, and included in his book a series of resources readers could use to gain a good night's sleep. Finally, imagining that some readers might continue to be insomniac (like some of the difficult cases he had researched), he included some very useful recommendations, in such a way that after reading the chapter on insomnia and lack of sleep, we can stop worrying about it and do what needs to be done.[332]

On November 2, 2008, I watched an interview with the neuroradiologist Dr. Edson Amaro Junior, who explained some efficient ways to improve brain function and to avoid brain maladies like Alzheimer's Disease, which affect five people out of every hundred. Dr. Amaro said that exercising the mind was very important, as well as breaking routines to change one's perspective. Other factors contributing to better brain performance are physical exercise and optimism. Dr. Amaro also shared research performed on basketball players who visualized shooting baskets and scoring. Performing this exercise increased their real point scores during games. Dr. Amaro couldn't explain the reason why positive visualization effectively improves results. Topics like these were broadly researched and described by Carnegie over six decades ago.

After finding that worries decisively impact our lives and, conversely, calm and tranquility sufficient for rest and consequent action can produce a full, happy, and long-lasting life, Carnegie listed the most significant worries as well as the worries that may not be as important, but leave us distressed nonetheless; he then showed examples of dedicated people who overcame their suffering and preoccupations and started to live better. We read the case of an aunt who lost her beloved nephew, whom she had raised as her own son, in the war; a person who suddenly lost his sight; another who lost all his real estate and became bankrupt overnight; a man who lost his hand, another who used to sell cookies but began to work with explosives on a ship; a writer (like Carnegie himself) who overcame the publishers' rejection of his novel after dedicating two years of his life to it; how Lincoln overcame his enemies' aggressions during the Civil War; artists surviving resentment and offenses that dragged through a lifetime; the marital turmoil between Tolstoy and his wife that made their lives a living hell; students worried about exams; an events planner reborn from the ashes... and so many other examples. In this way, Carnegie made a study of interesting characters and was able to develop and propose successful ideas for a fuller and richer life. He also studied the habits of kings, university deans, writers of short stories, presidents of chain stores, artists, teachers and so many real-life characters who learned lessons about worrying and resulting maladies and in turn developed 'systems' for their lives that, being so special and practical, were presented to the reader in detail. Here we see, for example, how Socrates dealt with being condemned to death, how stockbrokers survived the personal and professional catastrophe of the Great Depression, methods Ambassador Benjamin Franklin used to avoid being too troubled by his troubles; life lessons a chemistry teacher imparted to his students; how the champion boxer Jack Dempsey dealt with two successive defeats that ended his career; how convicts endure the daily hardships of prison, and many more.

Carnegie also studied popular proverbs and analyzed them carefully, trying to imbue them with new meaning or recognize their empirical value through examples. From such a well-known saying as 'If life gives you lemons, make lemonade', he writes an interesting chapter demonstrating how many people transform adverse situations into magnificent personal triumph. And in these situations there are two possibilities: either we continuously complain and create a negative environment or we roll up our sleeves and go to battle. If we act with determination and enthusiasm, we have all the tools we need to change the situation to a much more favorable one. But his versatility on the subject was such that he could look out the window, observe the calm of birds, cows and dogs and make a lesson out of it: animals don't spend their lives worried about whether it is going to rain the next day, which is why they don't go mad or die of anxiety. As you can see, he did everything possible to demonstrate the problem (worrying and the resulting maladies it caused to mind and body), the solution (how to avoid or eliminate preoccupations), and the result (a better life); all was presented in order to honestly help the reader. When asked about the book, Carnegie was again modest, saying that "All you have to do to stop worrying is remember two little proverbs:

'Don't cross your bridges before you come to them' and 'Don't cry over spilled milk.' What's so hard about that?" [333] But we cannot be deceived by his modesty, for he organized a system of human and individual relations. Actually, when you read *How to Stop Worrying,* it seems you have a great sage contributing to your life, trying to help you through the steps, making your life happier and sweeter. I think about the number of people that were saved by reading *How to Stop Worrying*, and how many could have their existences completely changed, being able to organize their day, their homes, their lives, their clothing, and constructively assimilate their experiences.

In a warm July of 2008, while researching some of Carnegie's lesser-known works, I visited the beautiful New York Public Library a few times. On the first visit, I gained access to the books I was looking for, once I had registered as a patron. The books were at my disposal, just like any other book in the library, free of charge and available to anyone. It is incredible how the legacy of a book is democratic and can be enjoyed by anyone. Carnegie's books are accessible in practically every library, bookstore, and second-hand shop in the world. But besides being widely available, Carnegie's formulas for living are easy to understand and very simple to apply to every day of our lives. With millions and millions of copies spread around the world, I think about the contribution *How to Stop Worrying and Start Living* made to a veritable multitude of people. People who had already lost hope, who could not find an escape from their problems and considered them hopeless, even fatal, people who could not organize their belongings, their work habits, their various commitments and necessary tasks and plans. By teaching how to live more calmly and confidently, Carnegie brought the reader to the next task: organizing one's professional life. But first, let's see more of the balance suggested in *How to Stop Worrying.*

Carnegie utilized a style of writing that resembled a frank and friendly conversation with the reader, in which he revealed his own personal failures, his efforts at improvement, his reading and interviews with people that suffered through hard times. It is possible for the reader to momentarily lose track of the fact that Carnegie conducted careful research in support of his precepts. An example is his assertion about the power of the mind and the importance of 'conscious monitoring' of thoughts.[334] In one passage, he described his friend Lowell Thomas, whose fantastic documentary about the Arab world and reports about 'Lawrence of Arabia' were very well-received and brought him fame. Suddenly after this high point, Lowell faced a fearful financial crisis, reaching such a low point that he lacked money for even food. Yet Lowell adopted a positive mental attitude, facing the hardship as something useful for learning lessons and evolving even more.[335] So how did Carnegie confirm and recommend Thomas' attitude? He mentioned work done by J. A. Hadfield, an English psychiatrist, that investigated the psychology of power, that is, how mental state can impressively affect even a person's physical strength. Hadfield measured the grip of three men under normal conditions using a hand dynamometer; the assessed average grip was 101 pounds. The men were then hypnotized and informed that they were very weak; upon retesting, they were only able to grip 29 pounds. Finally, they were hypnotized again and told that they were strong. A final test measured an average grip of 142 pounds.[336] This is an example of the broad research on which Carnegie based his affirmations. One of these affirmations concerned forgiveness; by urging the reader to not avenge wrongs, Carnegie shows the benefits quick forgiveness can bring to our health. The desire to retaliate over unfair aggressions can cause various illnesses, so forgetting about annoying provocations can be considered a great remedy. Hate disturbs our own happiness. Isn't this method of leaving our enemies alone and moving on with our lives interesting? By acting in this way, we can continue undisturbed towards our goals. Of course Carnegie also shows other advantages to pushing hate aside. For example, we get a better view of reality, we can see the serious mistakes we make and can even take advantage of this view. Instead of wasting our time on our enemies, we can dedicate our time to a nobler cause, our most relevant personal projects. By better understanding human nature, we become more ready to deal with human actions and reactions, and are in a better situation to face the many things that disturb us. One of these things is ingratitude. Why do we place so much emphasis on the approval of others? This expectation can cause unhappiness, as it is common for people to not acknowledge the favors we do for them. In this case, we can think of the lawyer who saved a client from the electric chair, or the boss who pays her employees better than most; in either case, it is rare to hear a 'thank you'. Even Jesus Christ, who healed ten lepers, only received one acknowledgment of thanks.[337] It is easier, then, to do things without expecting any sort of gratitude. Personally, I feel that if I do something good in this universe, I receive a credit that will always be available if I need it later. This thought is comforting; after all, the universe always shows itself to be governed by the laws of cause and effect. Waiting for the gratitude of a specific person we helped ignores the infinite intelligence of nature, since we can only pretend to take in all the ramifications of cause and effect; even the best candidates for understanding, like Newton, Einstein and Max Planck, only scratched the surface. I remember a story by Malba Tahan that described a very evil person who, after death, was sent to the most terrible places a soul could be sent. However, in his weeping and regret, he asked if there was no other option for his condemned soul. He was answered that if he could remember one good deed he had done in life, he would be spared. After thinking hard, the poor soul remembered he once had saved a spider from death. A spider web then appeared from the skies so he could escape the abyss. As the wretched soul started to climb the web, the other souls being tortured there rushed towards it to climb and escape with him. Afraid the web would break, and he would lose his only chance to escape, he began to yell at the other escapees. Because he had not really reformed his spirit, and did not want to help the others, the spider web broke and they all fell back into the darkness. We can never know for sure how a good deed can return to help us. When I was a teenager, I kindly lent out all seven of my books by Malba Tahan, among them *The Man who Counted* and *Legends of the Desert*. The woman vanished with all my books and never even thanked me for them! But at this moment, I look around me and see hundreds of books all around, as if they speak to me. When I lent my books to her, I only had about twenty books in my collection. Who knows what nature really wants of us? Many times, when we think we have lost something, we gain so much more. How many people have tried to harm us and, without realizing it, helped us? To those people that were petty and disturbed us so much, thank you! They only hurt themselves by being evil, but gave us even more strength. Thank you very much! Besides this, there is a feeling of happiness we get when we help someone. Who knows what forgiveness can bring us in terms of health. On the other hand, the feeling we must have is gratitude for the gifts we receive each day. Whenever I recall something that upset me during the day, I use a technique I learned in Carnegie's book: remember the blessings I received on the same day. Surprisingly, I always find more reasons to be thankful than to complain. This perspective makes me calm: count your blessings and forget your troubles.

But Carnegie went beyond this and addressed the complex topic of suicide. He had come very close to suicide himself, and there is always a need to approach this polemic subject carefully. But he opened his heart and fearlessly confronted the problem that tortures many, that is, the total lack of will to go on. So again he sought a series of examples, people who had been in that difficult place and recovered, and were grateful for their inability to complete their act of self-destruction. It can be noted that one incisive point for Carnegie is sincere prayer, to stop worrying about things around us and surrender to the mercy of a supreme being that supports us. Carnegie bases this on countless testimonials, from generals like Robert E. Lee to boxers like Jack Dempsey; from people who lived in extreme poverty like

Mary Cushman[338] to lawyers turned booksellers who could not manage to close a single deal, like John R. Anthony; from Admiral Richard Byrd, stuck in the immensity of glacial ice, to the philosopher Immanuel Kant. Carnegie gives prayer such power for reasons that run the gamut from the intuition that there is something greater in this world than what we see, to logical aspects: first, because praying helps us to express in words exactly what troubles us. Second, because we no longer carry the weight of the world on our shoulders. And third, because praying is the first step toward action.[339]

We might be surprised to know that many people who were laid out in hospital beds or knocked down in various corners around the world, thinking they had no strength to get up and carry on living with head held high, could change overnight to become heroes, warriors and leaders during crises that would leave half the world beaten down and with no strength to react. Why do I say this? Because the history of human civilization shows it. We underestimate the power of the people around us, but inside each one lies a latent and hidden strength waiting to be tapped. In that person hides an actress or a singer, someone who can help others survive tough times, someone with a special gift of painting or teaching, a police officer or a doctor, postman or author. What matters is that there is a spectacular potential. How do I know this? Well, how do we survive in the wild, how do we find shelter and defend ourselves from animals much stronger than us? We are sons and daughters of the survivors, we descend from those brave ones who fought the most devastating forces of nature, cleared forests, drank water from streams and hunted to survive. We are the children of brave warriors who fought one another. We are the ones who survived the birth, growth and decline of the empires. We saw seemingly indestructible things destroyed, and the victory of underdogs. We beat the plagues, the impetuous forces of nature, lies and hunger. We beat every challenge, every time, and we are here. The most important sentence I have ever heard in my life was comes from Papillon, the escaped prisoner. When he finally breaks free from his accursed prison, and floats in the ocean in an improvised boat, he shouts: - *I am still here, you bastards!*

We are the children of Socrates and Jesus, of Alexander the Great and Julius Caesar, of Newton and Einstein, of Joan of Arc and Helen Keller, of Marie Curie and Elizabeth; of Mary and Joseph, of water and fire, of earth and the air; of the fight against the shark in the sea and against thirst in the desert; of the cold of the boundless snow and the intelligence to improvise. We are children of nature and here we are. So, what do we fear? Our most ancient predecessors faced ghosts, monsters, beasts and armies for us to be here today. They fought against murderers and the peddlers in the temple for us to be here. And here we are. What are we afraid of? Debt? Being unable to close a deal? Of walking down the street? Of changing jobs? Of what people might say? Seeing someone we like say goodbye or leave? It all seems unbearable, but it's just superficial. We are here to make our own way, and we have all the forces of the wilds and the oceans to help us live, see and discover new ways, new paths, new people around us. What can be done is just take one step after another, like Jack London's sea wolf; so sure of its strength, even immobilized with sickness, it manifested monstrous strength. Mother Nature is proud of each one of us because, no matter what we do, we are winners. If she knows it, then why can't we accept our power?

One of my favorite topics is the criticism we receive.[340] An editor once told me he heard authors criticize things every day, but few dared commit their criticism to paper. To what did he attribute this apprehension? To the fear of being criticized themselves. Many disregard the possibility of writing great books because they fear the inevitable rain of criticism. And this is a reasonable concern; people's life experience shows them that criticism is frequent and often unfair. Carnegie was aware of this and developed a method for analyzing criticism:

1) If criticism is deserved, we should learn from it.

And that is true. Over my fifteen years of teaching, every time

I return corrected exams, my students immediately hone in on the questions they got right. This is great, but I try to explain to them that beyond the right answers, they should focus on the ones they got wrong. Learning from one's mistakes is an excellent way to improve. I explain that they already understand the topics they answered correctly, but should know why the wrong answers were wrong, so they can avoid making the same mistakes again. Carnegie writes about Benjamin Franklin's interesting method for dealing with mistakes: at the end of the day, do an analysis of what was done wrong, and try to correct these mistakes afterward. Some of Franklin's mistakes were: wasting time, stewing over trifles, arguing and contradicting people.[341] I see I share these faults with Franklin; do you also see yourself in Franklin's list? Carnegie finishes the topic with: *Instead of waiting for our enemies to criticize us or our work, let's beat them to it. Let's be our own most severe critic. Let's find and remedy all our weaknesses before our enemies get a chance to say a word.*[342] When rereading these observations I decided to try a new tactic with my students. I asked them to take out a sheet of paper and write, anonymously, what they expected of a good teacher. I did this so that I can correct my faults, and it is very important to me. I try to get one or two of these pieces of feedback every day; here are a few I have received: "The teacher must use didactic material, be respectful, stick to the syllabus and be organized". Another: "The teacher must be humble". And another: "Deep knowledge of the topic and provocative methodology, which shows good preparation, availability and accessibility to students, and application, punctuality and good class planning." It's not easy!

2) The second point is also crucial and refers to undeserved criticism; we all know how often that shows up.

People make up stories, belittle others, speak aggressively; eventually, it gets to us. But Carnegie was also familiar with this truth and, thankfully, suggests that we not waste our time on it. If we do something, we will be criticized; if we don't do it, we will be criticized just the same. Therefore, we need to keep on with our work, gaining time, and not waste one moment worrying about unjust criticism. If we were as righteous as Christ, we would still probably be crucified; if we were as smart as Galileo, we would be sentenced to house arrest. Criticism should not get us down. Carnegie concluded about unjust criticism: *Do the very best you can: and then put up your old umbrella and keep the rain of criticism from running down the back of your neck.*[343]

Now imagine the amount of criticism that our friend Dale Carnegie received. During the recession he was well known, getting richer by the day and selling millions of books. It's not hard to guess what happened. Of course the criticism began. Our question is whether this criticism was justified or not, as we shall see next.

# CHAPTER 10

# CRITICISM

*While Carnegie and his practices are often maligned by
those who know of him only through his public image and
have little or no experience with the man or his ideas,
those who have studied Carnegie hold a different opinion
with respect to his significance as teacher and speaker.*
(Stephen E. Kirkland)[344]

## 1) HE QUOTED SUCH CONTROVERSIAL HISTORICAL FIGURES AS NAPOLEON AND JOSEPHINE

Carnegie came from humble country roots, but soon became a household name. Of course he became a target for aggression; this serves as a warning for the reader, since well-known people attract heavy criticism. Carnegie expected critics to appear, and they certainly came. Some of their complaints were so trivial that they hardly bear repeating, for example that Carnegie discussed Napoleon and Josephine[345:] certainly these were polemic characters in history, but don't diminish his work in any way. What is the problem with mentioning Napoleon? The days of being burned at the stake for discussing ideas or books are over. Criticizing an author's repertoire seems like ideological policing, a vision that prescribes 'correct authors' or 'correct characters' for study or discussion obviously flies in the face of intellectual freedom. Furthermore, we know that Carnegie didn't cite Napoleon in order to praise his politics or his tyranny, but only to comment on a peculiarity of his life. I present an excerpt in which Carnegie mentions the two:

> *If we merely try to impress people and get people interested in us, we will never have many true, sincere friends. Friends, real friends, are not made that way.*

*Napoleon tried it, and in his last meeting with Josephine he said: 'Josephine, I have been as fortunate as any man ever was on this earth; and yet, at this hour, you are the only person in the world on whom I can rely.'*
*And historians doubt whether he could rely even on her.*[346]

In another passage, Carnegie compares Napoleon's life with Helen Keller's. He makes the case that despite Napoleon's power and Keller's own challenges, Keller's self image was better than that of the Emperor.[347] We can conclude that many of his critics did not actually read his books. But some other complaints deserve a more detailed analysis.

## 2) HIS MARRIAGE WAS NOT SUCCESSFUL

It is said that one chapter of *How to Win Friends and Influence People* was removed from the book. It was supposed to be about "Seven Rules to Make Your Life Happier". These rules ranged from tips on maintaining patience with a loved one, to suggestions on buying books about sexuality in marriage.[348] It is not clear if Carnegie really intended to publish this chapter.

One of Carnegie's critics stated that despite creating rules for better conjugal living, his first marriage was a dismal failure.[349] Not much is known about this marriage, but Carnegie probably made a mistake. However, doesn't he have a right to make mistakes and learn from them? This is just one of millions of relationships, marriages, and partnerships that for some reason failed. Carnegie recognized it had been a mistake; many times he said so to Dorothy, with whom he had an excellent marriage. Demanding perfection from anyone contradicts human nature. Unfortunately, this brings us to comment on another of Carnegie's virtues, which was his conviction that one must recognize one's own mistakes; he often discussed his shortcomings, and many can be found in his books. Carnegie's silence about his failed marriage, though, appeared to many to be an omission. However, public discussion of the relationship would have contradicted some of his other principles, such as not criticizing others; discussing his divorce would involve criticizing his ex-wife, whether directly or indirectly. He also would be 'crying over spilled milk', complaining when it was too late to change or take action. By not wanting to contradict his own values, Carnegie once more demonstrates good judgment. But there is something in Carnegie that goes beyond normality, which is his authenticity and sincerity. One day, when all I knew about Carnegie was only gleaned from the books he had written, I saw a television show that impressed me greatly. The program portrayed Dale Carnegie's life, talking about how his way of life exactly matched the principles he espoused in his books. His modest life did not correspond to his financial wealth. He lived in a quiet neighborhood in Queens, in a simple house like any other (I visited the place, which, by the way, is very peaceful), with humble habits...

What we tend to see is exactly the opposite: hundreds of artists, athletes, executives with eccentric habits, spending fortunes to impress public opinion or to simply to attract more attention. They live immersed in drugs, lacking responsibility or respect for others or themselves; they are not good examples of how to live. Meanwhile, Carnegie showed people that they could progress in life, regardless of who they were and what type of situation in which they found themselves; whether in business or public life, they could live without entitlement or snobbery.

## 3) HE NEVER BECAME AS GREAT A PUBLIC SPEAKER AS DEMOSTHENES

Did Carnegie fail because he never was a 'public speaker as grand as Demosthenes'?[350] Well, I would not jump to this conclusion. It is certain that the critics of that day only knew one type of public speaker, from the way they described him in their books and events in which they participated: the emphatic, pompous, proud, and shall we say, the 'demagogue politician' style. But Carnegie's suggestions were innovative, more suited to the new way of living that was emerging in New York: people hurrying along the streets, no time to lose, ruining their health with big city stress. Carnegie created the simple, direct, frank, authentic and honest public speaker. And he was able to attract crowds to his lectures and courses, and persuade millions of people to believe in themselves, to be confident enough to know they had just as much potential as those idols they held close to their hearts. With time, Carnegie was able to make his Course into something more than just an oratory course. It could be said that Dale Carnegie was a great public speaker, a great seller for his classes and courses and books. The critics of that era looked for, in Carnegie, a type of public speaker that was already a thing of the past, which Carnegie himself had already surpassed.

## 4) SOME INTERVIEWS WERE CONDUCTED BY PAID ASSISTANTS; ON THE OTHER HAND, OTHER CRITICS CLAIMED HIS STUDY ON STRESS WAS NOT BASED ON STATISTICS[351]

Some criticism of Carnegie seems more of a compliment than anything else. To state that some people Carnegie interviewed were actually interviewed by his employees[352], in my opinion, only confirms the reputability of his work. It means he wanted to know more, listen to more people, add value to his research. It also means that he invested time and money in broadening his scope and in collecting valuable information that was not widely available at the time. It certifies his scientific dignity. Many scholars conducting research hire people to interview different people to obtain diverse statistics or opinions. It is an honest job. Dishonesty would entail fabricating facts and opinions, interviews that were never conducted, words that were never said. In other words, lies. Carnegie never hid the fact that he had assistants. Let's be honest, the task of interviewing dozens or even hundreds of people is overwhelming; even if we were able to do it, if we felt the results to be insufficient, wouldn't we invest a bit more and hire more people to conduct more interviews in different areas to complete the project? This is really an example of the persistence and responsibility necessary to truly engage in the subject of writing or study. Many of us could do better in our jobs and lives if we followed Carnegie's example: really get into the challenge. In this way, the argument that his studies about worry 'do not take into account statistics' is invalidated, because when someone invests significant time and money in research, they certainly are building a solid foundation to form a broad sample for study. As we have seen, Carnegie's citations of scientific research are extensive, not to mention the countless interviews he conducted.

## 5) HIS STUDIES ON STRESS ONLY TOOK INTO ACCOUNT THE NEGATIVE ASPECTS, WITHOUT ATTEMPTING TO SEE THE POSITIVE EFFECTS[353]

I have the impression that if Carnegie were still alive, he would love to receive fair criticism and utilize it in order to improve his work. However, it seems that some comments about his work are really out of context. This one, for example, is interesting since it posits that Carnegie discarded the positive aspects of stress when he talked about overcoming worry. Of course we know that adrenalin, for example, is a defense compound used by our body to enable quick reactions to dangerous situations, such as a quick jolt of fear felt before dashing to the sidewalk to avoid being hit by a car. But let's face it, this wasn't what Carnegie wanted to help his readers with; he wanted to help those on their way to premature deaths, some even terminal cases that needed, I repeat, needed a radical change in order to be saved. People with heart disease, cancer, intestinal problems and many others who arrived at this point because of unorganized lives, anxiety, stress, nerves and a desperate need to change their attitude. No! Carnegie was one of the pioneers in alerting society to the ravages of stress. Of course, a bit of stress is beneficial, but Carnegie referred only to the unbalanced part, the nervous and restless life of people like him, like you and me. But even the positive aspects of stress weren't ignored or forgotten by him. He himself would tell a young sportsman or public speaker that being a bit nervous does have its positive side. But Carnegie also dealt with those who were essentially blocked and unable to function in public situations due to excess stress. That was one of his stated goals, to get as many people as possible to have the self-confidence and strength needed when in public and stressful situations.

## 6) SHOWING INTEREST IN OTHERS IS 'CYNICAL' AND 'MANIPULATIVE'

One criticism of Carnegie claims that while he told people to be sincere, he taught 'tricks' to influence others.[354] Well, the first thing that comes to my mind is the fact that speeches, dialogues and talks are all essentially ways to convince or persuade; it is intrinsic to dialogue. Even in the humblest of situations, when we ask someone something, we insinuate that we don't know about the subject, and would like more information about it. In this way, we would be persuading the other person to give us information. As such, if Carnegie developed methods of persuasion to be used in conversation, I don't see any contradictions. From the statement 'convincing someone, yes; lying to them, no', it can be concluded that we can persuade people without lying, we can be involving without being fake or attempting to trick someone. Persuasion has always been taught in school; after all, what more is 'publicity', 'marketing', 'business', 'economics', etc.? But, as Kirkland wrote, when 'persuasion' ceases to be academic, we start to doubt it. But a sincere smile can bring another sincere smile; persuasion is not necessarily a way to flatter or coerce, but a means to attain through sincerity.[355] When we persuade a child to go to school without using violence, are we cynical? Is being persuasive a way to manipulate people? Coincidentally or not, Carnegie talks about persuading children, but at the same time he shows parents and guardians how important it is to give children respect and attention. He refers in his book to a story that, without a doubt, is one of the most touching things I have ever read: *Father Forgets*, by W. Livingston Earned.[356] Every person, parent or not, should read this short text to learn how to deal with and truly respect children. After *Father* Forgets, Carnegie concludes: "Instead of condemning people, let's try to understand them."[357] This he follows with: "To know all is to forgive all"[358]. One must comprehend the context of his thoughts before having grounds to criticize him.

One of Carnegie's golden rules for a good relationship between people, and for attracting attention to yourself and consideration from others is that one must show interest in others. Critics say that this method is 'cynical' and 'manipulative'. Taking an interest in others, asking about their favorite hobbies, or just paying compliments would signify gratuitous adulation and manipulation of others, according to this attitude.[359] Tom Sant offered a very interesting response to this accusation: it depends on the person who applies these principles, for if the main intention is to get someone do something for you, or buy something from you, and you simply discard the person afterward, that would be cynical and manipulative. However, if being interested in others becomes a lifelong habit, in which admiration is encouraged, is becomes a virtue that decreases tension between people, and improves everyone's mood.[360] In all of Carnegie's writings, the reader can see how much he developed his vision for seeing others. It is almost like magical glasses that allow us to truly see other people and the good things they do, filtering out our own tendency to criticize everything we encounter. We could argue: "But people make mistakes, and they are this or that…" Carnegie would have replied with something like: "But if we were in their place, wouldn't we act the same way?" Being interested in others is a principle that goes back to Socrates and Jesus; we see it in the Golden Rule, in Kant and John Ross.

In this aspect, I do consider this criticism of Carnegie to be malignant,  but simply as a consequence of not closely reading the text, and not understanding the entirety of his thoughts. Carnegie never encouraged nosy people who only remember us when they need a favor (and are usually very predictable when calling us, seeking us out only when they need something). Instead, he preached that we should really take an interest in others, to offer help and be at their service if needed. After all, isn't that what this sentence from his book really means? "If we want to make friends, let's put ourselves out to do things for other people – things that require time, energy, unselfishness and thoughtfulness."[361] Evidently what we see here is not a selfish or opportunist philosophy, but the idea of dedication to others. If this method can improve people's lives, especially with regards to relationships, and it benefits them, isn't this acceptable? Knowing how to accept the good in people can be a sign of humility; after all, if I try to participate in the lives of others, why would I prevent them from participating in my life? Wouldn't the person that assists, gives attention and dedicates him or herself to others actually be presumptuous and proud if he or she did not accept other people's help? Even more, those who follow Carnegie's suggestions and dedicate themselves to others would benefit from the well-being this dedication provides. We know little about the laws of the universe; however, everyone has heard of karma and bad deeds punished and good deeds rewarded. Is this a fantasy? Have you ever found the same thing? Why does it happen? Here we have a pragmatic topic; if it is real for us, the fact that we are unable to explain or prove whether the laws of action and reaction apply to behavior, whether it is a matter of the collective unconscious, or of the action of God or Gods upon us, it cannot stop us from acting in the best way possible.

Another sample of what we express in discussions of Carnegie's feelings about interest in others can be seen in the following phrase from *How to Win Friends and Influence People*:

*A show of interest, as with every other principle of human relations, must be sincere. It must pay off not only for the person showing the interest, but for the person receiving the attention. It is a two-way street – both parties benefit.*[362] From reading this, I developed an idea that I always share with my friends: two-way friendship. The good in a true friendship must go both ways. I do not mean that if we do something for our friend, we should receive the equivalent. I am talking about the <u>concept of friendship</u>. If we are talking about real friendship, friends help each other. This does not mean that must agree with each other on every point. No! It is possible to disagree about things, whether serious or trivial. But if a friend needs help, how can we abandon her in her hour of need? If we turn our back in hard times, then we never had a real friendship. A friend once told me: "If my friends abandon me in my time of need, they weren't really my friends." I say this not to judge anyone, but only to state that if someone helps us and we never help them back, we received their generosity, but we were never friends.

But Carnegie is wiser than my prejudiced judgments on friendship; maybe he wanted us to be better and more detached, instead of habitually judging of others. He observes:

> *If you want others to like you, if you want to develop real friendships, if you want to help others at the same time as you help yourself, keep this principle in mind: become genuinely interested in other people.*[363]

I confess it is not easy to accept such magnitude and grandiosity, but I try to do my best; sometimes when I see Carnegie talk about the difficulty he had in following his own teachings, I feel comforted. It calms me to know that Carnegie carried around and read his principles every day, because if it were easy to follow them, then I would be in serious trouble when facing my own difficulties.

## 7) SHOWING ENTHUSIASM IS RIDICULOUS?

According to the research of behavior specialists, our attitudes influence our actions and vice-versa; this in turn influences the opinions and behavior of others.[364]

Accordingly, I cannot agree with attempts to demoralize Carnegie's encouragement of displays of energy, enthusiasm and joy, for enthusiasm is the spark of life. When Carnegie's methods began to be successful with people of all social standing, defamatory accusations also appeared, arguing that the methods were ineffectual. Yet other brave voices were raised in support of Carnegie, including many scholars who tried to prove his theories, who were convinced that these theories were not only right, but also within reach of many. Professor William A. D. Millson of John Carroll University, for example, wrote an article declaring that many college students benefited from Carnegie's methods. While conventional teaching used obsolete and mechanical techniques, Carnegie developed emotion and trust. With that, Professor Milson concluded that "Perhaps we have yet to discover that our students have emotions as well as brains, and voice and body".[365] Students themselves wrote course evaluations stating that the Carnegie Course gave them what they wanted, while college level oratory courses were not what they had expected.[366] People had some idea of the enthusiasm technique before taking the Course, but only after did they understand that the technique went deeper than they had imagined.[367] In the field of music, I imagine it is what Wynton Marsalis called 'playing with feeling'. We all need to do things with feeling; in everything in life, in every moment and every activity, enthusiasm is what makes the difference. Brazilian soccer players say that when they played well, they 'played the game of their lives' and 'gave their blood to the game'. In this complex concept we can find the essence of human expression. In his unholy and wonderful travels with no set destination, Jack Kerouac tried to explain enthusiasm in his own way:

> Now, man, that alto man last night was IT – he held it once he found it; I've never seen a guy who could hold so long.' I wanted to know what IT meant. 'Ah, well' – Dean laughed – 'now you're asking me impon-de-rables – ahem! Here's a guy and everybody's there, right? Up to him to put down what's

*on everybody's mind. He starts the first chorus, then lines up his ideas, people, yeah, yeah, but get it, and then he rises to his fate and has to blow equal to it. All of a sudden somewhere in the middle of the chorus he gets it – everybody looks up and knows; they listen; he picks it up and carries. Time stops. He's filling empty space with the substance of our lives, confessions of his bellybottom strain, remembrance of ideas, rehashes of old blowing. He has to blow across bridges and come back and do it with such infinite feeling soul-exploratory for the tune of the moment that everybody knows it's not the tune that counts but IT.*[368]

Of course not every critic knows these 'imponderables'. But let's see how Carnegie manifests his IT, when he gives guidance to those responsible for working with course participants, in the instructor's handbook:

*I beg of instructors not to think of this as a public speaking course. Think of it as a course in destroying fear and building self-confidence. Think of it as a new way of life. For it often is just that. When a man banishes fear and develops confidence, his ceilings will become higher and his visibility unlimited…*

*Fear causes more physical illness than germs. Jesus condemned fear more than he condemned sin. Fear is probably the greatest of all sins. It is a sin against the abundant life we should be living. It is a sin against our health. Above all else, it is a sin against our children, for if they are brought up by fearful, shy, self-doubting parents, they are almost sure to go through life only half-living because of timidity… Above all else, we are developing skills in acquiring courage.*[369]

This was one of the many ways Carnegie showed enthusiasm!

## 8) BEING KIND MAY NOT CHANGE THE REALITY OF THINGS

Margaret Marshall was a columnist for *The Nation,* and her overflowing pessimism was on display in a bitter article about Dale Carnegie. She said that when an employer fires an employee or refuses to accept a complaint, it does not change the employee's situation; whether the employer fires them kindly or rudely, the result is the same: unemployment. Margaret also claimed that Carnegie was more concerned about the employer than the employee.[370]

Margaret's criticism seemed more neglectful of the book *How to Win Friends and Influence People;* she wrote in 1938, when the book was already successful and there were many unemployed people in the United States due to the stock market collapse and resulting economic crisis. However, it is evident that Margaret did not read the full book, nor analyze its context, for Carnegie was concerned for both employees and job-seekers, developing topics that would help the worker keep his job, progress in his job and help the unemployed gain employment, to the extent that he discusses how to write a letter to a prospective employer and so on. Furthermore, Margaret did not notice Carnegie's sensitivity; in his recommendations on how to be kind at the most critical moments, Carnegie puts himself in the place of the person being fired. He shows that, even if the person is no longer employed, he should still continue to be respectful; he teaches that employees are not disposable, and always deserve respect from the employer. How many people wouldn't prefer to have the employer's consideration when confronted with an inevitable dismissal? Refusing a complaint with a loud and arrogant NO, or accepting that one can naturally be dismissed, with no consideration, this wouldn't be considered a lack of sensibility? It seems ruthless, and is exactly the opposite of Carnegie's tenets. Dismissal is not the problem Carnegie is trying to solve; anyway, it is not realistic to expect someone to come up with a catalog of clean answers to all of humanity's problems. If we analyze the context of his work, even in this aspect Carnegie did not neglect his readers; when he taught about human relations and the best mechanisms for dialogue, he also helped the candidate to get an honest job. After all, how many employers nowadays pray (or even beg) for candidates with qualities Carnegie espoused to appear? We can see this from the many companies around the world that enroll their employees in Dale Carnegie Training.

But let's focus on the technique of praise, which was used on Carnegie's students almost from the beginning. In his study on the Carnegie Courses, William Longgood showed that the cruel critic (even the most subtle one) is banned from the course. Instructors focus on the positive aspects, not on negative ones. Mistakes are corrected in an impeccable technique that doesn't block the apprentice by criticizing her faults, but by instead focusing on her merits. How does it work? It is a complex technique that Carnegie's instructors are prepared to use, just like bearers of some magical potion, but one they utilize in an impressive way. It is based on 'inspiration'. It shows how to be more effective and how to do better, and focuses on the person as a whole.[371] As a result, it corrects positively, constructively, eliminating the "little mistakes" that reverberate inside our heads. But wait, let's hear the precise words of one of the best interpreters of the technique. Dr. L. Gray Burdin, who was vice-president of the Dale Carnegie Institute, and also a teacher of oratory at Butler University in Indianapolis, said:

> *Academic people always think it is impossible. They say, 'How can you train without criticizing?' We say, 'You can inspire'. Does this mean you don't correct? No! We do correct, but there is more than one way to do it. This is the root of the Dale Carnegie philosophy of teaching: 'We never criticize; we show you instead how you can become more effective. That is the secret of our success. We tell you how to be more effective and then show you how. We don't just tell you what's wrong, but immediately show you how to do better. We concentrate on the whole person, not just the one*

*thing he may not be doing the best possible way. We want no one to sit down with the feeling that he failed. For that reason we use praise and inspiration as our teaching tools.*[372]

Carnegie took this so seriously that even if a student requested it, criticism was not given. Carnegie knew the devastating effects of criticism, of obscurantism, and the harmful damage it caused. On the other hand, he reminded his instructors he did not want adulation. Anyone who fawned on the students would be fired. Longgood reports the phrase Carnegie fervently repeated to his instructors: "There is no place in this course for anything but unswerving integrity".[373] Actually, the method was much more sophisticated than some critics even imagined.

## 9) HE DEVELOPED 'VERBAL SIGNS THAT SUFFOCATE INSTINCT'

One of the most curious criticisms of Carnegie that I have read was written by Gail Thain Parker, in an article entitled *How to Make Friends and Influence People: Dale Carnegie and the Problem with Sincerity*. Parker's complaints were sharp; I will refrain from commenting on all of the issues she mentioned, as it seems that she did not define her topic very well, and rambled with various unfounded complaints. Yet, when she discusses Carnegie's discoveries, such as the support groups[374], she does not emphasize their merits, which seems skewed even from a dispassionate critic. In any case, the criticism most deserving response is Parker's comment that Carnegie developed 'verbal signs to suffocate people's instincts to react aggressively in everyday situations'.[375] Yet, according to Parker, 'sincerity is spontaneous'.[376] Reading this brought to mind Goethe's comment that he could see himself committing horrendous crimes every day; thankfully, this was only in Goethe's thoughts, and the great poet is honored to this day. Yet Goethe was not 'spontaneous' when he smothered his aggressive instincts, instead channeling his energy into writing. How many times do we regret being 'sincere' when criticizing someone close to us? Sincerity is spontaneous, says Parker, but she does not consider how often we open our mouths to be 'sincere' and then come to regret it. I, for one, would take back ninety-nine percent of the criticism and complaints I uttered throughout my life, which I regretted, thought better of, and reconsidered as inopportune or even groundless. It is better to think before judging people. Parker also says that *In contrast, Carnegie was convinced that the human mind consisted of separated faculties and that intelligent self-interest should govern the instincts and feelings.*[377] When I finished reading Parker's article, I felt that she must live in a place where society is pure, every man on the street tells the truth, and no one practices deception. Where is Parker headed with the notion that everyone should expose his or her instincts, and immediately say what comes to mind? Even more, who said our first impression of something or someone is correct, and immediately should be passed on to third parties? Carnegie never defended insincerity; he implores readers to seek truth countless times. I do not intend to bore the reader with further repetitions of Carnegie's thoughts, but I will convey one more thing he said about sincerity: "Above all, remember this: acting with sincerity, you will feel sincere."[378] We have also seen that Carnegie calls for reflection on how we should envision and fully respect the other, as if we were in their shoes. This goes quite beyond any discussion of 'suffocating instinct', for Carnegie calls his reader to exhibit rationality, good manners, moderation, respect and, without a doubt, the sincerity that comes from thinking instead of instinctual violence and aggression. Many times, I have seen a beautiful stranger on the street and wished I could hug or kiss her, but if I did such a thing, I would soon find myself in jail or an asylum. Just as I would not like to see my own sister, partner or lover approached and touched by some stranger on the street, I must also control my 'sincere instincts' and think before acting. This is completely human and reasonable. I was impressed by Parker's superficial criticism of Carnegie, although she disguised her comments as 'academic criticism'. On the other hand, I confess that her scattered approach to Carnegie's themes made me think. One of the points she addressed was Carnegie's name change, a topic we have already discussed. However, even Parker yields a bit despite her nay-saying, when she literally states: *If you sincerely wanted to improve your ability to do well with people because you sincerely wanted to survive, you were, according to Carnegie's way of thinking, for ever safe from being accused of hypocrisy.*[379] Parker's words contradict her thoughts: 'improve ability', 'do well with people', 'survive', are things that Parker herself would like to improve, are they not? If not, I am starting to wonder about her sociability; or perhaps she is the purest version of Candide, described by Voltaire as someone who only saw the purity in people. No! Parker started with the wrong assumptions. If she had considered what people who acted on impulse could do to her and her family, she would certainly reconsider and defend the filter of rational thinking, of courtesy, of the easy smile, of balanced consideration suggested by Carnegie. Without this cordiality and the benefits Carnegie elaborated, life would be a terrible hardship and, why not, even a 'human wilderness' in which everyone ends up like a cat that is trod on accidentally, but still bites the friendly hand that is only trying to help.

## HOW DID CARNEGIE REACT TO THE CRITICS?

Well, we know what Carnegie said to his readers on the topic of how to face deserved and unjust criticism. It was explained well in *How to Win Friends and Influence People* and *How to Stop Worrying and Start Living.* In these books we find some other formulas to better understand why people criticize us, what's behind the criticism, and what should be done with these malignancies, whether done consciously or not. However, I think about how this could have bothered Carnegie, to the point of upsetting his life. Let's remember that he cared about his writing career, but when he published his big successes, he did not expect to be successful as a writer. However, after impressive sales figures, the hail of criticism was close behind. Did Carnegie follow his own advice, opening his umbrella and letting unjust criticism roll off his back? It is hard to say, but there are some sign that can lead us to a conclusion. First, Carnegie's personal investment in his work, and in everything he did, was impressive. Even when he was on vacation, or during his leisure hours, he took advantage of the information available to produce something useful for his course and writings; an example was his trip to China. It is also well known that the intensity of his dedication and focus was really singular. The effort of being put on the spot all the time by some critics, often for superficial reasons, can no doubt affect even a soul who is aware of his merits. Secondly, wouldn't someone with such a privileged vision of how to treat others feel the ruthless blows of people who could have cared less about anything other than themselves? Certainly Carnegie's public image as the grand master of how to treat people could have caused his detractors to think that Carnegie did not need as much consideration as any other person. This can be noted at times in the cold or indelicate approaches of some critics, who did not analyze the theme carefully or express their opinion in a truly academic form. What I want to say is that some critics did not lack an air of superiority, and underestimated Carnegie's enormous capacity to confront criticism.

From what is known, even those interested in the course were a bit put off by the critics, and by ignorance of the course's content. Hesitant, some people enrolled under fake names, thinking that the course was only for people who had  some problem that needed 'fixing'. According to Longgood,  people realized over time that those who wanted to improve their abilities in a competitive society were, in fact, minds focused on success. Some people turned the dust jacket of *How to Win Friends and Influence People* inside out so others wouldn't know what they were reading.[380] What I have noticed was that everyone, from the academic to the man on the street, adopts a certain air of superiority when referring to Carnegie. It is an understandable disregard considering the multitude of books labeled as 'self-help' that stand in comparison to the purity and simplicity of Carnegie's work.

What damage did the critics cause? I think that it  upset Carnegie at the very least. However, I believe he was more affected by the lack of academic recognition of his contributions. Maybe scientists, politicians, sociologists, pedagogues, psychologists, philosophers and historians were careless about the depth of Carnegie's work because his books were found on the 'self-help' shelves, not on the shelves of their subjects. Or maybe they all just thought that Carnegie wouldn't mind not being complimented...

# CHAPTER 11

# THE STIGMA-LIBERATING CHARACTER
# OF HIS THOUGHTS

*Stigma acquired two dimensions: one objective (signal, use, skin color, origin, illness, nationality, alcoholism, poverty, religion, sex, sexual orientation, physical or mental challenge, etc.) and the other subjective (bad or negative attributes given to these states, for example: if you are physically handicapped you are bad, inferior or worse, etc.). Where the derivation of rules for the stigmatized function as a way to harm their daily lives and also generally weaken human contact in general, the so-called "normals" are also harmed in the relationship. They are false rules that have no connection with reality.*
(Carlos Roberto Bacila)[381]

How can prejudice be conquered in a society that is so complex? One character of Dale Carnegie's books always draws attention: he does not stigmatize and promotes the appreciation of difference, respecting all people equally. He utilized studies of mental ability to disseminate the value of every human being. So, in the 1940's, at a time when women were considered second class citizens or worse, he cites Mary Baker Eddy's biography, acknowledging the immense cruelty she suffered before founding Christian Science. Carnegie follows this by emphasizing that she was the only woman to ever create a religion.382 He takes advantage of Mary Baker Eddy's experience with mental strength to show her feminine talent. How many writers did that back then? The point is that, in the way he expressed himself, such realities sounded great, because he did not use a tone inspiring 'a challenge to men' or something similar. I was impressed by the liberating manner of his speech, which he used in his work as a researcher and promoter of data on human behavior, making it sound natural. But the beauty of it all is the diversity of stigmas that he discredits in one passage: Mary Baker Eddy was 'homeless', 'poor', 'had disturbed thoughts', 'was abandoned by her second husband' (the stigma of the woman not being married), she was 'sick' and a 'vagabond', etc. But even then, Carnegie saw Mary Baker Eddy for a the heroine she was. More than by words and empty speeches, women's emancipation was built on, and is still built on action. Another passage that shows what could be done was described by someone who knew him well, his secretary Marilyn Burke. She said that in 1955, when Carnegie was already suffering from the illness that he would succumb to later that year, he was invited to give a lecture at the Brooklyn Rotary Club. He asked if Burke could accompany him. Unlike today, at that time women were not permitted to attend rotary meetings, and the directors declined his request. Carnegie responded that he found it ridiculous, and would be unable to attend without Burke. The club made an exception, and finally allowed a woman to participate.[383]

In another situation, and after studying case after case, he showed that the child who leaves home is often looking for personal enlightenment and means to improve his or her life[384], and is not necessarily an 'ungrateful son', a 'rebel without a cause', or anything similar. To Carnegie, what matters is not what we are or what we have, but our mental attitude. This is good for our peace of mind, but it is also good for avoiding stigmatization, which corresponds with the way he lived: simply, free of excessive social etiquette and at the same time, with depth. Let me repeat Carnegie's words on the topic: "I am deeply convinced that our peace of mind and the joy we get out of living depends not on where we are, or what we have, or who we are, but solely upon our mental attitude."[385] How often is the 'place we are' responsible for stigma? 'Foreigner', 'outsider', 'hillbilly', 'Latino', 'gringo', 'African', 'Arab', and so many others are systematically discriminated against because they come from another country, or live in a different state, or they live in the suburbs, or reside in a house that is not 'up to standard', etc. 'How much we have' is an object of the stigma of poverty, which is responsible for many cruelties from personal offense to unfair criminal convictions against the economically disadvantaged. 'What we are' can also provoke an endless parade of stigmas: 'woman', 'homosexual', 'bachelor', 'single mother', 'liberal', 'special needs', etc. If this is the case, both those who discriminate against others and the stigmatized parties can benefit from Carnegie's message: get rid of the stigmas, improve your thoughts and live better. If this philosophy were better understood and adopted socially, how many disasters and wars could we have avoided, how much suffering could we have been spared, how much evil would not exist. Leading a whole nation based on stigma brought the German people and the world to misery during the era culminating in World War II. In the early 1930's, Hitler came to power in Germany and started to implement one of the cruelest regimens of stigmatization of our times. Politicians, scientists, police officers, jurists, and the adepts of national-socialism started a campaign of battle, persecution, intolerance and violence against many stigmatized peoples. Almost every person that did not fit the 'pure race' concept (a flawed concept, for every nation has a mixture of races) fell victim to the Nazi regime. Beggars, prostitutes, Gypsies, Poles, Ukrainians, Russians and other immigrants, people with criminal records, people with distinctive physical features, people with mental problems, people of Jewish descent, black people and the multitude of people that fell under the category of 'asocial' were targets of persecution and brought to concentration camps. The concept of 'asocial' was so broad that it included those who did not agree with the dictatorship and allowed them to be removed from society and killed. Such 'asocials' included 'single mothers', people who had liberal sexual conduct, homosexuals, people who had sexual intercourse with people of different races than their own, those who were addicted to drugs or alcohol, etc. The stigmatized were brought to concentration camps such as Auschwitz, Buchenwald or Dachau, subjected to medical experiments of all kinds (some fatal), and then were murdered en masse in gas chambers, and then were incinerated. So you can have an idea of how vague the criteria were, the only thing necessary to seal one's fate was physical difference.

For example, let's look at the conclusions of the Attorneys General of Bavaria, who met in Bamberg in 1944, right before the end of the World War II:

> In different visits to the penitentiaries recluses can be observed who, due to the formation of their bodies, do not even deserve to be called people; they look like abortions from hell. It would be desirable to photograph them. Their elimination should also be considered, no matter how grave the felony and sentence received. Only the exhibition of photographs clearly showing their deformity should be allowed.[386]

When the war ended, the battle-hardened Allied troops wept when they entered the concentration camps. In Dachau, for example, American soldiers invited the Germans to see for themselves what had been happening inside the camp. There were survivors, adults weighing less than sixty pounds; there were piles of bodies, ovens to incinerate the dead. The German civilians got sick, cried, refused to believe that all this could have happened in their town. All this and more was presented as testimony at the Nuremberg Trials[387], in which some Nazi leaders were tried and sentenced to death, others sent to prison, and some absolved. The result of is all was that, at the end of the war, the enormous stigmatization process, officially embraced by the German state, ruined the country. Germany was basically destroyed, its principal constructions, lives, pride and all. Germany had to start over from nothing, with the help of the ones that were so abused: the different ones. The stigmatization of people brings only this: loss.

Meanwhile, Carnegie's book was full of examples that valorized stigmatized people's lives: the passage telling of the hanging of the 'convicted' (stigma of the criminal convict) John Brown, who incited slaves to rebellion[388], the passage quoting Milton when he wrote despite his blindness (stigma of the blind) : "The mind is its own place, and in itself can make a heaven of Hell, a hell of Heaven."[389] Another example was Borghild Dahl, who was practically blind for half a century. Carnegie recommends her book I *Wanted to See* as very inspiring.[390] He also mentions Helen Keller, (stigmatized for being deaf, blind and mute) who lived happier than Napoleon despite all his power.[391] People who were institutionalized due to emotional and physical problems and madness were also mentioned (stigma of the sick, the mad and the depressed) to explain that many reached this point as a result of leading lives full of stress, as we all do.[392] He revered the Englishwoman Edith Cavell for not feeling resentment upon being shot on October 12, 1915 by German soldiers; she had been nursing French and English soldiers and helping them to escape, debunking the stigma of enemies of war. He praised Dr. Laurence Jones, a black teacher who worked with illiterate people and lived in miserable conditions, and who was nearly hanged for unfounded accusations that he stimulated black people to fight against their country during World War I, facing down the stigma of race.[393] He also discarded the stigma of race when he quoted a prayer from the Sioux Nation, showing that we should not judge others hastily. This beautiful prayer should be known to everyone: "O, Great Spirit, help me never to judge another until I have walked in his shoes."[394] But Carnegie also admired good facets of the very rich, as in the case of Andrew Carnegie, Ford and Rockefeller, putting aside the stigma of the rich and thus avoiding cursing the material things we depend on, recognizing the good aspects of those people. In Rockefeller's case, he highlighted his change of attitude and focus, which brought him to contribute to humanitarian causes, and improve his quality of life exponentially compared to before, when he had not realized there were more important things in the world than making money. Carnegie also mentioned politicians and their virtues, as with Winston Churchill and Theodore Roosevelt, opposing the <u>stigma of the politician</u>. He mentions the elderly, including his parents, valuing their experiences and teachings, discarding the <u>stigma of old age</u>. In a historical era – and what a long-lasting age it was – where women were assigned the role and the <u>stigma of the housewife,</u> and when women's needs and concerns were invisible, Carnegie told the story of Thelma Thompson, who went to live in the Mojave desert with her husband, who was serving in the army during wartime. After initially suffering from the tedium and roughness of the desert, Thelma adopted a philosophy of social integration, made friends with the native people, studied the cacti and dogs of the region, and looked for signs of nature's beauty, such as seashells that had been there for millions of years. Finally, she wrote a book.[395] How many writers at that time cared about what 'housewives' thought, felt or wrote? And what kind of stories do we find in Carnegie's book? Here is one: *His name is Ben Forston. I met him in a hotel elevator in Atlanta, Georgia. As I stepped into the elevator, I noticed that this cheerful-looking man sitting in a wheelchair in the corner of the elevator was missing both legs.*[396] He goes on to tell an interesting story about this person's life, for he talked to Ben and wanted to know more about him. How many of us – and I include myself in this question – would start a story saying that, upon entering an elevator, we met a man named Ben and we noticed he had lost his legs? Wouldn't it be more usual to say we met a person who had no legs? But in this last case we would just be reinforcing the <u>stigma of the handicapped,</u> because when we meet someone, we simply meet someone, but in the case of a stigma, we usually refer to them by their names along with their stigma: 'woman driver', 'a blind man called Paul', 'a paralytic', 'Remo, a homosexual', 'Drusila, who is a lesbian', 'John, an ex-convict'... But when we do not give the stigma any importance because we treat people equally, we say: the driver is waiting; I met someone called Paul; I was helped by a salesman named Remo; I have a friend called Drusila; etc. You may note that Carnegie gives people the chance to tell the full story, no matter what stigma they are given by society. He recognizes their value as human beings, and comments about amputation or their problems in a way that we can learn from it, but not as an identifying characteristic of the person, as something that is so integral to the person that they will always be associated with such a stigmatizing characteristic. Eliminating stigma was not the goal of his book, but he does it in such a natural manner, which should make the reader take notice. It is genius! Someone who, in the first half of the twentieth century, did not see people in a stigmatizing way, but simply talked about people. The writers that preceded him in this manner – seeking out virtues in stigmatized people or even just treating them equally – were rare at that time. One of the few writers that broke the routine of propagating stigma was Jack London. He was born in San Francisco in 1876. In a compilation of stories called *War,* London takes stigmas and uses them to give full lives to his characters, showing, for example, a beggar and ex-convict who had an interesting and dignified life, but suffered from social mechanisms which led him to be arrested. The title of this story in particular is *The Hobo and the Fairy*. In it we hear the tale of a youth of seventeen named Ross Shanklin, who served fourteen years in prison on false charges of stealing seven horses. When he was released from prison, he went to live in the great outdoors. One day he was approached by a frail waif of a girl, Jane. Ross was surprised and thought he was dreaming when he saw such a beautiful child speaking to him, a man who had seen nothing but evil in his life. Afterward Jane's mother, a good woman, also treats Ross with respect and consideration. The wonderful dialogue they have changes Ross' life; he in turn seeks a job on a farm to work with what he likes best, horses. Ross thanks the farmer for the opportunity given to him: "All right. I'll make good. Where can I get a drink of water and wash up?"[397] The fact is that, at a time when economic liberalism made the successful millionaire a hero and the hobos wandering the streets invisible, London gave the hobo a story full of life! Moreover, it discusses situations common in the penal system, the stigma of the beggar, the ex-convict, and the importance of social contact, no matter how simple, showing that a gesture of interaction bring a potentially great person out from under the bridge. At that time dialogue about how to 're-socialize' convicts was sorely lacking, while London shows it simply yet profoundly: by treating them with dignity and respect. In the same way, Carnegie wrote without expressively emphasizing human rights, yet placed so many stigmatized people in conditions of equality, and held them up as examples to be followed, that his work could be considered revolutionary! Instead of giving empty speeches, purely theoretical and lacking realistic vision, Carnegie inserted the stigmatized into his writings, showing how the other should be treated: the way we would liked to be treated, equally and with respect. Carnegie also gave the stigmatized stories and, by doing that, made them equal, because everyone who has a life story is human. How did Ben Forston lose his legs? In 1929 (coincidentally, the same year that many became poor and received the stigma of the poor, confirming that stigmas follow no logic or reason), Ben went to cut walnut branches to build a trellis for the beans in his garden. When he was driving back home in his Ford "...one pole slipped under the car and jammed the steering apparatus at the very moment I was making a sharp turn. The car shot over an embankment and hurled me against a tree. My spine was hurt. My legs were paralyzed. I was twenty-four when it happened, and I have never taken a step since."[398] Now, let's think, does this fact allow Ben to keep living? Is he still a human? Is he a human being? Should we keep greeting him and treating him like a human being, despite the accident? I'd like to think so. Now, what happens to him on the streets? I'll tell you, because I saw someone going down the street in a wheelchair. It was 1988, I was studying law and had applied for a temporary job working on a mayoral campaign in my hometown, Curitiba. I started to coordinate the team that handed out pamphlets on the street. One employee quit with no explanation. I talked to a woman who worked with him and she said that he saw a neighbor pass by: he feared the neighbor would see him handing out pamphlets and tell everyone he knew. To demonstrate that there was no shame in working an honest job, I took the young man's place and started to hand out pamphlets myself. Some time went by and a man passed in front of me. Naturally, I gave him a pamphlet for our candidate, but he just stayed there. He was a guy in a wheelchair. He looked at me and said: "I'd like to tell you something. The city has hundreds of people handing out pamphlets, but you are the only one who gave me one. The others didn't give me pamphlets because I'm in a wheelchair, but you treated me like a human being. I don't know your candidate, but I will vote for him." Why wouldn't the other people who were handing out pamphlets talk to him? Because he is stigmatized, only because of the fact that he needs a wheelchair to move around. It is not necessary to treat others in an overly dedicated manner or to another extreme, as if the person were invisible-- just simply treat them like the human beings they are. But Carnegie's examples are so numerous that unconsciously, the reader begins to get used to seeing nothing more than exterior or behavioral characteristics, without these characteristics creating a human 'subspecies'. No, Carnegie did not think like that, he actually turned many stigmatized people into examples to be followed. Let's look at some of his conclusions:

> *Yes, it is highly probable that Milton wrote better poetry because he was blind and Beethoven composed better music because he was deaf. Helen Keller's brilliant career was inspired and made possible because of her blindness and deafness. If Tchaikovsky had not been frustrated –*

*and driven almost to suicide by his tragic marriage – if his own life had not been pathetic, he probably would never have been able to compose his immortal 'Symphonic Pathetique'. If Dostoevsky and Tolstoy had not led tortured lives, they would probably never have been able to write their immortal novels.*[399]

As you can see, it isn't just one quote here and there from which we can extrapolate Carnegie's thoughts, but strong characteristics of his thoughts about eliminating stigma can be found throughout his writings over decades, with repercussions until the present day. We can see, for example, a quote from President Barack Obama's autobiography, referring to the way his grandfather tried to relate well to everyone:

*Thus the legend was made of Hawaii as the one true melting pot, an experiment in racial harmony. My grandparents – especially Gramps, who came into contact with a range of people through his furniture business – threw themselves into the cause of mutual understanding. An old copy of Dale Carnegie's* How to Win Friends and Influence People *still sits on his bookshelf. And growing up, I would hear in him the breezy, chatty style that he must have decided would help him with his customers. He would whip out pictures of the family and offer his life story to the nearest stranger; he would pump the hand of the mailman or make off-color jokes to our waitresses at restaurants.*[400]

And so we find conceptions like this one of non-stigmatization in *How to Stop Worrying*, *Public Speaking* or *How to Win Friends…* It does not matter which one of Carnegie's works it is; his thoughts are consistent, radiant, without pretensions to become a doctrine but actually a doctrine in the best sense of the word.

At this point, we return to a main theme of Carnegie's thoughts that was seen in *How to Win Friends and Influence People*, and again in *How to Stop Worrying and Start Living*. I'm talking about the full vision of the other; Carnegie brings back the topic to show that thinking about other people's well being reflects in ourselves. He does not do this in a mystical or religious way, but develops a study about the consequences of 'me' seeing 'you'. Carnegie starts with a study of depression, a malady that plagues millions of people. To Carnegie, one of the most efficient treatments is a very objective change of attitude. One of Carnegie's inductive starting points is research done by specialists, normally psychiatrists or other professionals who have intensive contact with depressed patients. These authorities then developed a technique based on making the patients be routinely interested in others' well-being. This treatment is applied in a friendly and persuasive way and leads the patient to gradually occupy him or herself with doing good things for other people in general, no matter who eventually benefits, and regardless of what the benefit might be. It seems simplistic but the results were impressive. And there is logic in the patient's improvement; while they are thinking about the other person, they forget to worry about their personal problems that only lead to unhappiness and disintegration. Moreover, depression can originate with difficulties in social interaction. Making the patient take interest in others gives him a new perspective on life, an occupation that both distracts and re-engages. Again, Carnegie's case studies shown in the book bring practical techniques, like doing a good deed, however simple. It snowballs, where actions keep growing, growing, and when we least expect it, we find ourselves in a more positive and vibrant place, not wasting time on useless and maddening thoughts. Carnegie titled the chapter on this topic *How to Cure Melancholy in Fourteen Days.*[401] I am sure there are many who completely healed their melancholy by applying this method, and others who diminished their depression significantly. Another resource that Carnegie teaches us, learning to see others, can be used by us all. He took this idea from a woman who was very sick, who thought she was so 'exclusive' that no one could be her friend. She was given a task: create a story about the first person she saw on the street. She was to imagine all aspects of that person's life. This exercise made her start to talk to others and take interest in other people's lives. It was so contagious that she became a friendly person and finally was able to heal.[402] It is incredible! An activity consciously developed to bring out interest in others and a vision of the other! And with such a personal improvement as a result. Why don't we all try this exercise one day?

But here is another point to which I would like to draw the reader's attention: while teaching a mechanism to improve mood and well-being, Carnegie at the same time developed a technique of being able to see social outcasts, treat them well and even be rewarded with the joy of living. When he urges us to treat everyone well, he uses this maxim:

> *What about the grocery boy, the newspaper vendor, the chap at the corner who polishes your shoes? These people are human – bursting with troubles, dreams, and private ambitions. They are also bursting for the chance to share them with someone. But do you ever let them? Do you ever show an eager, honest interest in them or their lives? That's the sort of thing I mean. You don't have to become a Florence Nightingale or a social reformer to help improve the world – your own private world; you can start tomorrow morning with the people you meet!*
>
> *What's in it for you? Much greater happiness! Greater satisfaction, and pride in yourself! Aristotle called this kind of attitude 'enlightened selfishness'. Zoroaster said: 'Doing good to others is not a duty. It is a joy, for it increases your own health and happiness. And Benjamin Franklin summed it up very simply – 'When you are good to others,' said Franklin, 'you are best to yourself'.[403]*

Helping to see the grocery boy, the newspaper vendor and the shoeshine man is proof of his increasing ability to see the other. Discovering benefits for oneself was another one of Carnegie's brilliant ideas that collaborate with his reader and with a life slightly sweeter for those who begin to be treated more humanely. Sometimes a greeting or a compliment to a stranger brightens their day, or their lives or souls. Everyone wins. Here we see that labeling Carnegie's books 'self-help' is not right, for the book also preaches helping the other. So we would have a work that does not limit itself to an egocentric vision of teaching the reader some tricks, but sees something beyond that affects all of humanity, especially if we take into account the millions of readers who have had access to his book. The dimension of his work is perceptible in countless passages and nuances. We will discuss the philosophical aspect in a separate chapter, but note the naturalness with which Carnegie inserts great thinkers in the two paragraphs above: Florence Nightingale, Aristotle, Zoroaster and Benjamin Franklin. We will see other examples.

If we carefully read the passage in *How to Stop Worrying* where he discusses Edith Allred's clothes and behavior, he analyzed the stigma of fashion and way of being, discussing differences from person to person and assigning value to the concept of being different, considering it to be a thing of beauty and not a flaw.[404] Now here is a relevant topic we could learn from Dale Carnegie; the need to be ourselves, find ourselves with our virtues and weaknesses, accepting ourselves as the different beings we are. Isn't it great that we are different than everyone else? Imagine if we were all the same: the same face, same attitudes, same tastes, what a flat, dull world full of the same mistakes. How would a conversation go? "What is your favorite color?" "Blue, like everyone else's." "What do you like to drink?" "Soda, like everyone else." No way! I accept different tastes, opinions, convictions. And thankfully, people think differently than I do. I will fight to maintain the right to think differently. It is said that a friend of Thoreau went to visit him in prison and asked him: "What do you do here?" And Thoreau retorted: "And you, what do you do out there?" Those who were able to accept themselves conquered the world! This does not mean that we should learn to live with our mistakes. No! This is different! Sometimes we do not recognize a problem that we suffer from but can conquer, as the case with drug addiction, for example, or alcoholism. A person suffers from pain and disease caused by alcohol, suffers ridicule from acquaintances, and their friends and family suffer, but they don't see themselves in this way, and believe they are in control of their actions. However, they are not, and the way they see themselves is different from how they are seen by the community. I call this factor the 'stigmatizing of the self'. First, because they do not see themselves as the stigmatized people they are, and then because they do not care and try to change what can be changed in the world around them, do not adopt an attitude of facing the world and living the reality of it, doing what is possible and accepting what is different and beautiful. What cannot be done is passive contemplation and acceptance of society's stigmatizing treatment.[405] This brings us to another of Carnegie's topics, the matter of accepting who we are. How many times do we make superhuman efforts to change our ways and be more like someone we admire, when in truth, what would have been best thing is to identify our own essence, our own style. Finding oneself is priceless. On the other hand, the will to be something other than ourselves can drive us mad or bring about anxiety.[406] Carnegie described his own mistakes in trying to be an actor and imitate great actors. Another mistake he almost made was trying to compile the written works of the best public speakers. When he abandoned this idea, and started to write about what he believed was the best way to speak in public, he wrote the best oratory book. From time to time, when I get upset with things, to find myself again, I try to revisit things that motivated me in my childhood and adolescence, so I register for chess tournaments, I play soccer, and so on.

I have in mind a song from the southern Brazilian countryside that says: "A friend for me is different... a friend is a friend without having to know why they are." Who does not need a friend? When we liberate ourselves from stigmas, we find true friends, as we see the other as he is, not as how he might be one day. By being ourselves, we see ourselves as free individuals.  Then we will see ourselves flying far from tedium, high in the skies that caress the blue sea.

# CHAPTER 12

## DALE CARNEGIE'S PERSONAL METHOD FOR STUDYING, WRITING AND BEING SUCCESSFUL

*O I could sing such grandeurs and*
*Glories about you!*
*You have not known what you are – you have slumber'd*
*upon yourself all your life;*
*What you have done returns already in mockeries.*
*But the mockeries are not you;*
*Underneath them, and within them, I see you lurk;*
*I pursue you where none else has pursued you.*
(Walt Whitman)[407]

It is not unusual to point out Dale Carnegie as the precursor of 'self-help books'. It must be true, for after the release of *How to Win Friends and Influence People* in 1936, more than 30 million copies were sold and this certainly brought out many authors writing about similar topics and publishing the most varied kinds of books as 'self-help'. But it is an illusion to stereotype Carnegie as a 'self-help author' or to stigmatize him as such, for this does nothing to reveal the essence of his philosophy and systematic studies. Whoever skims through the pages of Carnegie's books might be forgiven for thinking, based on the clarity of ideas and the many examples given, that he wrote in an improvised way, not very carefully, without scientific or logical consideration, or with research methods unacceptable in the academic world. One could assume he wrote as if he were improvising all the time, with no accuracy. One would be mistaken. Maybe the reader would like to know what methods Carnegie used to study, write and give his lectures and classes. How did Carnegie behave when he was preparing his books? Well, it is known that no content appears randomly, and we can agree that there is a lot of content in his teachings and concepts. Although Carnegie did not have a college degree, he was the exception to the rule that only those with a traditional education can teach well, for Carnegie brought about a new way of communication. Some critics, without knowing the subject very well, believed that this alone was a disqualifying factor.[408] However, his preparation was superior to that of countless 'academics'. What was his secret? I can assure the reader that I came across an interesting discovery about Carnegie's success in his writings: he used every single one of the methods to write a thesis. I know what I'm talking about, because I wrote one to earn my doctorate in law, and I can tell you, it is not easy. In order to become a professional in this area, I carefully studied the process of elaborating a thesis, and researched various approaches. Carnegie's self-taught genius is evident here, the power to discover paths not taught in conventional settings. Researching things by himself, investigating and discovering methods of study and biographies of successful people led Carnegie to develop a system of study comparable to the methods of the greatest academic researchers, which evidently gave a propriety and quality to his writings that shot him to number one with the themes he debated and taught about. He truly became a complete author, for he overcame his initial lack of academic training, but he did so in such a way that left behind many researchers who used only one method or another to obtain their knowledge; on the contrary, Carnegie became a scientist of human relations, a philosopher of American pragmatism and a perfect salesman for the product he discovered. I keep imagining if Carnegie had studied any other scientific topic: I believe he would have succeeded in that as well. Academia needs organized people and ones that act according to procedural handbooks; however, without creative, self-taught, innovative and unconventional people, there would be no attraction, production, or useful critics in academia. Actually, in this aspect, I am a bit mystical, believing that the Alma Mater chooses her children. When he was studying an unusual topic, without making pretense to obtain an academic title, few realized that Carnegie was developing a new philosophy and mechanisms of human relations that would have far-reaching consequences. One of them was a type of literature called 'self-help'. The other was the proliferation of professional development courses in business administration. Another consequence was the application of Pierce and James' philosophy, and some of the principles of Jesus and the Buddha. A new oratory arrived, a new approach to stress, a new codification of practical language... Carnegie did not worry about labeling his thoughts or naming what he developed. Maybe he was smothered by the overblown criticism of his writings. But something new was going to happen in writing. What I intend to show now is that nothing that happened was random, and that his method of research and divulging ideas through a clear and precise style was not by chance. On the contrary, it was the result of elaborate research on the topics he addressed.

I selected a few methods of research and writing not only to confirm Carnegie's seriousness, but as a useful model to those who intend to progress professionally. I believe that the mechanisms used by Carnegie can be adapted to whatever the reader does for a living. Let's look at the methods.

**Field Research.** As the name states, in field research the student infiltrates a subculture, and we take this expression to mean that it could be a non-conventional or predominant culture, but never an inferior culture. Examples of subcultures include teenage cliques, artists, drug users, prisoners, immigrants, peddlers, police officers, people in asylums, nuns in convents, etc. The researcher 'goes into the field' and does the research directly with the integrants of the subculture, often stigmatized people. This interaction can be done in such a way that the researcher secretly infiltrates the subculture, not to betray nor contradict it, but to know exactly what its members think and how they act. For example, we know that drug users have more sincere conversations with those who also do drugs, and do not communicate certain things to strangers who do not do drugs. So, infiltrating as if one is part of the subculture implies getting more information more authentically. Carnegie conducted intense field research on everything he wrote. In public speaking, he faced challenges since he started from scratch in adolescence, first losing and then winning speaking contests, eventually attaining prestige. After the contests, he applied oratory to sales, sometimes with success, sometimes not; finally, he started to teach public speaking to what was probably the toughest crowd he could have chosen. Then he started to develop methods that would apply even to people who did not have much time or money to improve themselves. As if that weren't enough, he graduated in drama when he tried to become an artist, and acted for a while. In this way, he realized how true artists use their best resources for communication. After years of practice, he started to participate in conferences in front of enormous crowds in grand auditoriums, he participated in television and radio shows, portrayed himself on TV and gave countless interviews on varied topics. Isn't this one of the most complete examples of field research? Regarding his other topic, he wrote 'how to win friends and influence people'; the experience was no less intense, for Carnegie had great difficulty making friends after being stigmatized for his poverty. After going to New York and again experiencing a solitary life, he was still a poor outsider who lived alone and had no friends. But he was able to change that, and, besides the change, he could think about the factors that allowed him to develop real friendship. On top of this, Carnegie was a profound people watcher, an observer of habits and behavior, actions and reactions, making his daily life a spectacular laboratory for interaction and conclusions. To learn 'how to stop worrying', Carnegie also lived the weary existence of a worried life, which he slowly overcame. He also learned how to take advantage of his interaction with worried people and with people whose lives ground to a halt from stress. Finally, on the topic of his management, leadership and sales courses, there is no doubt that his previous professional life taught him a lot. His three jobs in sales showed him how difficult the topic was, the importance of conviction, and the importance of doing it well. Carnegie noticed that selling is not a one-sided process, in which the salesperson only 'sells', but a two-way path, in which the buyer 'buys'. Carnegie visited countless companies; he got to know entrepreneurs, salesmen and complex sales processes, in a way that he could freely discuss the field in his writings and courses.

**Interviews.** Another important way to obtain knowledge is from interviews. Interviewing people uncovers information, straight from the source, about the topic being researched. Carnegie was one of the greatest interviewers of all time; he spoke with the greatest personalities of his day and, to satiate his desire for further information, he hired people to interview more and more people who were knowledgeable about subjects of interest.

**Realism.** We are not usually interested in abstract and vague things; descriptions are more attractive and interesting when they are close to our reality. Carnegie's work is full of real facts and full of life, and these facts and anecdotes are closer to us than we might think. We just have to leave the house and talk to the letter carrier, the saleswoman, the newspaper vendor about people's lives to see that they are full of stories rich in content. The excellent logic of this method is that every person has individualized approaches and particularities that they use to overcome their challenges in a unique or unusual manner, and their testimonies can be a source of enlightenment for all of us. Of course, Carnegie selected such anecdotes very carefully so that they would fit perfectly into the topic he discussed. But this realism is so important that many academics who tend to avoid using practical cases related to their research cannot imagine the benefits they are missing. To show how people solved serious problems, one of the anecdotes he relates is the story of C. J. Blackwood, who one day realized he was surrounded by problems: 1) the business college that was his source of income was on the verge of financial disaster; 2) his son had enlisted to fight in World War II; 3) he was being evicted from his house so that an airport could be built; 4) the well on his property had gone dry, and he had to carry buckets of water for his animals; 5) he couldn't afford to buy a new tire if he suddenly got a flat; 6) his daughter had graduated early from high school and he did not have the money to send her to college.[409] We become curious to learn how Blackwood solved his problems, which brings us to Carnegie's next technique.

**Arouse interest.** One technique that Carnegie always uses in his writing is to arouse constant interest in the reader, making her want to know more and more about what is to come. This makes reading pleasant, and stimulates the reader to continue. Further, learning is easier, because it creates mental images that elucidate the subject. Let's see an example from the beginning of a paragraph found in Carnegie's book, explaining how to banish depression: *When I find myself depressed over present conditions, I can, within the hour, banish worry and turn myself into a shouting optimist.*[410] Then, Roger W. Babson explains an original method he uses to solve his annoyances. He goes into a library, closes his eyes, and walks towards… well, the rest of the story is in *How to Stop Worrying and Start Living.* Would the reader like to know more about this story? Well, besides being a real story, it awakens our interest and encourages us to keep reading and learn more, to investigate other lives and other mechanisms to eliminate depression. This technique of Carnegie's, which he applied like no one else could, is only successful where there is content, substance and wisdom. If the reader continues reading only to discover that the story is weak and has no message, then the effects are contrary, decreasing interest. However, in Carnegie's case, he worked so hard to really contribute to the theme that reading it is continuous and stimulating.

**Debates.** Carnegie participated in radio shows where he debated the topics he studied, listened to thousands of students discuss their problems and solutions, and commented in newspaper columns, television shows, and public expositions. This process of talking and listening, being challenged, answering, agreeing or disagreeing with critics is a fabulous path towards scientific growth and evolution. Ideas that are discussed become clearer, and previously obscure ideas appear.

**Systematic reading.** Carnegie was a persistent and investigative reader, a researcher, a frequenter of libraries and bookstores. This thirst for reading is necessary to academic growth and elaboration of a good thesis. Carnegie's citations are plentiful and varied, showing that he not just read about his targeted themes, but also historic, philosophic, sociological and psychological studies. The more complete a researcher's reading, the more resources he can draw on for his own writing. Reading increases everyone's horizons. As a natural consequence of this reading, Carnegie's thought constructions are perfect, analyzing texts in detail and presenting valuable interpretations, as with this interpretation of the words of Christ:

> *Many men have rejected those words of Jesus: 'Take no thought for the morrow.' They have rejected those words as a counsel of perfection, as a bit of mysticism. 'I must take thought for the morrow,' they say. 'I must take out insurance to protect my family. I must lay aside money for my old age. I must plan and prepare to get ahead.'*
>
> *Right! Of course you must. The truth is that those words of Jesus, translated over three hundred years ago, don't mean today what they meant during the reign of King James. Three hundred years ago the word thought frequently meant anxiety. Modern versions of the Bible quote Jesus more accurately as saying: 'Have no anxiety for the tomorrow.'*
>
> *By all means take thought for tomorrow, yes, careful thought and planning and preparation. But have no anxiety.*[411]

**Writing.** When writing, Carnegie used all his abilities to attract the reader's attention and convey his messages accordingly. One of his favorite techniques was to personally enter the text and talk about his experiences, or those of people he met, some of whom he knew so well that he could draw deeper conclusions. This conferred authority on the subject as well as a natural feeling, an incentive to curiosity and the authentic practical anecdote. It was not rare for him to talk about his own parents and their virtues and mistakes which had taught him a lot in life. For example, when he talked about ways to avoid worry, he mentioned methods used by his parents. When his father was so stressed about the farm's mortgage and seemingly endless financial difficulties, he became so sick that the doctor gave him six months to live; he considered throwing himself into the dark waters of the One Hundred and Two River. But Carnegie's father thought about the words of his wife, who believed that if he fulfilled his duties and believed firmly in God, things would end well. And his father overcame that moment and lived happily for another forty-two years. They found the strength to overcome adversity in religion, which Carnegie explained in detail.[412] This realism is convincing and touching, for the text is not flat and cold, it portrays years of blood, sweat and tears. How many writers should pay more attention to that? But how did he reconcile the fact that he didn't feel the same level of intensity about the religion of his parents? Well, he explains it using pragmatic philosophy of William James to visualize the point, and he mentions James himself: 'Of course, the sovereign cure for worry is religious faith'.[413] The reader can note the decisive style of this conclusion, for many might ask about those who do not have a religion, or who doubt the truth or benefits of their beliefs, so the final touch of pragmatism gives another way out apart from dogma. Following this, Carnegie exposes his own doubts and fears, showing his sincerity in writing about them and courage in facing them. This humanizes his texts, making him just like any of us. So he describes his point of view, which as I understand it, affirms his philosophical support of Pragmatism. The reader can see the clarity, the simple style and the beauty of the writing: *Do I profess to know the answers to all these questions now? No. No man has ever been able to explain the mystery of the universe – the mystery of life. We are surrounded by mysteries. How your body works is a profound mystery. So is the electricity in your home. So is the flower that grows in a nook in the wall. So is the green grass outside your window.*[414] He continues with more scientific and interesting examples that prove his words about the infinite mysteries we encounter in life, and he concludes: *The fact that I don't understand the mysteries of prayer and religion no longer keeps me from enjoying the richer, happier life that religion brings.*[415] Doesn't this passage welcome all kinds of readers? From those who do not espouse any religion, to the person who adopts one? This is a subtle way to write, a method that offends no one. But this does not mean that he himself did not have an opinion. On the contrary, he adopts a pragmatic understanding that accepts all religions and people who do not have a religion. It is what I call denying the religion stigma. We can believe in divine spirituality or not, adopt a determined religion or not, we only have one obligation: to treat people that do not share our opinions without contempt or animosity, which would create enemies. Can the reader imagine the results of this on our planet? How much enmity would be undone, how many lives saved, how many wars avoided, how much miraculous progress would have been brought about? It boggles the mind. Comprehension of such thoughts reveals infinite problems not just in front of us, but often inside our own homes. Under the pretext of abiding by the law, in truth we try to adapt the laws to our own religious concepts, and accordingly we chase out the 'evil' we see in some people or their behavior. Beyond matters of legality and the state, conflicts multiply every day, but many still do not notice that the issues all revolve around the question of imposing one's religion on others, and treating those who don't adhere to one's own religion as inferior. I call it the 'stigma of religion'. During a time in his life, Carnegie said he was a protestant[416], but the reader can see how he explained his own vision of religion: *I have gone forward to a new concept of religion. I no longer have the faintest interest in the differences in creeds that divide the Churches. But I am tremendously interested in what religion does for me, just as I am interested in what electricity and good food and water do for me. They help me to lead a richer, fuller, happier life. But religion does far more than that. It brings me spiritual values. It gives me, as William James puts it, 'a new zest for life... more life, a larger, richer, more satisfying life.' It gives me faith, hope and courage. It banishes tensions, anxieties, fears and worries. It gives purpose to my life – and direction. It vastly improves my happiness. It gives me abounding health. It helps me to create for myself 'an oasis of peace amidst the whirling sands of life'.*[417]

Maybe this is one of Carnegie's great secrets for attracting, captivating and motivating crowds of people to read his books. His language is universal, it is ample, and accepts all who listen. It shows his point of view without his necessarily "owning" the truth. It also shows the reader how to reconcile personal views with a better quality of life, regardless of the opinions they hold. In this way, Carnegie does not create enemies, but reaches those who are disposed to read him, showing a readiness to learn more and to evolve. This subtlety in writing is an outstanding characteristic in his work.

Another point to be observed, still close to the topic of religion, is the call to reflection. We know that the process of knowledge, education and learning that can lead one to creativity is not the one-sided process of an informer, of a professor chock-full of knowledge who teaches, and a receiving vessel, a well-mannered student who learns everything. No! Carnegie discovered an important bilateralism when he urged his students to talk about their experiences. As a result, in this process students gain not only information, but the calling to individual reflection, a unique phenomenon that forces one to evaluate one's existence, reach one's own conclusions and follow a chosen path. In one quote, he encourages the reader to take a detour into a dialectic investigation of his or her own. He quotes Francis Bacon: "A little philosophy inclineth man's mind to atheism; but depth in philosophy bringeth men's minds about to religion".[418] With this, he transfers part of the responsibility to the reader, who in turn formulates the question: Why did he say this? Is it true that if I go deeper in philosophical thoughts, I can reach different conclusions, or confirm my own? More philosophy is needed to continue in this vein, and the exercise Carnegie provokes is further thought. What a great suggestion we gives us: let's think more, no need to fear it.

**Humility.** There is a well-known quote by Socrates: "I know nothing except the fact of my ignorance". Being sensible means being aware that we know so little, and that even in our own areas of specialty, we can always find something new to learn, or someone who can do things better than we can. Every person has a special gift, an ability that distinguishes him or her from everyone else. The gift may be hidden, but it exists. Let's look at someone who had a special gift, who recognized the magnitude of the universe and how this magnitude dwarfs the little we know. In 1642, the world was compensated for the death of Galileo Galilei with the birth of Isaac Newton. Newton was a thin man with a fat cat, which ate the food that Newton was too absorbed in his studies to pay any attention to. Bubonic plague had been terrorizing Europe since 1348, and hit London in 1665, forcing Newton to take refuge on a farm. It is said that those were the two most important years for science. Among other things, the young man discovered a mathematical procedure that became very useful to scientists: differential calculus. I will not try to explain it, but Einstein talked about it at length.

By age twenty-five, Newton was already a presence in the world, teaching his ideas at universities, but he began to draw heavy criticism and was tortured by personal crisis. Eirik Newth[419] correctly states: "The tendency is to believe that the great thinkers are strong and exemplary people, but it is frequently not the case. It can be really difficult to be as different from others as Newton was." He became reclusive and refused visitors for years, until an astronomer named Edmund Halley – who later would predict regular passings of a comet every seventy-five years – provoked Newton, asking for help in calculating planetary movement. Three months later the answer was ready, and one of the most important problems in astronomy was solved. Halley asked Newton to publish his theory. Newton not only did so, but wrote a book entitled *Mathematical Principles of Natural Philosophy*. Its importance? It changed the history of the world. As Pope paraphrased in his eulogy of Newton: "Nature and nature's laws lay hid in night; God said, 'Let Newton be!' and all was light"[420]. Although he elaborated aspects of physics that only began to be surpassed in the twentieth century by physicists like Einstein and Max Planck, if we were able to ask Newton how he felt about his achievements, he might have replied with: "I don't know what the world will make of me. But I see myself as a child playing at the beach who found some beautiful seashells and stones, while the infinite ocean of truth remained unexplored before me."

Carnegie always taught how to be humble. Although he had written his own biography of Lincoln, every time he spoke of the biographer Ida Tarbell, he referred to her as 'the most famous biographer in the United States'.[421] Though he could have taken credit for developing a system about human relations, he always took an attitude of serenity. He only used his knowledge to strengthen his ideas, never to showcase his own erudition or superiority. He could have named his theories and philosophies so that they would be studied with a scientific rigor. But Carnegie was not like that, he kept himself humble and serious, focused on his work and on the progress of his students and his readers. This attitude brought him better results than if he had wasted time with useless activities, if he had tried to demonstrate his superiority. His modesty led many to criticize him for having no depth. This criticism would have been evaded if he had adopted an arrogant pose and wrote in a more complicated manner, but this would have hindered his message, so he kept his writing simple; the result was that he achieved not only reason, but touched the very souls of his readers and students of the course. Being humble is not being submissive. It may take a lifetime to understand the difference between the two. But, instead of talking about it, let's see how Carnegie did not skimp on humility when he recognized all the details and virtues of others, and affirmed that he owed his life to others, as in the following passage where he discusses Rockefeller's change of attitude and work in the community, especially after he changed his philosophy on life and instituted the Rockefeller Foundation:

> *I speak with feeling of this work, for there is a possibility that I may owe my life to the Rockefeller Foundation. How well I remember when I was in China in 1932, cholera was raging all overthe nation. The Chinese peasants were dying like flies; yet in the midst of all this horror, we were able to go to the Rockefeller Medical College in Peking and get a vaccination to protect us from the plague. Chinese and 'foreigners' alike, we were able to do that. And that was when I got my first understanding of what Rockefeller's millions were doing for the world.*
>
> *Never before in history has there ever been anything even remotely like the Rockefeller Foundation. It is something unique. Rockefeller knew that all over the world there are many fine movements that men of vision start. Research is undertaken; colleges are founded; doctors struggle on the fight to a disease – but only too often this high-minded work has to die for lack of funds. He decided to help these pioneers of humanity – not to 'take them over', but to give them some money and help them help themselves. Today you and I can thank John D. Rockefeller for the miracles of penicillin, and for dozens of other discoveries which his money helped to finance. You can thank him for the fact that your children no longer die from spinal meningitis, a disease that used to kill four out of five. And you can thank him for part of the inroads we have made on malaria and tuberculosis, on influenza and*

*diphtheria, and many other diseases that still plague the world.*[422]

If Carnegie had been solely concerned with showcasing his own goodness, he would not have been able to see such a simple yet important and even lifesaving act as this. Recognizing how important others are to one's own existence is a sign of humility, for without life, the wisdom of the world means nothing-- we wouldn't even exist to contemplate it. Many act as if they own the truth. If they were to experiment with humble behavior, they would feel happier, especially when criticized or upon seeing their theories being surpassed by superior or more interesting ideas. The important place in the circle of life is guaranteed to all, and everyone collaborates in his or her own way; with this attitude, we all can find our place in the universe.

**Notes.** Another technique used by Carnegie consisted of writing down thoughts on what he was reading at any given time. Because he had a plan for his classes, when he needed to write a book, the material was already organized. He also used to consult his notes often in order to remember them and to strengthen the principles he believed would be useful to people. His intellectual honesty is evident when he writes and recommends the reader to reread the most important principles, as he himself did. One of the thoughts I read in Carnegie's work and taped to the bathroom mirror was: "The north wind made the Vikings". I liked to read this sentence and think that difficulty would make me stronger. Writing down favorite quotes and spontaneous ideas can be advantageous when an opportunity arises. When we register our creative thoughts, we can return to them later and develop projects that can be important to our lives. With regards to writing, for example, at any moment we might have to quote someone, discuss a topic, look for a different approach and there it is, we have already done the research or considered our position. On this point, personal organizers are very useful; I don't know how people survive without one. Carnegie said that even if we were lost on a desert island, we should have a schedule. If we are lucky enough to not be marooned, we can buy an organizer and write down our daily, weekly, and annual events, extending years into the future. We can also register important thoughts. If these thoughts are written down somewhere, we can savor them even while we are stuck in traffic, or waiting in line for movie tickets. Some subjects I copy from an old agenda into a new one; a favorite is Sibyl F. Partridge's text that Carnegie transcribed in his book *How to Stop Worrying and Start Living*. I refer to it constantly, but most especially when I am a little lost and need some orientation from above:

JUST FOR TODAY

1. Just for today I will be happy. This assumes that what Abraham Lincoln said is true, that 'most folks are about as happy as they make up their minds to be.' Happiness is from within; it is not a matter of externals.

2. Just for today I will try to adjust myself to what is, and not try to adjust everything to my own desires. I will take my family, my business, and my luck as they come and fit myself to them.

3. Just for today I will take care of my body. I will exercise it, care for it, nourish it, not about it nor neglect it, so that it will be a perfect machine for my bidding.

4. Just for today I will try to strengthen my mind. I will learn something useful. I will not be a mental loafer. I will read something that requires effort, thought and concentration.

5. Just for today I will exercise my soul in three ways: I will do somebody a good turn and not get found out. I will do at least two things I don't want to, as William James suggests, just for exercise.

6. Just for today I will be agreeable. I will look as well as I can, dress as becomingly as possible, talk low, act courteously, be liberal with praise, criticize not at all, nor find fault with anything and not try to regulate nor improve anyone.

7. Just for today I will try to live through this day only, not to tackle my whole life at once. I can do things for twelve hours that would appall me if I had to keep them up for a lifetime.

8. Just for today I will have a program. I will write down what I expect to do every hour. I may not follow it exactly, but I will have it. It will eliminate two pests, hurry and indecision.

9. Just for today I will have a quiet half-hour all by myself and relax. In this half-hour sometimes I will think of God, so as to get a little more perspective into my life.

10. Just for today I will be unafraid, especially I will not be afraid to be happy, to enjoy what is beautiful, to love, and to believe that those I love, love me.[423]

**Substantiation.** Because of the rigor that is the foundation of his writings, Carnegie's opinions bring trust and security to the reader. Speaking scientifically, the modernity of his thoughts prevails until today. It was not uncommon to hear interviews in 2008 that came to the same conclusions that Carnegie reached over sixty years before. Let's look at an example of what I mean. When he talked about fatigue and boredom as factors that generate worries, and proposed methods for attaining a more dynamic and joyful life, he mentioned medical opinions from Dr. Edmund Jacobson, Dr. Walter B. Cannon of Harvard Medical School, from the psychiatrist Dr. A. A. Brill, Dr. Rose Hilferding and others. From specialized literature, he pointed out work in the field of management from Frederick Winslow, J. A. Hadvield's work on psychology, and other specialized texts usually written by specialists in the medical and psychological area; he also mentioned the manifesto written by the director of the University of Chicago Laboratory of Physiology, which was used by the United States Army to optimize their recruits' productivity, methods that also enabled well-known personalities to successfully overcome fatigue during extreme situations, as in the cases of Winston Churchill, John D. Rockefeller, Eleanor Roosevelt, Gene Autry, Henry Ford, Horace Mann, Jack Chertock, Thomas Edison, Sam Goldwyn, General George C. Marshall, Vicki Baum, Galli-Gurci, Helen Jepson, etc. He mentions an experiment in which the engineer Frederick Taylor discovered a way for metalworkers to be four times more productive and yet less tired than they had been before. He mentions guidance of insurance companies, and conclusions from the Medical Congress of Boston, where Dr. Joseph H. Pratt developed a way to deal with cases of gastric ulcer, headaches and backaches, arthritis, chronic fatigue and other vague illnesses that did not manifest exterior symptoms. Dr. Pratt gave courses periodically for years to people suffering from such ailments and got excellent results. These opinions and reports, whether from specialists or from the people themselves who triumphed over worries and fatigue, all come together to form a demonstration of ample preparation on the topic. This method of preparation for writing, and inclusion of opportune, interesting quotes that lend credibility to the theme made him a trustworthy and inspiring author, besides, of course, providing the reader with many tools that contribute to improvement of quality of life and personal satisfaction. All those quotes occur in a space of less than twenty pages![424] And they are interesting because they are well organized and contain maxims that can be valuable for the reader's well-being. If we continue reading the book, we will see even more interesting and well-founded quotes. I do not remember ever having read another book with such substantiation and such well-placed citations from other authors. Even scientific books lack such craft. If Carnegie's bibliography were situated at the end of the book and citations not scattered throughout the text, we would see hundred of authors and books listed as references. Even so, it is a smooth read and flows naturally and attractively. Problems with self-help writing came after Carnegie and even as a result of his success, when many people decided to write about personal progress, without realizing that they would need heavy preparation. I don't mean to say that writing should be restricted to an elite group of well-studied people, but good content is necessary even when writing a personal story. A critic might include Carnegie in the group of authors who can craft a catchy title, but who don't have the preparation to write consistently. Someone who has read weak books and only glanced at Carnegie's titles could carelessly classify him as a mere self-help author, whose books lack such content. The important thing is to understand that Carnegie's success in literature is the fruit of seriousness, research, work and intellectual honesty. The lasting presence of his books in bookstores and their continuing sales occurs because of their content, their message, their utility and their relevance to readers' lives.

**Personal Organization.** Reading and researching about personal organization and efficiency in business taught Carnegie to be an organized person who wrote down his thoughts, read books, and constantly worked on improving himself. He developed a method in which organization became a part of every hour and every square foot of a person's life. Here, again, he substantiates his point of view when he says that the desk and work space must be kept clean and organized. An unorganized desk generates worries. It generates the feeling that there is too much to do, and this feeling in turn is a factor that generates stress and nervous disorders. He comes to this conclusion with opinions of specialists that will form the list of experts who support his thesis.[425] But let's think about the utility of this point. Besides the pleasant feeling we get when things are in order and we are organized (and we really are), when our house is clean, our desk is in order and we are dressed appropriately and carefully, it reflects directly on our image of good people and good professionals, which builds self-esteem and confidence in oneself. At this point it can be argued that freedom and less personal discipline would be better for spawning creativity. But truthfully, if our things were messy and our clothes torn or dirty, would our performance improve? I doubt it. Another important detail Carnegie related is to not keep things on one's desk that are not directly related to the topic we are working on at the moment. So if we are doing research on chemistry, all the related books can and should be spread all over the desk, no problem. But after we are done using them, do we benefit from leaving them on the desk?

The method of personal organization he put together for his readers also contributed to Carnegie personally and professionally. In photographs, Carnegie was always neatly dressed, well-combed and wearing a happy expression. This attitude positively impacted his job. The daily observations he wrote down, his constant strides towards personal development and his reflections on how he could improve more had a direct impact on his work. Everything he had read, researched or asked about was applied to his writings. He was well-prepared to write, and his organization propelled him to excellence. For years I had secretaries and assistants that made decisive contributions to my own work. The book I always gave them and asked them to read was *How to Stop Worrying and Start Living*. Of course my intention had been that they would learn how to leave the office clean and organized, but when they really got interested in it, the book contributed to a better and more professionally successful life. Of course, the impression you give when you hand someone a book and ask him to read it is that you are trying to teach them, to make them change their behavior. But let's think about it, this book does not tell you what to create, which religion to follow, which profession to choose or even if you should pick one at all. The book teaches how to be organized, how to respect others and one's own personal space. It offers tools like the ones used by a carpenter: screwdriver, hammer, saw, pliers, all of which enable you to do the best job possible, but which don't tell you what to make, or what your job entails. It is very different. Ideological control of others is manipulation, it is trying to create other people just like you. But organization, cleanliness, neatness, a responsible attitude to time and commitments, this seems logical to someone who is disposed to work. Even so, many of the people to whom I give *How to Stop Worrying* do not read it, or are not even interested in reading even the first chapter. I suppose this is due to four factors: 1) people think that the book is a stereotypical self-help book. We already saw that even though Carnegie's literature spawned books labeled as 'self-help', he himself does not fit this stereotype; 2) People are vain and think they do not need to read about how to stop worrying and start living, since reading such a book could be seen as admitting to having problems; 3) Many times we envision a hero as a rebel, with unruly hair or radical clothing, a 'nothing to lose' type. Well, there is an exception to every rule. Perhaps what is good for millions of people is not good for others, and we must pay attention to this. More specifically, about our heroes; do you think they became successful because of disorder, mess and disorganization, or their success is related to other factors, not just the way they dress, or the way they walk, but other merits? This deserves investigation, because perhaps their success was not due to their dress, the food they ate, the drugs they used, their addictions, aggressiveness, etc. It could be that the person is going through some problem. At the end of the story, it is their life to live, but should we emulate them for the sole reason that they are our idols? 4) People are not in the habit of reading. Why not change this? Reading transforms people. Whatever happens, no soul is lost forever, as Papillon taught. Personal organization brought Carnegie splendid success. His image as an organized, winning and responsible person lends his books and course credibility to this day, a century after he began his work. I again insist that reflection on detail was what made his work great, so let's clean our desks and read about why specialists believe this brings positive emotions. It is worth a try.

**Like your public.** The author who loves his public has much more to say to it. That is intellectual honesty. Really wanting the best for his readers was characteristic of Carnegie. He worked hard to contribute in any way he could to improve the quality of life of the men and women who read his books. At some moments, he takes the role of the father figure, at others the friend, at times the altruist appears, but in general what leaps out at the reader is the friendliness and respect he shows for the reader. The advice he gives would be the same advice he would have given his daughter Donna, or a dear friend. So when Carnegie suggests we read history books to experience the perspective of someone who lived ten thousand years ago, in order to realize the insignificance of our own troubles,[426] we can be sure that he really believed in this method and wanted to share it with the reader. Reading Carnegie's books also develops the reader's culture. The fact that he is a very well prepared author who illustrated his ideas superbly allows anyone that reads his work to develop intellectually. In this way, those who do not like to read can slowly develop an interest in it and improve their knowledge. These qualities are directly owed to Carnegie's ability to see the other, as we have already discussed. But if we think only of the benefits we can obtain by loving our public, we can mention a very simple example. Nowadays, some sales methods are based on observation of the client's preferences, their tastes, their problems, their priorities, religion, politics, sports, weight, height, birthday, and so much more data, all collected with the aim of collecting clients and building lasting relationships with these clients in order to do more business. We may find that some clients are different, some more objective and decisive, others more analytical, others dreamers... But the fact is that if we learn to 'love our public', it all becomes natural. We tend to listen more to the people with whom we are in constant contact at work; we know their interests and particularities, and this surely brings us better results. The goal is to know the client better, and to never trick them into buying. Establish a relationship of trust, but do not sacrifice loyalty for a tempting one-time sale. Honesty and the will to become a respected professional is valued. Deep down, this is the Christian philosophy of doing to others what you would like done to yourself. Love others as you love yourself... and suddenly, it yields impressive professional results. As a result, it is also necessary to accept these fruits, because the process compounds itself: other people (our 'public') will also achieve self-realization by doing something good for us. Then we must have the grace to naturally accept kindness of others, for this benefits both parties. We do not have to say: "Oh! You shouldn't have!" It is better to simply say: "Thank you for your kindness!" To summarize: do good because you respect others. Accept kindnesses from others because we are all equals: not above needing anything from others, and not inferiors to the point that we don't deserve anything from others. Simply: equals. Different as individual beings, equals in the greatness of mankind.

**The study of victories.** Reading biographies was, without a doubt, one of the factors that brought Carnegie to excellence in human relations and personal improvement. The purpose of studying the lives of the well-known is not to copy them, but to learn their methods and life lessons. Carnegie went beyond that, writing biographies such as *Little Known Facts about Well Known People* in which he recounts interesting things about such famous characters as Einstein, Cleopatra, Garbo, Marconi and so many others.[427] But what do we learn about famous people? How they solved problems we all share, such as overcoming stigmatization? In Einstein's case, for example, how did he reconcile the fact that he had been stigmatized as stupid or delayed, that is, right up until his theories became known? But that's not all; from important people we learn simple things like the importance of personal effort, organization, persistence, fighting spirit, self-confidence and so many other subjects. In another book called *Dale Carnegie's Biographical Roundup*[428], he selects no less than forty biographies of world-famous people. The portrayals show that well-known people have just as many problems as we do, if not more. Let's look at some examples: Madame Curie at one point was sleeping under a chair to keep warm; Clark Gable was timid around women, although after he became famous they would spend half a day waiting just to catch a glimpse of him; Mussolini commanded the Italians to live dangerously, but was afraid to return home in the dark; The Wright Brothers made history in twenty seconds; a reward of 200 thousand dollars was offered to whoever captured General De Gaulle, dead or alive. One of the most interesting stories is of George Bernard Shaw, a man who attended school for only five years but became one of the most important writers, winning a Nobel Prize for Literature.

How did he overcome his lack of education and become an author? Well, one of his secrets was to have a plan: write five pages a day while working as a bank teller. The pages he slaved over for nine years brought him a total of thirty dollars, a cent a day. But Bernard Shaw persisted with his plan and his will to win: "I only have one life to live," he said. "and I won't waste it behind an office desk."[429] Isn't that stimulating? Examples like these make us stop complaining, start dreaming our deepest dreams, and then start believing in them. Yes, we can plan our lives and fight to get what we want, even though we find ourselves in an unfulfilling place. That can be changed. These great lights of humanity passed through the same daily trials and tribulations that we also deal with every day. And so Carnegie studied biographies, or better yet, the lives of real people who endured as many problems as we do-- or more. Sometimes, he would select a small passage of someone's life from which to extract simple lessons useful to all, as shown in the following passage:

> *Charles Luckman, the lad that started from scratch and climbed in twelve years to president of the Pepsodent Company, got a salary of a hundred dollars a year, and made a million dollars besides – that lad declares that he owes much of his success to developing the two abilities that Henry L. Dougerty said he found almost impossible to find. Charles Luckman said: 'As far back as I can remember, I have got up at five o'clock in the morning because I can think better then than any other time – I can think better then and plan my day, plan to do things in the order of their importance.*[430]

Of course his most profound biography was Lincoln's, which we have already discussed. But we always must take into consideration Carnegie's most important message about biographies, in the sense that we must learn from them and still be ourselves. Yes, we can learn from others without copying them, following our own path. But first we must acquire content, learning, life lessons. No one makes his or her own way entirely from scratch, ignoring everything that came before. For starters, this hypothetical independent person would be unable to even communicate. Yes, we owe a lot to our environment and the giants upon whose shoulders we stand. The correct order of things is then: 1) Learn and 2) develop your own style.

If the reader allows me, I would like to recommend two biographies I have in my library, two rare jewels that I keep displayed and consider to be divine gifts written by enlightened people that show how it is possible to reach the farthest dreams and loftiest ideals. If I had to start again, to read all the books I have read and build my library anew, I would, without a second thought, include two magical books. I keep them in a specific section of a shelf that has books written by my friends and dedicated to me. It is as if they were my friends giving me advice. These books are *Yes, I Can: The Story of Sammy Davis Jr.* [431] and *Papillon: the man who escaped from hell*, by Henri Charrière. [432] The book about Sammy Davis Jr. enabled me to truly understand racism. In *Papillon*, I was able to comprehend the true meaning of freedom. As I write this now, I am listening to the movie soundtrack. The singer begins: *You, who see the sea...* The word 'papillon' means 'butterfly' in French. The butterfly wants freedom, but at the beginning of its cycle, it must undergo a metamorphosis, the transformation we all have to go through to reach freedom...

**Kill your fear.** After teaching public speaking to thousands of students (when this anecdote took place, Carnegie had already listened to and oriented over ten thousand public speakers), the worst case of fear he saw was Bryan, a student who was so afraid of speaking in public that he fainted. Despite the gravity of the situation, Carnegie assured Bryan that not only would he conquer his fear and speak in public, but he would even enjoy speaking in public. And some weeks later, it was true. How often do we give up on our dreams for fear of failure? Fear can paralyze us to the point of immobility[433] and, if so, our plans are left unfinished. Whatever it is you want to do, as long as it is honest and legal, Carnegie's advice is to do what you fear, as if you were not afraid. Stop thinking about yourself and think about the subject at hand. Quoting Emerson, he says: "Do the thing you fear most and the death of the fear is certain."[434]

**How to choose your topic.** When selecting a subject on which to speak in public, Carnegie's recipe for making the right choice is infallible. You should select a topic you know well, for example: preparing lasagna or coffee, how to wrap presents, the origin of a martial art, whatever it is that you know well. However, if the subject is assigned and we have no choice, then we must dive into it, until we know it well and it is a part of our personal experience. To prepare a lecture, you must inventory your own experiences, talk to people, ask about what they have found. Interview merchants, dentists, doctors or managers about the subject. Write to national associations asking where you can obtain further material for research. Carnegie said that the next step should be a trip to the local public library to collect more material. Finally, spend an hour preparing for every seven seconds of speaking, and collect ten times more material than what you will use. "You will have an internal incentive, a conviction, and your speech will flow almost by itself."[435]

If we think about it, Carnegie's magnificent formula for choosing a speech topic or speaking on an unfamiliar topic can be adapted to assist us in choosing a profession or an art. We just adopt the same criteria: if we intend to choose a profession, why don't we start with something familiar, easy, and pleasant? Recently I read a book, a book so good that I gave it to a very dear friend – I can't recall the name of the author – that told the story of a very special teacher who suggested that her students ask themselves the following question in order to discover what field appealed to them: "If you were rich, really rich, and did not have to do anything else to make money, what would you like to do?"

**Live enthusiastically.** In his biographical studies, Carnegie mentions George Bernard Shaw's recipe for living with enthusiasm: "I have one life to live and I will not spend it behind an office desk."[436]

And Shaw had enough enthusiasm to endure many refusals from publishers.

When I was a child, I used to stay in the street all day playing soccer with my friends (soccer being very serious business, not just a game). For hours I would put my whole heart into the games, which could last all day. I only stopped after repeated calling by my mother or father. But when it was time to study, well, time dragged by slowly... Studying was boring. Playing on the streets was not. And this is true for you, for me, for everyone. We feel tired and annoyed when we do something we are not interested in. And this was another finding of Carnegie's. He realized that we were made to express emotion and live intensely, but not to do anything with which we cannot identify, or in which we have no interest. Carnegie talks about this with great propriety, citing research, records of mountain climbing and military expeditions and even fishing. He mentions authorities on the subject and concludes: we should practice intellectual or physical activities, subjects that engage us and that we enjoy doing. But, and here is the heart of the matter, it seems like most people don't do exactly what they want to do. Then there is only one alternative: make what you do interesting. This is a way to survive, at least until you can manage to do what you love, or figure out what you enjoy so you can make a plan, carry it out  and finally realize your dreams. But what if your job is too boring? This is another reason to make it interesting. I will cite an example formulated by Carnegie based on the experience of his second wife, Dorothy. In this real-life example we see that even a simple thing, competing with oneself, can make a monotonous job bearable, at least for as long as it lasts, and such an attitude can be life-changing, as we will see. Let's see how Carnegie looks for impressive life lessons in all his experiences:

> And so what? What can you do about it? Well, here is what one stenographer did about it – a stenographer working for an oil company in Tulsa, Oklahoma. For several days each month, she had one of the dullest jobs imaginable: filling out

*printed forms for oil leases, inserting figures and statistics. This task was so boring that she resolved, in self-defense, to make it interesting. How? She had a daily contest with herself. She counted the number of forms she filled out each morning, and then tried to excel that record in the afternoon. She counted each day's total and tried to better it next day. Result? She was soon able to fill out more of these dull printed forms than any other stenographer in her division. And what did all this get her? Praise? No... Thanks? No... Promotion? No... Increased pay? No... But it did help to prevent the fatigue that is spawned by boredom. It did give her a mental stimulant. Because she had done her best to make a dull job interesting, she had more energy, more zest, and got far more happiness out of her leisure hours. I happen to know this story is true, because I married that girl.*[437]

And here is the main point: we can make something interesting out of a necessary activity. So, at this moment we can draw two conclusions: 1) seek out what you enjoy to keep your spirits high; 2) until this can fully take place, do what you have to do to make it interesting.

One of the things I most enjoyed in my youth was playing chess. After years without playing a single game, I came to the conclusion that I needed to return to studying and playing chess. So I started studying chess and playing in tournaments again. It cheers me up, even when I often have to fill my hours with activities I'd rather not be doing. Another thing I adore: soccer. So I am starting to gather people to play soccer with, preferably people unrelated to work, so that I can feel more at ease and we can discuss other things in our leisure time. The dear reader might be thinking, "what about this method of being enthusiastic about what needs to be done?" This is indeed the question, and maybe I left it for last because I consider it to be the most important: if we bring energy and enthusiasm to an activity, the chances of it working out successfully are immense. Let's think about this method and Carnegie's career. In the beginning, he sold cars, but he did not like cars. Even so, he held fast until he was able to deal with something he liked, and then his career took off. I had to deal with this too. Most of us have to deal with it. It is necessary to endure what we need to do, so in the future we can do what we like to do. In this way we gain our freedom, just as Papillon did. When we smile at the world, the world smiles back at us too. Carnegie's words seem like a prayer teaching us how to evolve: *Keep reminding yourself that getting interested in your job will take your mind off your worries, and, in the long run, will probably bring promotion and increase pay. Even if it doesn't do that, it will reduce fatigue to a minimum and help you enjoy your hours of leisure.*[438]

**Establish connections.** When we look at *How to Stop Worrying,* we see that we should change our problems into opportunities. Make lemonade out of that lemon. Carnegie tells the story of Harlan A. Howard, a student who decided to take more interest in his job at an ice cream counter, where he sold ice cream, cleaned tables and washed dishes. He started to study ice cream, reading everything he could find on the topic, up to and including its chemical composition. Because he already knew a bit about the subject, he stood out in his chemistry classes in college, where he worked on the chemistry of ice cream. As he continued learning about ice cream, he won first place in a contest at the New York Cocoa Exchange for his project using cocoa and chocolate. He opened a lab and, well, suffice it to say, his career progressed.[439] Although Carnegie did not label it, I call this sort of realization 'establishing connections'. The first time I heard this expression was from the jazz musician Wynton Marsalis, whom I admire not only for his professionalism but also for the good role model he is for his students and fans. Before he was forty (he was born on October 18, 1961), Wynton Marsalis was already considered the greatest jazz musician of his time. He sold millions of albums, won eight Grammy awards in the jazz and instrumental solo categories, and gave about a hundred and twenty concerts a year. He won a Pulitzer prize for music, and *Time* magazine featured him in 1996 as one of the most influential people in America.

Despite his success, Marsalis does not behave eccentrically. When he was criticized for dressing too well for an artist, he replied: "How can you get the respect of the public if you go on stage dressed like a tramp?"

Respect. This word seems to match Marsalis: he respected discipline, study, dedication, and especially the touch-points of the jazz world, the references for his own growth and stylistic development, until he too was someone to be 'respected'. How is it possible to develop something new and substantial, not eccentric or fraudulent, when you don't know the meaning of what is old? Would we have reached the moon had we not understood Newton's physics?"

When teaching his students, the master asks them how they intend to truly play jazz if they don't know John Coltrane or Duke Ellington: their lives, their histories, their music…?

It is a shame that the method Wynton Marsalis developed for study of the trumpet is not followed by all those who aim for progress in arts, science, sports, professionally… He developed twelve steps to effective practice:

1. Seek out the best private instruction you can afford.
2. Write/work out a regular practice schedule.
3. Set realistic goals.
4. Concentrate when practicing
5. Relax and practice slowly
6. Practice what you can't play. - (The hard parts)
7. Always play with maximum expression.
8. Don't be too hard on yourself.
9. Don't show off.
10. Think for yourself. - (Don't rely on methods.)

11. Be optimistic. - "Music washes away the dust of everyday life."

12. Look for connections

It is interesting that Marsalis tried to learn the best from the best in the field yet has not lost his own personality. He interpreted the classics using his own style. He became, through the years, a force unto himself.

The idea of 'establishing connections' is important, and refers to developing connections between what we have to do and what we like to do (which could be our projects). We can illustrate this using the following example: Cecilia got a job behind the counter at a coffee shop. Drusila took the same job, in the same shop, so she could work with her friend Cecilia. Neither of them wanted the job. They would have preferred to work as assistants in a big company, since they both studied to be executive assistants. But each one acts in a completely different manner: Drusila's work lacks energy and interest; she claims that no matter how much coffee she serves, or how good it is, she'll take home the same paycheck, so why bother. Cecilia, on the other hand, applies Carnegie's techniques, and is enthusiastic, smiles and takes an interest in her work. In this case, she reads about coffee in order to understand it. She serves her clients well and attentively, and takes a genuine interest in them. She acts with optimism. In this way she reaches a level of competence in what she does, and the people who frequent the cafe begin to notice her. Because she takes interest in others, others reciprocate. Executives, managers, security guards, janitors, salespeople, teachers and others begin to admire this person, this professional who serves their coffee. All these people who drink her coffee have some influence in hiring people, and could be of help when an executive assistant is needed in the workplace, which is the position Cecilia is aiming for. Meanwhile, Drusila the pessimist emails her resume to many companies, looking for an opportunity to show how well she can do her job.

So, what is the connection that Cecilia established? She needed to find an opportunity to work in her chosen field. In order to do this, she worked efficiently and optimistically, showing off her qualities in a place where she was constantly on public display and always monitored. She even got paid to show off her abilities!

Connections are infinite. A factory worker lived far from his factory. His dream was to run competitively. So he established the connection: he would dress in his practice gear and run to work. He would shower there and put on his uniform; after work, change again and run home. The connection was his need to go to work. For work, he needed to get from Point A to Point B, but he took advantage of this and, at the same time, trained for championships. He reaped these benefits: 1) First and foremost, the practice time he needed so badly in order to reach his goals as an athlete; 2) he saved money on transportation, always a good thing; and 3) he improved his physical and mental health, because he felt like he was saving time. The result: he won a national competition. I know about it because he commented about it in an interview on television.

There is no chart of connections, for they all depend on what must be done and what you would like to do, according to your own life and work. If you have to wait hours in line, you can read a book. If you spend hours stuck in traffic, you can study a language. I got this idea from a law professor in Germany, when I asked him how he came to speak Spanish so well. He replied that he listened to the course during his daily commute. It is necessary to think about your own situation in order to establish connections. To academics who tell me they work in a tough job, I usually reply: "You're doing field research, take advantage of it." What are the connections you can make? Have you thought about them? How many things could be better in your life? When I clean my house I don't think: "Ugh, what a boring job!" No! I think: "What a great opportunity to exercise." I can guarantee you, if it weren't for the connections I established in my life, I would still be trying to get into college. I like this subject so much that I could teach about it for a year. Who knows, maybe one day I will. I've been known to tell friends who are farmers or bricklayers: "And you get paid to exercise. I know people who pay a lot to go to the gym and don't get the results you do!" Or then, I tell a friend who works at a coffee shop: "You are paid to meet interesting people who come in just to talk to you!" When I say this, my friends start thinking, seeing seeing the advantages of their activities. The fact is, the 'teacher of connections' was Dale Carnegie. The courses advertised his books, and his books advertised his courses. He took his students experiences to develop the doctrine in his books. He took his personal experiences to give life to the ideas he defended in his writings. If we look carefully at his trajectory, we see that he was always establishing connections. With them, he was able to reach his dream of being a writer: by establishing connections.

**Some other 'secrets' for writing well.** I can assure the reader that there are no shortcuts to a job well done that will achieve success. I would like to repeat one of Carnegie's phrases, given its importance to personal improvement: *I will tell you a secret that will make it easier for you to speak in public immediately. Did I find this in a book? No. Was it taught to me in college? No. I had to find it out gradually, and slowly, through years of trial and error.*[440] Carnegie was an example of a life dedicated to learning and work. Even after studying oratory extensively, participating in (and eventually winning) contests, after trying out a career in sales, with results that were first disastrous and then successful, after studying drama and having fought like a madman to become an artist-- with no success, after going back to sales, this time with automobiles and still no success, he started the public speaking course... but even then, he kept up his dream of becoming a writer. This entire time, he kept upgrading himself, kept improving. In 1913 he took a composition course at the College of Journalism at Columbia University, and in 1914 he took a course in short story writing at New York University, for which he earned an A and great recommendations from the professor. In 1916 and 1917 he attended B.C.S. Baltimore's school of business and finance.[441]

But for each drop of theory he learned, Carnegie did ten times as much immersion in the real world and reflection on the topic. According to Ormond Drake, who knew him well, Carnegie capitalized on every experience, no matter how simple. Months might pass by, but these experiences would show up via his analytical thoughts in an article, a comment in a lecture or on the radio. Still according to Drake:

> *Over and over I saw it happen. He would go visit someone, and there's another chapter; watch his dog, and there's another. Once at an NBC radio studio we judged a speaking contest. To me it was just another contest and soon forgotten. To Dale it was an experience for his filing card cabinet. Months later I heard him deliver a speech in the Murray Hill Hotel. By this time that studio experience had become a five- or six- minute talk; he called it 'A Chunk of Life.' Everything had a lesson for Dale.*[442]

It is necessary to reaffirm the importance of another of Carnegie's 'secrets': honesty. Honesty in the broadest possible sense of the word. Honesty, meaning speaking the truth to people, saying what you really think or believe. Intellectual honesty: stating the truth, never attempting to cheat or harm others. Drake noticed this trait in Carnegie and remarked: "He was a happy man. One of the most honest persons I ever knew." And, "I learned that he believed everything he said 100 per cent".[443] At one point in Carnegie's life, he was invited to speak to the Dutch Treat Club of New York; his friends tried to talk him out of going to the event, saying that this would be a tough crowd. Carnegie replied: "If you've got truth and honesty on your side, you've got a good shield and buckler".[444] Honesty is an indispensable requirement for true success. The things and ideas we have should be legitimately fought for and earned. If belongings or ideas do not belong to us, we should declare and recognize the fact.

How much personal investment, how much will to improve. How many people who should see that nothing is built by chance. Intellectual construction is like that, step by step, always forward. And Carnegie's attempts moved forward from his books to the newspapers. As the course he developed for adults became successful, he was asked to write. The writing process exercised his abilities and his style improved. According to Giles Kemp and Edward Claflin[445], the formula Carnegie used for writing consisted of this sequence: 1) start with something interesting, tell a good story[446], start dramatically to grab the reader's the attention from the start. Carnegie teaches this technique in *Public Speaking*, but in truth, it is one of the most impressive writing techniques and possibly even the number one secret of his books' success: catching the reader's attention at all times. He does this masterfully, and anyone who has pretensions of writing should read each chapter carefully and study the techniques with which Carnegie begins his compositions. Of course, without personal consistency, a great start won't help a story too much. Personal and constant preparation is necessary. As we have seen, preparation does not always imply formal courses of study, although it could. 2) Draw a conclusion. Apart from story-tellers – and even they should make conclusions – the story you tell is a preparation for developing a point of view, a conclusion that brings us to reflect on the topic. 3) Finally, show the benefit. This simplified formula demonstrates to the reader that if they act in a certain way, they will reap this certain benefit. This writing style seems to be the best for various ends, whether scientific, entertainment, romance or business.

## COMPARISON BETWEEN CARNEGIE AND JACK LONDON

Returning to the first point, starting with a story that grabs the reader's attention, we can formulate a comparison between Carnegie and another very successful writer of his time: Jack London. London also developed his narratives with a story to catch the reader's attention from the start, creating mental images that make the reader anxious to know what will happen. In *White Fang*, for example, the adventure takes place in the snow, creating a deadly crash involving Bill and Henry, two friends who lead their sled dogs on one side, and on other side, a pack of evil and savage wolves led by an enigmatic she-wolf.[447] London is also innovative. While wolves were being hunted to extinction in the world, seen as villains and monsters, London focused the story on White Fang, a wolf-dog mix who has all the aggression of his wild forebears but, in the end, becomes a hero and a life-saver, contrary to all expectations. London created this trip to the stereotypical "wild" that all people know, later transforming the mentality that ignores the true essence of things, showing that the wolf is the dog that saved people, and that even the wolf has a story! Yes, London brought the reader into an adventure in which they see the wolf's point of view, and are allowed to recognize the wolf as a being worthy of respect. By writing in this manner, London created an ecological conscience; after all, he really liked the wild. But the value of his writing is the fact that we are talking about the time between the nineteenth and twentieth centuries, a time when it was unusual to have an ecological conscience. Considering the large impact *White Fang* made when it appeared, it is hard to estimate what repercussions it had in terms of ecology, but it must have been important. By making the reader enter the stigmatized character's (the wolf's) world, and creating for this character an interesting and worthy story, London presents a unique style. If we think about it, London's novels bring us conclusions, messages and often benefits extracted from conduct that could be designated as examples to follow. In the story of the hobo and the fairy, another example that occurs in London's short stories is the benefit the reader gains from recognizing some stigmatized other as a full-fledged being, seeing thrilling life experiences and liberating knowledge without having to personally experience the dark streets, gloomy ships, dead-end alleys and the death on the battlefield that London himself saw throughout his life.

Here we have another common point between Jack London and Dale Carnegie: both drank from the same well, running body and mind along paths of desperation, hunger, humiliation and hope and disbelief living together side by side. Jack London was unemployed for a time, later working as a sailor, factory worker, gold miner and journalist. London also had the dream of being a writer. A plank was found in a cabin  in Alaska, on the gold field where Jack London had lived, bearing the inscription: *Jack London, gold miner and writer, January 27, 1898.*[448]

Now, let's continue with this duo. London also entered subsequently dropped out of college. At a time where women were not yet able to vote, London defended women's suffrage.[449] As we have previously seen, Carnegie was a defender of women's rights, being the first to bring a woman into a Rotary luncheon at a time when women were not yet welcome. London was born in a poor home, was self-educated and wanted to become successful to help his family...[450]

Jack London had been in London and was inspired to write *The People of the Abyss*, which was based on his experiences exploring poor regions of the city and living with people who were unable to find ways to support themselves. Carnegie wrote part of the Lincoln biography in London.  Even at the height of his fame, London continued to be simple and accessible, with even beggars frequenting his home.  A newspaper of the time noted: "...he is a person with a singularly magnetic force of attraction.  Anyone else would have been ruined by the adoring legions that surround him.  His life is that of a movie star.  Yet despite this, he lacks any personal vanity."[451]  He enjoyed interviewing all types of people to hear the stories of their lives, which later entered his stories, or simply enriched his knowledge.

In the end, London and Carnegie gained public recognition and conferred upon their readers the ability to see this treasure map of knowledge and entertainment, passing along a path that was all at once safe, toilsome, illustrated, explained, victorious, masterful, sublime. Another commonality: there are no blocks or shields in their language, it flows crystal clear. It is easy to understand them, because they like the reader. No, not like, they love the reader. They talk to their public like loving parents who tell a charming story to explain serious things, and to reward the children who pay attention. To write like Carnegie and London, one needs to be able to love the reader. As if this weren't enough, they are magicians that belong to some other world, a world where you can talk with every being, living or not, material or immaterial. They speak to every kind of energy and inertia. They sense beings and see life in non-beings. They lose their fear of storms. They wave amicably to the investigating vulture. They hiccup until they laugh, and laugh until they hiccup. They see the confused child inside the atrocious monster, and cynical ceremony in the purest saint. They learned the secret of the universe.

# CHAPTER 13

## PHILOSOPHY AS A MEANS OF SUPPORT

*The import of the difference between pragmatism and rationalism is now in sight throughout its whole extent. The essential contrast is that for rationalism reality is ready-made and complete from all eternity, while for pragmatism it is still in the making, and awaits part of its complexion from the future. On the one side the universe is absolutely secure, on the other it is still pursuing its adventures.*

(William James)[452]

When she learned that I was writing this biography, a friend by the name of Cecilia asked: why do you believe Carnegie is a philosopher? I responded: because he created a system of ideas. A coherent, complex system of rules of communication based on themes of learning, the objective of which is to obtain practical and functional results. If we look at a phrase from one of today's exponents of Pragmatism, Richard Rorty[453], we see an affirmation that "...all our knowledge exists within descriptions adjusted to our current actual social conditions..." As such, Carnegie was a philosopher. He sustained himself with philosophy, because this knowledge is legitimate, and he practiced science as well in the development of means to achieve desired social goals. Carnegie is the original base of pragmatic, practical and functional knowledge.

One of the most important themes of philosophy is truth. For William James, truth is what works. This is a new philosophical model, one which is a recent development in history. Two passages from Rorty[454] show the development of a new concept in philosophy: "If we face knowledge not as something with an essence, something to be described by scientists or philosophers, but instead, as something that we believe to be right according to common standards, then we are well on our way to viewing dialog as the ultimate context in which knowledge should be understood."

And more: "To see a conversation progressing as an objective sufficient for philosophy, to see wisdom as something which is made up of the ability to sustain dialog, this is to see human beings as producers of new descriptions, instead of beings who hope to be capable of describing in an exact manner."

Carnegie applies such knowledge to the way he created efficient rules for communication, rules which are directed at real people who then come to reproduce this knowledge. In this latter sense, science is the end result. Let's look at an example of philosophy, followed by science: Carnegie develops his "Formula for Enthusiasm" which basically consists of acting energetically in personal or professional situations. This formula has deep roots from its original source, the Chautauqua Institution, to Carry Nation's movement. As we have seen, things became clear to Carnegie when he witnessed people flocking to the speaker who spoke with genuine enthusiasm in Hyde Park in London. From there Carnegie maintains that we always perform better, whether as a salesperson, an orator, or as simple human beings interacting individually, if we do it with enthusiasm.

Currently, the formula is, "Act with enthusiasm and you will be enthusiastic." Up until this point, we have a philosophical affirmation because people don't exactly know that acting with enthusiasm will bring them greater benefits; Carnegie systematically develops this idea, which despite being extremely simple, has staggering results. Without a doubt, when Carnegie applied ideas such as these to his books and courses, providing examples and exercises on how to act with enthusiasm, this was social science.

Many other themes were then developed by Carnegie, first philosophically and then later scientifically, applying such concepts to his course and as suggested exercises in his books. Let's look at some principles and rules: act fearless to conquer fear, establish hermetically sealed compartments during the day, carry out tasks according to the order of their importance, etc. If these and so many other principles developed by Carnegie were already known as "making lemonade when life gives you lemons", without a doubt they would not have received the fundamental treatment and subsequent systematic application that Carnegie gave them. Previously these proverbs had been known to some degree, but after Carnegie, they took on another meaning.

"So," asked Cecilia, "why isn't Carnegie cited in works of philosophy, sociology, psychology, or history?"

Great question! In 1984, Steven B. Hobart wrote his history thesis on Dale Carnegie; after researching in depth, he was surprised at how rarely Carnegie is mentioned in history courses, considering that from the 1930s Carnegie was one of the most read authors in the world.[455] This is nothing new. Herman Melville did not receive recognition for his now-famous book *Moby Dick* until after he had passed away. It took until after World War I, when critics began to discover indications that Melville's book was not just a whaling adventure, but a work with much grander dimensions. Today *Moby Dick* is known around the world as a classic. In Carnegie's case, it is also necessary to investigate the value of his writings and the dissemination of his philosophy so that his thinking can be discussed at an academic level.

In any case, to return to Cecilia's question, in my opinion Carnegie is not treated as a philosopher because he is stigmatized as the author of a self-help book. When Peter Drucker, named by *Business Week* as "the man who invented Administration", affirms "there is nothing so useless as doing efficiently that which should not be done at all"[456], specialists took this to heart. Yet when Carnegie said that it was necessary to do things according to the order of their importance, people said that was common sense. It can only be concluded that Carnegie was stigmatized as a self-help author and his philosophical and scientific thought was pushed to the side, a product of prejudice.

Prejudices bring about war, catalyze individual acts of violence and suffocate the thoughts and good readings of thinkers such as Carnegie. This stereotype about him is so strong that even people who have adopted and benefited from Carnegie's work feel embarrassed to admit that they have read him, or say "what he said was really common sense, things everybody knows but nobody does".

The problem is purely one of prejudice. When Socrates stated that his advantage was that he knew that he knew nothing, this was philosophy. But Socrates has been studied for 2000 years, while studying Carnegie as a philosopher, which I imagine has not been done before, leaves us with a wide open field of study.

Carnegie not only created new ideas in philosophy, he revitalized consecrated thinkers such as the Buddha, Schopenhauer, Epicurus, James and others, linking his thinking seamlessly with his philosophy, not an idealistic philosophy that believes that the thinking subject creates the thought object, but a pragmatically philosophy which was developed, in a certain sense, exclusively by his own style.

We will now look at some philosophies which were revisited by Carnegie and transformed into concepts for contemporary life.

**Marcus Aurelius** and **Epictetus**[457] did not appear in Carnegie's citations by chance. Both were part of a philosophical legacy called *Stoicism.* It is said to owe its origins to Socrates passing through Athens, observing the number of superfluous wares for sale and remarking: "How many things the Athenians need to live!", meaning that people did not truly need so much.[458] This was the beginning of the school of *cynicism,* people who understood that happiness does not depend on external factors such as health, possessions or power. These social tools are temporary, and freedom from such addictions was the root of true happiness, which one found could no longer be lost.[459] The most famous *cynic* was Diogenes. There is a famous passage by him that always springs to mind, especially when I see a person living on the street. It is the dialog he had with Alexander the Great, one of the greatest conquerors of nations of all time. It went something like this: Diogenes lived in an old empty wine vat, and his only possessions were the clothes on his back and a sack of bread. Alexander, hearing of Diogenes, went to visit him. He asked if Diogenes knew who he was, but Diogenes did not respond. Alexander said he was Alexander. He received this response: "And I am Diogenes." Alexander replied: "You should know I have an empire and thousands of men bow before me." Diogenes: "For me, I have enough, which is this vat. As for the men, many look for one but find him not." Alexander: "You are everything they say indeed, an extraordinary person. Ask anything and I will make sure your wish is fulfilled." Diogenes: "I wish you to step aside, you are blocking the sunlight." Alexander: "If I were not Alexander, I would wish to have been born Diogenes." But we must remember that Alexander had a deep grounding in philosophy that enabled him to understand Diogenes' greatness; after all, Alexander had been Aristotle's student between the ages of twelve and fifteen. Nowadays the word *cynicism*, derived from cynic, has a different meaning than the original, for it does not express its Socratic heritage, which defended the ideas of self-sufficiency and a changed understanding of the world, but only the cynics' disregard for the suffering of others, just as they did not care about their own suffering. So, in popular use the word 'cynicism' has a negative sentiment and does not demonstrate its philosophical significance.

From the original cynics came stoicism. It was founded by Zenon, who gathered his friends in the covered doorway of a building, a gateway in Greek called a *stoa*. The stoics considered each and every person to be a small world completely connected to the larger universe. This unique essence makes our relationship with nature impervious to time, space and conventions; from this springs the notion of *Natural Law*. Nature governs the lives of all people, who in turn should try to understand its laws. There is logic in every part of the universe, and there is a connecting point that could be described as *sympathy*. *Sympathy* is a connection of proximity to reality – not of identity, but of proximity. The connections are infinite, such as the movement of tides and the moon, the relationship between people and nature,[460] actions and omissions and their consequences, our thoughts and the lives we lead. In order to understand such laws, the stoics gave great importance to interpersonal relationships, and made the human being the center of philosophical concerns. From this sprang the concept of *humanism*, which gave a more extensive vision of what the *cynics* had developed.[461] The expression *stoic tranquility* means that a person naturally and serenely accepts things that would seem to be negative (only seem) as well as good things.[462] In Dale Carnegie's texts, we see a constant flow of stoic ideas: 'if life gives you lemons, make lemonade', 'no one kicks a dead dog', 'do not worry about unfair criticism', 'be yourself', 'don't be bothered by the buzzing of mosquitoes', and so many others. Of course, Carnegie presents other topics that approach stoicism, like the idea of living enthusiastically and joyfully, which no doubt would be in harmony with the universe's own ideas. Personally, I think that comprehension of the messages of the universe might just be, in the end, a request for a nice smile. What Carnegie adds could bring a new reading to stoicism.

Another observation to be considered is that stoicism goes beyond one's own backyard because it contemplates the entire universe, creating another adjective for this vision: *cosmopolitan*. Carnegie's concepts are universal, they apply to every situation we experience regardless of race, sex, religion, or way of life, which again brings Carnegie close to stoicism. Maybe stoicism's cosmopolitan vision explains its appeal to people in varied political and economic conditions, such as Epictetus and Marcus Aurelius, eventually mentioned by Carnegie. Marcus Aurelius Antoninus reigned as emperor of Rome between 161 and 180CE; at this time Epictetus was a slave living in Rome. Marcus Aurelius understood that as a citizen he was a Roman, but as a man he belonged to the world. Good could only be good if it was intended for Rome as well as the entire world. Marcus Aurelius tried to see people's souls and not their outward appearances.[463] To him, evil did not live in souls, or as a modification of the physical body, but in the self. Even if the body was wounded or burned, the thinking interior should remain calm. Difficulties do not exist outside but inside the being and his opinions.[464] Epictetus (50-130BCE) was a slave who later won his freedom. Similar to Carnegie, Epictetus tried to separate things that depend on us from those that do not. For things which depend upon us, we should try to do what is right. For those that do not depend on us, we are left with only indifference. And it is here that we can find happiness and peace for our souls. Things that do not depend on us are, for example, the body into which we are born, wealth, others' opinions of us, the posts to which we are nominated. Things that depend upon us: our point of view, tendencies, desires, aversions.[465] Carnegie formulates a more modern list of the two categories, making Epictetus' separation a bit more relative. But in citing Dr. Reinhold Niebuhr's well-known prayer, Carnegie shows the presence of Epictetus' thoughts in his writings: *God grant me the serenity to accept things I cannot change; The courage to change the things I can; And the wisdom to know the difference.*[466] So, to the stoic, the true path was the absence of passions, impassivity. Slave or emperor, the one who could separate himself from his passions would reach freedom.[467]

Another thinker Carnegie mentions is the famous pessimist **Arthur Schopenhauer**.

Do you think you know someone who is a pessimist? Well, imagine the most pessimistic person in the world. Done? Now multiply it by a million, no, a trillion times! But you may as well give up, what you are now imagining is nothing close to Schopenhauer's pessimism. He wasn't just a pessimistic person, he was pessimism embodied. Am

I exaggerating? Look at how Schopenhauer expressed his gratitude to God for creating the world:

> *If it is true that a God made this world, I would not like to be this God; the pains of the world would tear apart my heart. If we imagine a demon creator, we would have the right to censor it, pointing at its handiwork and saying: 'How dare you disturb the sacred rest of nothing, to create this world full of anguish and pain?'"*

Perhaps this negativistic prism that colored his vision can be explained by the miserable life the philosopher led. Perhaps he was influenced by another great pessimist: Voltaire, one of the pillars of the French Revolution.

I don't believe any of it. Schopenhauer was a true genius. He observed things as they were, and he said so. What is shocking about him is the naked truth: having the courage to speak it, no matter what offense it may cause. It is his truth after all. He observed things and explained them, and this could cause trouble... are you ready to hear them?

I do not mean that Schopenhauer was always right. That's not it! Sometimes he is wrong (but he makes us realize that we never considered things from his point of view, which shows the depth of his thought) and sometimes he even <u>created</u> contradictions. After all, one of his most important affirmations would be found years later, in the twentieth century, at the core of the theories of the most practical, optimistic expert in public relations, Dale Carnegie: "a way of pleasing me is to let everyone talk about themselves." "Do not fight others' opinions: consider that if we wanted to correct every silly thing they believe, even if we lived as long as Methuselah we would never finish." Seems like a phrase by Carnegie, doesn't it? But it is from Schopenhauer.

Beyond this, you can catch a glimpse of hope in one born in the century of light (February 22, 1788, in Dantzig), but it is rare.

So, what would you ask Schopenhauer? Would you ask him about marriage? About finding the ideal woman? About death? Let's see all this and more. Just don't forget, he is going to answer.

(What is marriage?) "Marriage is a trap nature lays for us." "Happy marriages are rare because their end goal is not reproduction".

(How to acquire virtues?) "Virtue, like genius, is not taught".

(What is the foundation of love?) "The foundation of love is the instinct to reproduce the species."

(When does a woman become undesirable?) "A woman causes us aversion when, due to her age, she no longer inspires in us the desire to procreate. Youth, even without beauty, is attractive; beauty without youth does not hold any attraction".

(Don't you fear death?) "Man's individuality has so little value that nothing is lost with death; there are a few important things in general characteristics of humanity, which are indestructible."

"If a man was given eternal life, it would become so repugnant to him that he would end up wishing for death, tired of the lack of change in his character and his unlimited understanding."

"If we demanded immortality we would perpetuate a mistake, because individuality would not exist, and the true end of life is getting rid of it."

(Should we have life after death?) "What is the content, almost unchangeable, of this conscience? A torrent of petty, sheepish ideas. It would be best to let it rest for eternity".

(What do you say about the sociability of people?) "In general, man is only as sociable as he is intellectually poor and ordinarily vulgar".

But the main question I chose was:

To you, *All those who live desire. Who desires, suffers. So, life is pain.*

Why did nature give us pain? What is the reason for this saga humanity must suffer through?

SCHOPENHAUER: "If men lived in a fairy land, where nothing demanded effort, and where partridges flew already cooked and stuffed into easy reach, in a country where every one could attract a lover with no difficulty, they would die of boredom or hang themselves, others would fall apart, causing bigger maladies than the ones caused by nature. And that shows us that there is no better place than the one we occupy, and no better existence than the one we have".

While Schopenhauer shows that human beings are insatiable, and always desire what they do not have, Carnegie goes back to eastern philosophy, taking views from **Buddha** and encouraging a different view of the world, a pragmatic view, showing that one can contemplate the gifts they have. Curiously, some of Carnegie's followers pass off one of Schopenhauer's quotes as if it were from Carnegie: "It matters little whether you view the sunset from the window of a palace, or through the bars of a prison."[468] Schopenhauer wrote this in his book *Will to Love* right after commenting that people in general are slaves to their desires, but those who free themselves from the 'oppression of will' can find a interior balance, and peace in its plenitude.[469] So if a convict finds his spiritual balance, he will be able to see in the sunset a magnificent work of nature that brings joy, just as much joy as he would have had if he were in a palace. It is impossible to say which of the two places would be harder to live in, for there are some who live in extreme wealth but suffer more than the poorest of the poor. Carnegie saw this for himself when he visited the Sing Sing Correctional Facility and concluded: ...*the thing that astonished me most was that the prisoners there appeared to be about as happy as the average person on the outside.*[470] When we understand Schopenhauer's philosophy, dissected by Carnegie's pragmatic thoughts, we can clearly see the scene narrated by Fred Cochran; on Christmas Eve, among the crowds swarming to finish their shopping in Chicago, during a gorgeous sunset, he watched a flock of geese fly through this scene of indescribable beauty, and noticed a beggar woman who was also observing the flight of the birds. The woman walked away, murmuring happily: "God spoils me." Cochran came to the conclusion that he envied the woman.[471]

Schopenhauer quotes **Epicurus**, another thinker who tried to find a bigger sense in life among the simplest things, like gatherings with friends and life in harmony, criticizing the clamor of materialism. Carnegie had a strong philosophical connection with Epicurus, Buddha and Schopenhauer. As a result, we can understand why some might credit Carnegie with Schopenhauer's words. I saw this happen on a website that propounds Carnegie's ideas and also in a master's thesis in the field of law. This would never harm Carnegie's credibility, because of his fantastic rigor in writing and because he always gave credit to authors whose ideas he cited. However, the irony of this confusion is that, as I see it, Carnegie not only updated Schopenhauer's thoughts that converged with those of the **Buddha**, but also made tangible to the greater public one of Buddhism's crucial points... well, let me explain it more clearly.

Approximately 1800 years before the Christian Era, various tribes lived in the Indus Valley (presently India). These tribes were attacked by nomads that came from the south of Russia, called Aryans. These aggressors imposed a new form of manipulation and power that was especially sustained by religious stigmas and externalized in law, which was represented by the Manu Code. The word 'aria' (of Aryan) came to mean 'noble' in Sanskrit, the language in which the Manu Code was written.[472] In truth, an artificial nobility was created, which separated people into vertical social strata: the social caste system. Of course, the organizers of this scheme reserved the best options for themselves; the privileged were known as Brahmins, practically above the law, they were akin to gods. In the second place were the kshatriyas, military leaders responsible for enforcing the system. In third place were the vaishya, who made up the working class, farmers and merchants. In fourth place were the slaves, and lastly the untouchables, who could only deal with dirty things: garbage, the sewer and the cemetery. But there was a subtext supporting these ideas, for the Brahmins preached that if an untouchable lived an obedient life, in their next life they would be reborn a caste above, stepping up to slave status. And so people conformed themselves to the social caste into which they were born. Besides the lack of freedom, the Hindu people suffered brutal misery and hunger, as well as the violence that was permitted under the Manu Code. In 563BCE, a Brahmin prince who lived in a luxurious palace stepped outside to see the reality of people on the streets. His name was Siddhartha Gautama. Shocked by the sickness and poverty that desolated his people, he began on his path towards illumination that eventually ended with his transformation into the Buddha[473]; he then turned his attention to helping the stigmatized people suffering around him. Buddha enunciated seven principles, all paths leading to peace: I) vision; II) intention; III) word; IV) action; V) life; VI) effort and VII) concentration. *Nirvana* is the dominance of self, the search for the truth, life with energy and serenity, concentration and generosity.[474] Here we can see that many of Buddha's themes are present in Carnegie's thoughts. For example: concentration. Carnegie dissects the sense, foundation, and the 'how to' of concentration. Of course, concentration goes beyond the mental image we get of sitting silently on a meditation cushion. Concentration is important in every step of the day. To this end, Carnegie developed ideas like 'day-tight compartments'.[475] This means full focus on your activities, not letting worry take over. Worries damage your professional and personal activities, and harm a person's very existence via illness and unhappiness. To convince the reader, Carnegie looks for arguments from various origins. One example is religion. The best known Christian prayer, the Lord's Prayer, teachers a request to "Give us this day our daily bread..." In the Bible, we can read in Psalm 118: "This is the day the Lord has made; let us rejoice and be glad in it." But this is not all, Carnegie uses poems, short stories, personal accounts, legends, novels, plays[476], philosophy; suffice to say he uses multiple didactic resources to support practical rules giving the reader greater ease of concentration. "Shut the iron doors on the past and the future"[477], affirmed Carnegie, in the sense that one cannot stop living in the present to mentally navigate the past or the future. Planning the future is important, and learning from past mistakes is also fundamental, Carnegie recognizes both, but what he supports is activity focusing on what you do and what needs to be done. Schopenhauer's philosophy never reached the point of translating these ideas from Buddha the way Carnegie did. For someone labeled as an author of 'self-help' books, Carnegie certainly made many consecrated philosophers envious. Philosophy itself poorly discusses the possibility of abandoning the search for answers and directing our strength towards solving more mundane problems. Would celebrated philosophers, the founding fathers of pragmatism, existentialism, philosophy of language and so many other intellectual movements be as reverenced if the greater public had access to them? Carnegie was brilliant at the art of communication, and as a result reading his thoughts became so democratic. He did not write an 'Advanced Course in Oratory', but instead taught how to speak objectively and sincerely in public in his book *Public Speaking: a Practical Course for Business Men*[478]. Keeping this in mind, we must attribute the clarity of Carnegie's books to his dominance of the subject, depth of ideas and especially, his life experience he returned to the community as wisdom.

His simple writing style could also have been inspired by **Montaigne**, a French thinker who, according to one historian, philosophized as if he were speaking with a group of friends, illustrating all the themes with concrete examples. Montaigne also disliked and even contradicted social conventions inside his castle, studying others in order to discover more about himself; learning more about the most varied people, rich or poor, healthy or sick, in life or in death. Montaigne died in 1592; one of his well-known quotes is: "Study my life by looking for my life in the lives of others."[479]

The book that Carnegie most often had in his pocket was **Benjamin Franklin's** autobiography.

Benjamin Franklin and his book have much in common with Carnegie's philosophy. Franklin was a genius and yet at the same time a humble person. He had about a year's worth of formal education, but taught himself extensively. He began his life in extreme poverty. When he left New York and went to Philadelphia, he only had enough money in his pocket to buy three loaves of bread. But he adopted a life fully dedicated to study, work and discipline. To Franklin, reading was a mandatory exercise limited to... "at Night, after Work or before Work began in the Morning; or on Sundays..."[480] He was such a lover of letters that he founded libraries and museums. He adopted the Socratic method, specifically the technique of encouraging his conversation partners to make positive affirmations until they were in agreement. Carnegie discussed this method in the third part of How to Win Friends and Influence People[481], masterfully explaining with arguments more suited to contemporary life. In Carnegie's style, Benjamin Franklin confessed:

> I continu'd this Method some few Years, but gradually left it, retaining only the Habit of expressing my self in Terms of modest Diffidence, never using when I advance any thing that may possibly be disputed, the Words, Certainly, undoubtedly, or any others that give the Air of Positiveness to an Opinion; but rather say, I conceive, or I apprehend a Thing to be so and so, It appears to me, or I should think it so or so for such and such Reasons; or I imagine it to be so; or it is so if I am not mistaken.[482]

Did this habit work? It practically moved mountains. Franklin modestly claimed that it enabled him to inform some people and persuade others, avoiding confrontation; combined with cordiality, this approach allowed well-intentioned people to do the right thing, giving them no reason to respond negatively to arrogant behavior or a 'dogmatic' attitude.[483] But we know that Franklin did wonders with his modesty. Just to show how far this method took him, in 1776 Franklin went to France in order to persuade the French monarch to provide material support to General Washington and become an ally in the fight for the colonies' independence from England! He met with success in his mission.[484] There are legendary accounts of the feats Benjamin Franklin accomplished. His biography is a veritable encyclopedia, but I believe that what attracted Carnegie was Franklin's method of personal progress, his overcoming of obstacles, and above all, his honesty, which was a characteristic Carnegie prized. Regarding this virtue, Franklin writes: "I grew convinced that truth, sincerity and integrity in dealings between man and man were of the utmost importance to the felicity of life; and I formed written resolutions, which still remain in my journal book, to practice them ever while I lived."[485] Upon reaching maturity, Franklin developed a method he titled *a project for achieving moral perfection.*[486] His method, without a doubt, could be used with admirable success. Let's look at the thirteen items Franklin detailed:

"**1. Temperance**
Eat not to dulness; drink not to elevation.
**2. Silence**
Speak not but what may benefit others or yourself. Avoid trifling conversation.
**3. Order**
Let all your things have their places; let each part of your business have its time.
**4. Resolution**
Resolve to perform what you ought. Perform without fail what you resolve.

### 5. Frugality

Make no expense but to do good to others or yourself; i.e., waste nothing.

### 6. Industry

Lose no time; be always employed in something useful; cut off all unnecessary actions.

### 7. Sincerity

Use no hurtful deceit. Think innocently and justly, and, if you speak, speak accordingly.

### 8. Justice

Wrong none, by doing injuries or omitting the benefits that are your duty.

### 9. Moderation

Avoid extreams. Forbear resenting injuries so much as you think they deserve.

### 10. Cleanliness

Tolerate no uncleanliness in body, cloaths or habitation.

### 11. Tranquility

Be not disturbed at trifles, or at accidents common or unavoidable.

### 12. Chastity

Rarely use venery but for health or offspring, never to dulness, weakness, or the injury of your own or another's peace or reputation.

### 13. Humility

Imitate Jesus and Socrates."[487]

Knowing that the task was difficult, Franklin decided to attend to one topic at a time; once this topic was dominated, he would progress to the next. His priority was temperance, and next silence, for he considered that the ability to listen was necessary in order to be accepted by more serious people.[488] Franklin had an planning book in which he organized every hour's activities. Carnegie adopted a similar system, suggesting that tasks be organized by hour to avoid scattering and waste. Of course, Carnegie suggested other more complete specifics and fundamentals, but it is worth looking at Franklin's agenda to see how he organized his daily tasks. A typical day showed a morning (from 5 to 7am) beginning with the question "What good shall I do today?" and the following activities: rise, bathe, prayer. ""Contrive day's business and take resolution of the day; prosecute the present study, and breakfast". Then work (from 8am to noon). Noon: "Read, or survey my accounts, and dine." Then work. (from 2 to 6pm). Evening: "Ask: 'What good have I done to-day?'; put things in their places. Supper. Music or diversion, or conversation. Examination of the day". Night: Sleep, from 10pm to 5am.

With this, Franklin said he was surprised ...*to find myself so much fuller of faults than I had imagined; but I had the satisfaction of seeing them diminish.*[489] Franklin reaped many benefits from using this method: good health, income, inventions and the contributions to his community (from instituting a new fire and police department and organizing the army to writing books); he founded the University of Pennsylvania, acted as a justice of the peace, participated in directing the English postal system, defended the abolitionist cause, contributed to the urbanization of cities, invented a heating stove, invented bifocal lenses and, let's not forget, invented the lightening rod. According to Bruce Bliven, *He was the first to identify the negative and positive poles of electricity. We owe it to him to have it and concepts like: battery, electrical charge, condensator and conductor.*[490] When he wrote a book on electrical phenomena and sent it to the Royal Society of England, he was ridiculed and mocked, but the book was eventually published in many languages and gained worldwide recognition, forcing the Royal Society to retract its criticisms.[491]

Looking for a model for success, Carnegie saw in Benjamin Franklin more than just practical counsel, he saw the pillars of his philosophy on life and his teachings.

Another philosopher Carnegie admired was **William James,** born in 1842 in New York. Let's see how Carnegie works with one of James' quotes:

*'The Lord may forgive our sins,' said William James, 'but the nervous system never does'.*

*Here is a startling and almost incredible fact: more Americans commit suicide each year than die from the five most common communicable diseases.*

*Why? The answer is largely: worry'.*[492]

Carnegie continues to develop means of reducing worry and increasing quality of life. I think that the appearance of William James' thoughts in Carnegie's texts is far beyond any quotes Carnegie might have picked up from reading a magazine. I conclude this for two reasons: first, Carnegie includes many quotes by the thinker. In *How to Stop Worrying and Start Living* alone, Carnegie mentions William James thirteen times.[493] In one of these citations, he comments on a passage by James:

> *William James said this: 'When once a decision is reached and execution is in order of the day, dismiss absolutely all responsibility and care about the outcome'. (In this case, William James undoubtedly used the word 'care' as a synonym for 'anxiety'.) He meant once you have made a careful decision based on facts, go into action. Don't stop to reconsider. Don't begin to hesitate, worry and retrace your steps. Don't lose yourself in self-doubting which begets other doubts. Don't keep looking back over your shoulder.*[494]

As such, Carnegie's conception of interpersonal relationships in *How to Win Friends and Influence People* and his explanation of relationships and the physical and mental effects of worry in *How to Stop Worrying and Start Living* constitute pure application of Pragmatism. Action is based on experience, but is not restricted to it, because it takes the observation of what is correct as a model;[495] experience is a main source of pragmatical truth, but not the only one. As we have seen, Carnegie takes any and all everyday events, for example winning a new friend through dialogue, the achievement of a good business deal due to a novel approach, hiring a new employee for a quality they exhibit, overcoming a disease by a change of attitude, physical improvement through exercise, even the behavior of a dog or bird as sources from which to draw conclusions that could lead to a secure path for action. The pragmatic philosophers that came after James and Dewey changed the focus of pragmatism from experience to the theory of language or of linguistic behavior[496], but this is another story, one that came after Carnegie's time.

We can effectively affirm that Carnegie practiced not just philosophy but science by his demonstrations, explanations of 'why' people act in certain ways, and explanations of the psychological reaction to interactions and dialog between people. What Pragmatism as a philosophy attempts after James and Dewey is, according to Ghiraldelli Jr., an explanation of our various responses to certain actions: "*Explaining our linguistic interaction is saying, in a relationship that involves the language, why there was an understanding, if there were an understanding*".[497] However, Carnegie kept science close to people's needs, providing what was needed to act better, to better understand the mechanisms of action and reaction in the world and in people, as well as methods for better expressing oneself to the world. We can compare Carnegie's developments as they relate to pragmatism with the following example: while pragmatism proposed the 'theory of the importance of warming up in the cold and cooling down in the heat' with regards to human relations, Carnegie created the 'air conditioner' for the actions and relationships between people. Louise L. Hay sums up what we are talking about: *I love 'how to's'. Every theory in the world is useless unless we know how to use them to change something. I was always a very pragmatic person, practical, with a great need to know how to do things.*[498]

So we can see that there is a deep relation between the thoughts of Carnegie and James. It can be said that Carnegie not only interpreted James, but perpetuated his work. The founding of the philosophy known as pragmatism was attributed to Charles Sanders Peirce (1839-1914), but William James formulated the doctrine of pragmatism in a different manner. James observed Peirce's method of the logical theory of meaning and transformed it into a practical, functional, empirical method... In William James' words: "What you want is a philosophy that will not only exercise your powers of intellectual abstraction, but that will make some positive connection with this actual world of finite human lives."[499] The word 'pragmatism' is derived from the Greek 'prágma', meaning 'action', the same root of our words 'practice' and 'practical'.[500] If an individual's religion improves his or her life, pragmatism recognizes truth and value in this.[501] While rationalism clings to logic, and empiricism to the outward senses, pragmatism takes advantage of both philosophies, and also takes advantage of anything available, the humblest and most personal experiences, even mystical experiences if they create practical consequences.[502] Do we need to improve anything? Can we learn something? Are we open to the possibility of evolving? If we can answer all three in the affirmative, then opportunities will appear and we will be able to add to our stockpile of knowledge.[503] James masterfully defended his method, but in doing so, he intended to found a philosophy, with a universal and an academic language. However, Carnegie differs from James on two points: 1) Carnegie's language is much more accessible and illustrated; 2) he creates a specific method of practical behavior. To use another analogy, if pragmatism were a complete and general course, Dale Carnegie would teach on work, behavior and a healthy lifestyle. Coincidentally or not, Charles Peirce begins the first lessons on pragmatism with an article titled *How to Make Our Ideas Clear* in 1878[504]; Carnegie was born in 1888; William James took up pragmatism again and presented it with a different face at the University of California in 1898, when Carnegie was ten years old. By this, I mean to say that Carnegie was born and grew up under the influence of pragmatism, which has an acute connection to the American way of life. The United States was recovering from the Civil War and making its way to grand progress. The country grew, pragmatism evolved at the same time that Carnegie did. *Let the devil carry the Absolute!'* said James, pointing at conduct and the construction of reality. The construction of the American was also being carried out alongside the philosophy that most closely approximated the America way of life. The historians Allan Nevins and Henry Commager referred to this moment in the country's history: *This new process of looking at philosophy and the entire social order soon brought about a revolution in American thinking. With it, it brought an irresistible change from the deductive to inductive, from the intuitive to the experimental, from principle to practice and from form to function.*[505] However, Dale Carnegie's originality will never allow him to be mistaken for Peirce or James. William James influenced him, but Carnegie is unmistakable. He was very serious about the concept that a person should 'be himself', a lesson that we all could learn from. If Beethoven, Edison, Einstein or Pelé had tried to be like everyone else, the world would not be the same. They were unusual, outsiders, and were subjected to stigma. But they followed their own paths, did things their way. They were themselves. Finding yourself is being able to complete a task of which only you are capable, making it look effortless, as if you always had the necessary abilities. All you needed was to find them. Like these great names, Carnegie too was stigmatized as a 'self-help author', but he endured the criticism and carried on with his work, even though he knew that he could have tried to adapt to fit himself into the categories of 'science' or 'philosophy' of the time. Without being perturbed by criticism, he persisted in the treatment of themes fundamental to mankind, fundamental to you and me. The key point of this philosophy is not endless discussion of very vague ideas, no matter how logical, but instead the effectiveness of its content. Many times, avid defenders of complex systems do not understand the full extension of the philosophies they proudly champion in hallway conversations and superb exhibitions of public speaking; they also do not know how to apply these ideas to real life. Sweet illusion, bitter illusion. You cannot choose any single system and elect it to be the only truth, but what you can do is recognize a philosophy that is truly beneficent and close to people, to your day-to-day life, to your otherness...

Who knows if much of Carnegie's style of writing about subjects using examples wasn't inspired by James? After all, for the American philosopher, "It is always best to discuss things by the help of concrete examples."[506]

William Longgood supports this in the following passage:

*Carnegie had little patience with theory or abstract thought. He wanted only the practical, the useful, the functional. But coupled with his pragmatism was an incredible ability to learn from everything in life. Ormond Drake said, 'He was a fantastic observer. He could capitalize on practical experience better than anyone I ever knew. He was always writing things down and asking questions. He was terribly dogmatic about some things but his mind was not closed.*

*He could not only observe but could capitalize on his observations. I used to be amazed how he could see some thing happen and six months later he came out in print with it. I myself didn't see right or I didn't see its application to people. That was the heart of Dale Carnegie's genius – to be able to capitalize on experience.*[507]

If I were pretentious enough to try to summarize Carnegie's philosophy in a few brief words, I would say something like this: *Carnegie developed a system made to function and to benefit its adepts (readers or participants in a course); this system consists of a program of personal and professional improvement based on pragmatism. However, he noticed his work could go beyond and reach people in general, who would have access to his thoughts and life practice. Besides that, by developing pragmatism, he indicated a direction for nascent philosophy: respect and amity for others based on thinkers such as Socrates, Buddha and Jesus Christ.*

But instead of restricting myself to my opinions, I looked for an elaborated thought by a philosopher who was also quoted by

Carnegie; his passage can certainly define his way of thinking more clearly. I am talking about **Ralph Waldo Emerson**. In truth, I was reading an inspiring book that quoted Emerson, and I came across a paragraph that is a true synthesis of Carnegie's work. In stating his own philosophy, Emerson seems to be foreseeing his successor:

"What is success?

To laugh often and much;

To win the respect of intelligent people and the affection of children;

To earn the appreciation of honest critics and endure the betrayal of false friends;

To appreciate beauty;

To find the best in others;

To leave the world a bit better, whether by a healthy child, a garden patch or a redeemed social condition;

To know even one life has breathed easier because you have lived;

This is to have succeeded".[508]

Emerson wrote the poem... and Carnegie showed how to achieve it.

# CHAPTER 14

## THE PROFOUND SLEEP

*I rejoiced in life for its own sake. Life is no 'brief candle'*
*for me. It is sort of a splendid torch, which I have got*
*hold of for the moment; and I want to make it burn as*
*brightly as possible before handing it on to future*
*generations.*
(George Bernard Shaw)[509]

In the early twentieth century, when Carnegie was a teenager, his horseback commute between his farm and the college was a contemplative one, during which he worried about his near future and grew anxious about the long term. Uncertainties prowled his mind, just as threatening as the ferocious cougar that had devoured people in the region and might be waiting in the shadows to attack him and his horse. He needed to overcome these barriers that appeared and stood in his way until he graduated. And there were many difficulties. First, he was the rarest exception as the one student who could not pay a trifling fee to live in college town of Warrensburg so he could better focus on his  studies. Secondly, he did not have anything to wear, for his only set of clothes was laughably small, drawing unwanted attention when the teacher called him up to write on the board. As if that was not enough, he had to do farm work to scrape together  some money. Another difficult moment was his struggle to stand out in something, demonstrate his value to others and also o himself. He mustered up some courage during his youth after great sacrifices and striving, made his triumph in public speaking at school. All this now passed before him like a film.

Almost half a century later on August 8th, 1955, a still-lucid Carnegie granted a newspaper interview in which he stated that oratory had given him a feeling of importance that influenced him throughout his entire life, and that his mother had taught him his first lessons.[510] Fifty years prior, when he was still a teenager, he could not have imagined that he would be giving media interviews, talking about his life and the methods he developed. But even as an adult he would have never imagined how his relationship with his beloved college would develop; yes, he would come to be known as the college's most famous student. Carnegie's academic records are carefully stored and displayed in a museum at what is now the University of Warrensburg. Did they ever think that the relics of such a poor student, his photographs, report cards, books, homages, newspaper articles, letters and so many other items would, a century later, be so diligently cared for as treasures? The weighty task of curating Carnegie's effects falls to Professor Vivian Richardson, who teaches in the department of History of the American West. In 2004, Central Missouri State University's centennial theme was *Central Missouri: Winning Friends and Influencing People,* a reference to Carnegie. What would that young boy from the beginning of the century say if he could have seen the ceremonies, seen his daughter Donna, now a woman, present on the university campus and watching the event?[511] And if he walked into any bookstore in the world and found that his books were still being bought by people and changing lives as a result, that the name Dale Carnegie is still a current reference at the beginning of the twenty-first century, that millions of people read his books, that Dale Carnegie Courses take place in almost every city in the world and yet there is still so much to be seen about how future readers will see his legacy? And if they told him that homage to him still continues, and that on September 13, 2006, his name was added to the Hall of Fame in the Jefferson City capitol, and that *Life* magazine named him as one of the one hundred most important Americans of the twentieth century?[512] To him, university was as important as a map and canteen are to a man lost in the desert. When he thought about the university, Carnegie's eyes shone, and the university eventually recognized him for his merits.

The relationship between Carnegie and the college he attended was always strong. A year after he released *How to Stop Worrying and Start Living*, on May 10 1949, George W. Diemer (president of the CMSC) asked Carnegie to participate in Founder's Day activities, during which he talked about the reasons that motivate only some few Americans to change their lives and life well. One of the questions that echoed through the auditorium was "Why the heck are we worried?", which was supposed to have been the evening's theme. But Hendricks Hall, where the event was held, instead bore witness to a very intense life story. At one point, Carnegie looked to the podium and stated that just below it was where he used to tether his horse before going to class.[513] I can imagine the emotions that filled him on this occasion. But this would not be his last visit to Warrensburg.

In the summer of 1955, in July, Carnegie received an honor that pleased him greatly. His presence had been requested a year in advance, and although he prepared his speech carefully, he kept forgetting his notes. As a result, he ended up solemnly reading a text he wrote, something unusual for the master of public speaking. Yet he still spoke with his usual firmness and content, keeping his audience rapt from start to finish, as was his style.[514] Central Missouri State University conferred upon him their first honorary doctorate, presented by Dr. George W. Diemer, dean of what was then known as Warrensburg State Teachers College. On this occasion, 162 students were graduating from the summer session. The speech given by the administration on what was probably the college's most solemn occasion revealed that college records showed that Carnegie's classmates graduated in 1907 knowing that he would certainly attain fame. When Carnegie finished his studies at Central Missouri University in 1908, the speaker said, he had not graduated, but had gotten a certificate that allowed him to teach. The speaker also noted that Carnegie had been a member of Irving's Literary Society, another honor, and among other feats, won first place in a declamation contest in 1907, the same year he was elected class vice-president. When he spoke on the solemn occasion, James Kirkpatrick, Chairman of the Board of Regents of the University and Editor of the *Windsor* newspaper, told Carnegie:

> *It is in the best tradition of the Central Missouri State College that we recognize outstanding achievement and so at this time the Board of Regents and the faculty of this college honor one of its most distinguished alumni: An individual who came to campus from his nearby farm home; who here, by his own efforts and determination, developed from a timid, reserved farm boy into a skilled public speaker who won contest after contest; who through difficulties and adversity became renowned as a teacher of public speaking and applied psychology and gained world recognition as an author in those fields; who has been welcomed in many parts of the world as a benefactor of mankind who has helped thousands to conquer their fears and develop their innate abilities and self-confidence; a man who is now known and will be remembered, almost as a legend, by the entire world as a contributor to human happiness and development...*

The speaker continued to compliment Carnegie and his works and noted 1908 as one of the College's best years. However, nothing compares to another event that happened at the same time, which was more touching... Carnegie's tribute to his mother, Mrs. Amanda Carnagey.

His mother had dreamed that he would follow a religious vocation. Even though he did not opt for the priesthood, he was invited to lecture in a church pastored by the minister and author Norman Vincent Peale. If I could choose to watch one of Carnegie's lectures, I certainly choose to go back in time and watch this occasion, for it was extremely intense and emotional. He talked about his boyhood poverty and his mother's unshakeable faith. When there was nothing to eat at home, his mother was calm and unworried, saying that the

Lord would provide. She sang hymns of faith like "What a friend we have in Jesus", and this protected him from hunger and need. Carnegie stopped talking, his voice choked up with emotion. The congregation sat hushed into silence while Dale struggled to regain his composure, tears streaming down his face. Finally, still choked up, he said: "My parents gave me no money nor financial inheritance, but they gave me something of much greater value, the blessing of faith and a sturdy character." According to Peale, it was one of the most moving and affecting speeches he had ever heard.[515] Ah, if only I could go back and see 'that speech'.

In July of 1955 the Dale Carnegie Institute Convention was another success, and Carnegie's participation left two participants, L.G. Bue and Bud Hogberg,  quite impressed. They got into the elevator and found themselves sharing it with the great man, Dale Carnegie in the flesh. Bue and Hogberg wanted to take advantage of this chance encounter to ask Carnegie some questions and, to tell the truth, they were very anxious. But Carnegie was not well, and they later learned that he had to be  taken to his room to rest. But although they did not realize it at the time, Carnegie's kindness in excusing himself left the two men feeling almost pleased that the great man had left.[516] At this time he was already feeling the symptoms of his illness. He felt sick and got increasingly annoyed because he started to forget things.  According to Longgood, the cause could have been hardening of the arteries and a series of small strokes, but there is no unanimity on the matter. Carnegie's symptoms are also typical of Alzheimer's Disease, which was not well known at the time.[517] Regardless of cause, he would start something and get lost, or go somewhere and then find he did not remember his destination. This was when he began to rely on notes in order to give speeches, but Longgood maintained that lectures still had the 'old magic' despite not being spontaneous.[518]

At that time, he suffered an attack of shingles and made a slow recovery. Carnegie, Dorothy and Donna went to Bermuda for a vacation, but he had to be brought back to a hospital in New York. According to Longgood, when Dorothy realized that Carnegie was not going to be able to resist any longer, she brought him home to Forest Hills where he had wanted to stay. Longgood described his final moment: *For nine days Carnegie fought desperately for life, but finally, on a Wednesday morning, November 1, 1955, he slipped quietly into the great void of death; he would have been 67 years old on November 24.*[519]

One of the causes of Carnegie's death was Hodgkin's disease,[520] a form of lymphoma that generates malignant abdominal tumors, most often in the spleen, diaphragm, liver or bone marrow. Other symptoms of this disease, the origin of which is unknown, are fever, night sweats, weight loss and shingles. It is most seen in men around twenty years of age or over fifty.[521] The recommended treatment is radiotherapy, chemotherapy, or both.[522] According to specialized literature, the chances of cure depend mostly on the stage of the disease. Nowadays the prognosis is more optimistic, indicating that detection in early stages can allow over a 90% chance of cure. In later stages, chances decrease to 50%.[523]

Georgette N. Drake was an instructor in the course and the youngest to graduate at sixteen. When saying her final goodbyes to her idol, she remembered the day she turned eighteen as if it were that very moment. It was December 8, and Carnegie had sent her a message engraved in metal with Lincoln's own handwriting, in which the statesman had referred to a pact celebrated decades ago, but which occurred on December 8, 1863, the same month and day as Georgette's birthday. At the funeral she saw someone familiar: Ormand Drake, also an instructor. Some time after that meeting, they married, and Drake commented: "Even in death, Dale Carnegie stroked her head and mine with blessings."[524]

One of the pallbearers was Norvell J. Brickell; he had met Carnegie in July of 1944 at the Murray Hill Hotel in New York. One of the reasons Brickell admired Carnegie was the kindness with which he had been received by Carnegie. His favorite memory of Carnegie during a course, when a student was trembling, desperate with fear about his foreign accent. Carnegie told the terrified speaker: *You should get down on your knees every morning and thank God you are different. Your accent adds color and emphasis to what you say. It gives you a power possessed by no one else in this room.*[525]

Brickell remembered the transformation created by these words: the student seemed to stand taller, his eyes glowed and he, inspired, strived for more and liked himself more, and in turn grew to like others more.[526] At one time, Carnegie said that 'Personality is the effect you have on others'.[527] If this is true, Carnegie's personality was beyond measure. But the grandiosity of his work allowed him something only accessible to those blessed by the gods, for in his final moments, his last months of life, when he began to forget things here and there, thinking it a memory problem, it wasn't. In truth, he was slowly falling asleep, until being generously greeted by his great friends that were awaiting him on the other side.

# THE TOWN OF BELTON

After the religious ceremony in New York, near his well known residence in Queens, Carnegie was buried in Belton Cemetery in Missouri, where his mother and father had already been laid to rest; his mother had passed away in 1939 and his father in 1941. Although Carnegie could have built a large mausoleum there, he desired to be buried underground, at the same level as every other person who rests there. It was his way of showing respect to everyone. Today, we can see an ordinary tombstone engraved with the names of Carnegie, his parents, and Dorothy.

More than 350 people were present in the flower-filed sanctuary. Reverend Arnold Prater from the Methodist church celebrated the funeral mass. In his farewell words, Reverend Prater reminded that Carnegie frequented that church, greeting friends as he walked down the main street and walked into the sanctuary to pray alone. "This was the church his mother founded," said the Minister, "founded and taught here for years. It was his father's church. It is the church where he said goodbye to everyone in the years that passed". Belton became the city that Carnegie adopted as his own. During his last forty-five years he visited the town as if it were his hometown. It was there that his parents had settled since 1910, when they bought a farm south of what is today Carnegie Street. In this town, his mother Amanda was part of the Missionary Society and led a group of women who organized the first Sunday school. In 1937, a "Watermelon Feast" was organized in honor of Carnegie. Everyone waited for him to make a speech, but faithful to his style and considerate of all who had gathered there, his only pronouncement was: "I'm sure you all are just as anxious as I am to get down to the business of eating this delicious watermelon".[528] A year later, he visited a high school to participate in a charity even for the Belton Lions Club, of which he was a member. He also contributed articles to the Star-Herald newspaper in Belton.

His cousins, Mrs. George Wernex and her son Russel Wernex, still live in Belton and Cass County.[529]

Harold Abbott, who had a close relationship with Dale Carnegie for years, stated:

> *The only times I ever saw Dale Carnegie angry were the times we would be driving through the country and we happened to pass a run down farm that had been allowed to erode and deteriorate. Then he would rise up in righteous indignation. He loved the land. He loved Missouri. Yes, he loved Belton.*
>
> *Every time I took him to Belton, Dale would ask me to drive down the main street. One time in a reflective mood he said, "My mother used to trade at that store," and a little farther down he said, "My father used to bank at that bank." Because of the memories it had, Belton was a very sacred place to him.*[530]

A month before his death, at a request from *American Home* magazine, Carnegie was interviewed by E. L. D. Seymour, who commented on the garden that Carnegie loved and visited so often in order to relax and gather inspiration to write. Seymour concluded that Carnegie was the living proof of what he taught. He was the kind of man that makes a good gardener. He would have been a good gardener, if he had not cultivated people and their possibilities.[531]

# EPILOGUE

*We have all the time in the world*
*Time enough for life*
*To unfold all precious things*
*Love has in store*
*We have all the time in the world*
*If that's all we have you will find*
*We need nothing more*
*Every step of the way*
*Will find us*
*With the cares of the world*
*Far behind us*
*We have all the time in the world*
*Just for love*
*Nothing more, nothing less*
*Only love*
(Louis Armstrong)

I walked up the grand entrance stairway of the monumental New York Public Library, a truly communitarian institution serving all members of the community, regardless of creed or race, marital or economical status. Carnegie was a frequent visitor, expanding his knowledge for his classes, or researching his books, as with *How to Stop Worrying and Start Living*, which would become a worldwide success...Of course the library was even more significant to me because the object of my own study had spent so much time there. When I first arrived there, a curious thing happened: I was attended by a friendly man, and when I told him what I was looking for he replied, "Oh, that self-help author! But you can find these books in every bookstore."

That was how everyone saw Dale Carnegie and his books: "self-help". But this is exactly what I didn't agree with, for I believed I could find something new. On that day, I had not really even begun to dive deeply into my research. Days and weeks passed by. One day, when I was feeling quite at home at the library of the city that never sleeps, I started to ponder the material I had found there and all that I had read, looking for answers to my questions about Carnegie. At a certain moment, a curious thought came to me. I was born over a decade after Carnegie had passed away, and knew of course that I would not be able to talk to him about my questions. However, I started to imagine what meeting him in person would have been like. Certainly I would have asked him many things, but what I would want most to do is to thank him for the books that contributed to my life, and the personal development that they represented to me. How many people who read *Public Speaking and Influencing Men in Business* also benefited in oratory contests or other more personal improvements, progress that meant so much to them all? The other books then, what to say... How many people would like to say something, ask something, or thank Carnegie? In my case, I owe my style of teaching and writing to him and to the lessons I learned through his work. Above all, I have no shame in speaking of the spiritual comfort I derived from his works and how great a blessing they were to me. I relied on masters, Dale Carnegie and so many others, for all that I have done right in life, taking lessons from books, from the classroom, from friendly conversations. In this way, I owe Dale Carnegie a lot, but I started to agonize over what Carnegie would say in response to this query. So I fell into endless perplexity, far from my research and questions, separate from my doubts and conclusions. I had the inexplicable sensation of being some other person interested in hearing Carnegie's opinion on all parts of his life, and this I could not even attempt to discover through effort alone.

My materials were spread out all over the table. I suddenly came back to awareness, realizing that I had been staring at a sheet of paper on top of the many  texts and books I had been using for research. I looked more closely and saw that the paper held a drawing of a friendly, smiling Dale Carnegie. Under his image was the one lone message: *Thank you!*

Thank you, my friend Dale Carnegie; thank you, dear reader. Thank you very much!

Carlos Roberto Bacila

# PHOTOGRAPHS

"He lived in a tiny room in 244 West 56th Street, in Hell's Kitchen, a neighborhood as dirty as it was dangerous... In the morning, when he grabbed a tie from a nail on the wall, cockroaches ran everywhere... I visited Carnegie's old address in July of 2008; today, this gracious building houses a hotel and a pub. I talked with employees there but nobody had any idea who had lived there over a century before, unsurprisingly. What used to be

Hell's Kitchen was now part of a more gentrified Manhattan, with astronomical property values".

# The Belton Museum

# Belton Cemetery

**The City of Belton**: "After the religious ceremony in New York, near his well known residence in Queens, Carnegie was buried in Belton Cemetery in Missouri, where his mother and father had already been laid to rest; his mother had passed away in 1939 and his father in 1941. Although Carnegie could have built a large mausoleum there, he desired to be buried underground, at the same level as every other person who rests there. It was his way of showing respect to everyone. Today, we can see an ordinary tombstone engraved with the names of Carnegie, his parents, and Dorothy. ... Belton became the city that Carnegie adopted as his own. During his last forty-five years he visited the town as if it were his hometown".

"The book that Carnegie most often had in his pocket was **Benjamin Franklin's** autobiography. Benjamin Franklin and his book have much in common with Carnegie's philosophy. Franklin was a genius and yet at the same time a humble person. He had about a year's worth of formal education, but taught himself extensively. Like Carnegie, he began his life in extreme poverty".

In his visit to Kansas City, MO, the author poses with a sculpture of Benjamin Franklin commemorating the bicentennial of the Bill of Rights.

"In the summer of 1955, in July, Carnegie received an honor that pleased him greatly. ...Central Missouri State University conferred upon him their first honorary doctorate".

Celebration of "Dale Carnegie Day", June 1938.

His class in Central Missouri State College, when he still went by the name Carnagey.

Thanks to the University of Central Missouri for providing the photographs.

Beautiful Central Missouri State College, which at the time this photo was taken was just recovering from a terrible fire.

"...yes, he would come to be known as the college's most famous student. Carnegie's academic records are carefully stored and displayed in a museum at what is now the University of Warrensburg. Did they ever think that the relics of such a poor student, his photographs, report cards, books, homages, newspaper articles, letters and so many other items would, a century later, be so diligently cared for as treasures? The weighty task of curating Carnegie's effects falls to Professor Vivian Richardson, who teaches in the department of History of the American West. In 2004, Central Missouri State University's centennial theme was *Central Missouri: Winning Friends and Influencing People,* a reference to Carnegie."

First Methodist Church of Maryville: ...Carnegie's greatest example of enthusiasm was likely his mother Amanda, a fantastic woman who was strongly influenced by Methodist thinking...

"The Carnageys lived in Harmony Church, a small town ten miles northeast of Maryville, Missouri, and on November 24, 1888 their second son, Dale Breckenridge Carnagey, was born. The Carnagey family lived in extreme poverty on a modest farm, ten miles from the railroad tracks".

"The problems were terrible: the One Hundred and Two River, a great flow of dark brown water, flooded almost every year, destroying the corn fields".

The author visiting Carnegie Hall in 2008, before its renovation.

"It is at this time that Carnegie changed his last name from 'Carnagey' to 'Carnegie'. One speculation is that he was motivated to associate his name with the name of the ballroom where his lectures were now taking place, Carnegie Hall... Similarly, others consider that he changed his name to link his name with that of the magnate Andrew Carnegie (the original Carnegie of Carnegie Hall)... Quite to the contrary, conversations with those who knew Carnegie led me to consider another motivation. Apparently, Carnegie felt that having to spell out his name hindered communication; his friends out East spelled his name wrong, and Carnegie said he wanted to spare them any embarrassment".

# ABOUT THE AUTHOR

Carlos Roberto Bacila is PhD and teaches at University Federal do Paraná. He is doing his post-doctorate at University of Ottawa – Canada. Bacila is a graduate of the Dale Carnegie Institute.

He is author of several books. These include:

- **Bob London Lê e Vira o Jogo.** (Translation: *Bob London Read and Reverse the Score*). 3.ed. Amazon. E-book.

- **Introdução ao Direito Penal e à Criminologia**. (Translation: *Introduction to Criminal Law and Criminology*). Editora Intersaberes.

- **Sem Destino, Com Destino: A História de uma Viagem entre a Califórnia e o Havaí**. (Translation: *Easy Rider and Destiny – A Journey Through California and Hawaii*). Editora Juruá.

- **Criminologia e Estigmas: um estudo sobre os preconceitos**. (Translation: *Criminology and Stigmas: a Study on Prejudices*). 4.ed. Editora Atlas.

- **Lei de Drogas: comentários penais e processuais**. (Translation: *Drug Law: Criminal and Procedural Comments*). 3.ed. Editora Atlas.
- **Nos Bastidores da Sala de Aula**. (Translation: *Behind the Scenes of a Classroom*). Editora Intersaberes.
- **Teoria da Imputação Objetiva no Direito Penal**. (Translation: *Objective Imputation Theory in Criminal Law*). Editora Juruá.

# REFERENCES

ABBOTT, Harold. *Dale Carnegie – As I Knew Him*. BELTON HISTORICAL SOCIETY. The First Hundred Years. 2nd ed. Belton: Dodie Maurer Editor, 2006.

ABRÃO, Bernadette Siqueira. *História da Filosofia*. São Paulo: Nova Cultural, 1999.

ADAMS, Ian e DYSON, R. W. *Cinqüenta Pensadores Políticos Essenciais: da Grécia Antiga aos Dias Atuais*. Tradução de: Mario Pontes. Rio de Janeiro: Difel, 2006.

ANDREOLI, Thomas E. *et. al. Medicina Interna Básica*. 3.ed. Rio de Janeiro: Guanabara Koogan, 1994.

AURÉLIO, Marco. *Meditações*. Tradução de: Alex Marins. São Paulo: Martin Claret, 2001.

BACILA, Carlos Roberto. *Estigmas: Um Estudo Sobre os Preconceitos*. 2.ed. Rio de Janeiro: Lumen Juris, 2008.

BELTON HISTORICAL SOCIETY. *The First Hundred Years*. 2.ed. Belton: Dodie Maurer Editor, 2006.

BERNARDINHO. *Transformando Suor em Ouro*. 2.ed. Rio de Janeiro: Sextante, 2006.

BLIVEN, Bruce. *O Incomparável Talento de Benjamin Franklin*. FRANKLIN, Benjamin. *Autobiografia*. Tradução de Sarmento de Beires e José Duarte. São Paulo: Martin Claret, 2005.

BYRNE, Rhonda. *The Secret – O Segredo*. Tradução de: Marcos José da Cunha, Alexandre Martins, Alice Xavier. – Rio de Janeiro: Ediouro, 2007.

CARNEGIE, Dale. *Como Desfrutar sua Vida e Seu Trabalho*. 6.ed. Tradução de Fernando Tude de Souza e Brenno Silveira. São Paulo: Companhia Editora Nacional, 2002.

CARNEGIE, Dale. *Como evitar preocupações e começar a viver*. 37.ed. Tradução de Breno Silveira. São Paulo: Companhia Editora Nacional, 2003.

CARNEGIE, Dale. *Como Falar em Público e Influenciar Pessoas no Mundo dos Negócios*; revista por Dorothy Carnegie. 25.ed. Tradução de: Carlos Evaristo M. Costa. Rio de Janeiro: Record, 1993.

CARNEGIE, Dale. *Como Falar em Público e Influenciar Pessoas no Mundo dos Negócios*. 46.ed. Tradução de Carlos Evaristo M. Costa. Rio de Janeiro: Record, 2008.

CARNEGIE, Dale. *Como Fazer Amigos & Influenciar Pessoas*. 48.ed. Tradução de: Fernando Tude de Souza. São Paulo: Companhia Editorial Nacional, 2000.

CARNEGIE, Dale. *Como Fazer Amigos & Influenciar Pessoas para Adolescentes*. Tradução de Claudia Gerpe Duarde. 3.ed. Rio de Janeiro: BestSellen, 2008.

CARNEGIE, Dale. *Dale Carnegie's Biographical Roundup*. Highlights in the lives of Forty Famous People. New York: Greenberg, 1944.

CARNEGIE, Dale. *Five Minute Biographies*. Today – Carry Nation. A Cyclone in Petticoats Who Startled America. 1937.

CARNEGIE, Dale. *Grab Your Bootstraps*. Collier's for March 5, 1938.

CARNEGIE, Dale. *How to Win Friends & Influence People*. New York: Galahad Books, 1998.

CARNEGIE, Dale. *Lincoln, esse desconhecido*. 2.ed. Tradução de Wilson Velloso. São Paulo: Companhia Editora Nacional, 1966.

CARNEGIE, Dale. *Little Known Facts About Well Known People*. New York: Greenberg, 1934.

CARNEGIE, Dale. *Simple Secrets of Public Speaking*. Coronet Magazine. February, 1949.

CARNEGIE, Dale. *Viva com Entusiasmo*. Dale Carnegie Training.

CARNEGIE, Dale. We Have With Us Tonight. *The Reader's Digest*. Novembro de 1936, v.29.

CARNEGIE, Donna. COMMEMORATIVE CD-ROM celebrating ninety years of the *Dale Carnegie Training*.

CARNEGIE, Dorothy. Introdução de CARNEGIE, Dale. *Como Falar em Público e Influenciar Pessoas no Mundo dos Negócios*; revista por Dorothy Carnegie. 25.ed. Tradução de: Carlos Evaristo M. Costa. Rio de Janeiro: Record, 1993.

CARNEGIE, Dorothy. Prefácio à Edição Revista de CARNEGIE, Dale. *Como Fazer Amigos & Influenciar Pessoas*. 48.ed. Tradução de: Fernando Tude de Souza. São Paulo: Companhia Editorial Nacional, 2000.

CARNEIRO, Marcelo Motta. *A expressão Verbal na Educação Permanente*. Curitiba: Vicentina, 1986.

CHALITA, Gabriel. *Mulheres que Venceram Preconceitos: Mulheres Célebres que Trouxeram e Trazem Benefícios à Sociedade*. Rio de Janeiro: Imagem, 1996.

CHARRIÈRE, Henri. *Papillon: o homem que fugiu do inferno*. Tradução de: Círculo do Livro. São Paulo: Círculo do Livro,____.

COBRA, Nuno. *A Semente da Vitória*. 91.ed. São Paulo: Senac, 2008.

COCHRAN, Fred Lloyd. *O Vôo dos Gansos*. Coordenação de CANFIELD, Jack e HANSEN, Mark Victor. *Histórias para Aquecer o Coração*. Tradução de Marilena Moraes. Rio de Janeiro: Sextante, 2003.

COMMEMORATIVE CD-ROM celebrating ninety years of the *Dale Carnegie Training*. Generously provided by Brenda Leigh Johnson.

CONDE, Francisco Muñoz. *Edmund Mezger e o Direito Penal do Seu Tempo*. Estudos Sobre o Direito Penal no Nacional-Socialismo. 4.ed. Tradução de Paulo César Busato. Rio de Janeiro: Lumen Juris, 2005.

CROM, Rosemary. *Dale Carnegie As Others Saw Him*. New York: Dale Carnegie Training, 1987.

DAVIS JR., Sammy; BOYAR, Jane; BOYAR, Burt. *Sim, eu posso*. A História de Sammy Davis Jr. Tradução de: Maria Antonieta Tróia. Rio de Janeiro: Bloch, 1968.

DURANT, Philippe. *Jack Nicholson*. Tradução de Alexandra Maria Sousa Salgueiral. Lisboa: Pergaminho, 1990.

EMERSON, Ralph Waldo. Coordenação de CANFIELD, Jack e HANSEN, Mark Victor. *Histórias para Aquecer o Coração*. Tradução de Marilena Moraes. Rio de Janeiro: Sextante, 2003.

FAZOLI FILHO, Arnaldo. *História Geral*. São Paulo: Editora do Brasil, 1981.

FERREIRA, Aurélio Buarque de Holanda. *Dicionário da Língua Portuguesa*. 3.ed. Rio de Janeiro: Nova Fronteira, 1993.

FOHLEN, Claude. *O Faroeste*. Tradução de: Paulo Neves. São Paulo: Companhia das Letras-Círculo do Livro, 1989.

FOUCAULT, Michel. *Discipline and Punish. The Birth of the Prison*. Trans. Alan Sheridan. New York: Pantheon Books, 1977

FOUCAULT, Michel. *Microfísica do Poder*. 20.ed. Tradução de: Roberto Machado. Rio de Janeiro: Graal, 2004.

FOUCAULT, Michel. *Vigiar e Punir*. 9.ed. Tradução de: Lígia M. Ponde Vassalo. Petrópolis: Vozes, 1991.

FRANKLIN, Benjamin. *Autobiografia*. Tradução de Sarmento de Beires e José Duarte. São Paulo: Martin Claret, 2005.

GAARDER, Jostein. *O Mundo de Sofia*. Romance da História da Filosofia. 17ª reimpressão. Tradução de João Azenha Jr. São Paulo: Companhia das Letras, 1995.

GHIRALDELLI JR., Paulo. *O que é Pragmatismo*. São Paulo: Brasiliense, 2007.

HAY, Louise. *Pense positivo todos os dias*. Tradução de Teresa Bulhões. Rio de Janeiro: Sextante, 2008.

HANDALL, Peter. COMMEMORATIVE CD-ROM dos noventa anos do *Dale Carnegie Training*.

HARRIMAN, Margaret Case. He Sells Hope. *The Saturday Evening Post*, August, 14, 193(7).

HEMINGWAY, Ernest. *O Velho e o Mar*. 15.ed. Tradução de: Fernando de Castro Ferro. Rio de Janeiro: Civilização Brasileira, 1973.

HOBART, Steven B. *Dale Carnegie: Missourian Who Made Good -1888-1955*. Warrensburg: Central Missouri State University, 1984.

HOCHENAUER, Kurt. *Carnegie Course Continues to Pass the Test of Time*. The Kansas City Times. Thursday, December 3, 1981.

HOLLYMAN, Thomas B. *Success Amazes Even Carnegie*. Warrensburg: Daily Star-Journal, 28;01;1938.

HUGO, Victor. *Les Miserables*. Trans. Norman Denny. London: Penguin Classics, 1982

HUGO, Victor. *Os Miseráveis*. Tradução de: Frederico Ozanam Pessoa de Barros. São Paulo: Cosac & Naify, 2002.

JAMES, William. *Pragmatism. And Four Essays from The Meaning of Truth*. New York: Meridian Books, 1969

JAMES, William. *Pragmatismo*. Tradução de: Jorge Caetano Silva. São Paulo: Nova Cultural, 1989.

KAYE, Joseph. *A Youth's Timidy Led Him to World Influence*. The Kansas City Star. Sunday, July 24, 1955.

KEMP, Giles and CLAFLIN, Edward. *Dale Carnegie: the man who influenced millions*. New York: St. Martins, 1989.

KEROUAC, Jack. *On The Road. Pé na Estrada*. Tradução de Eduardo Bueno. Porto Alegre: L & PM, 2008.

KIRKLAND, Stephen E. *Dale Carnegie: The Man and His Ideas*. Detroit: Wayne State University, 1993.

LONDON, Jack. *Antes de Adão*. Tradução de Maria Inês Avieira e Luis Fernando Brandão. Porto Alegre: L&PM, 2007. p.07-14

LONDON, Jack. *The Call of the Wild*. New York: Viking, 1996.

LONDON, Jack. *Caninos Brancos*. Tradução de: Antivan Guimarães Mendes. São Paulo: Melhoramentos, 2002.

LONDON, Jack. *História de um soldado*. Tradução de Carlos Rizzi. São Paulo: Hemus,___.

LONDON, Jack. *O Chamado da Floresta*. Tradução de William Lagos. 2.ed. Porto Alegre: L & PM, 2008.

LONDON, Jack. *O Lobo do Mar*. São Paulo: Martin Claret, 1998.

LONGGOOD, William. *Talking Your Way to Success*. The Story of the Dale Carnegie Course. New York: Association Press, 1962.

MAROIS, André. *História dos Estados Unidos*. Tradução de: Godofredo Rangel. São Paulo: Companhia Editora Nacional, 1946.

MARSHALL, Margaret. *Dale Carnegie*. Columnists on Parade. The Nation, March 14, 1938.

MARTELL, Hazel Mary. *O mundo antigo*. 5.ed. Tradução de: Antivan Guimaraens Mendes. São Paulo: Melhoramentos, 2001.

MELVILLE, Herman. *Moby Dick*. London: Penguin Books, 1994.

MELVILLE, Herman. *Moby Dick*. Tradução de: Berenice Xavier. Rio de Janeiro: Tecnoprint, 1981.

MEYER, Adolph E. *How Dale Carnegie made friends*, Etc. In: The American Mercury.

NELTON, Sharon. *Nations Business*. December, 1988.

NEVINS, Allan e COMMAGER, Henry Steele. *História dos Estados Unidos*. Tradução de: Henrique Correa de Sá e Benevides. Rio de Janeiro: Bloch, 1967.

NEWTH, Eirik. *Breve Soria della Scienza*. La Ricerca della Verità. Firenze: Salani, 1998.

OBAMA, Barack. *A Origem dos Meus Sonhos*. Tradução de Irati Antonio, Renata Laureano e Sonia Augusto. São Paulo: Editora Gente, 2008.

PARKER, Gail Thain. *How to Win Friends and Influence People: Dale Carnegie and The Problem of Sincerity*. Burlington: The Johns Hopkins University Press, 1977.

PHILBRICK, Nathaniel. *No coração do mar: a história real que inspirou o Moby Dick de Melville*. Tradução de: Rubens Figueiredo. São Paulo: Martins Fontes, 1999.

POLITO, Reinaldo. *Assim é que se Fala: Como Organizar a Fala e Transmitir Idéias*. 5.ed. São Paulo: Saraiva, 1999.

RANGEL, Paulo. *Tribunal do Júri: Visão Lingüística, Histórica, Social e Dogmática*. Rio de Janeiro: Lumen Juris, 2007.

SANT, Tom. *The Giants of Sales: what Dale Carnegie, John Patterson, Elmer Wheeler, and Joe Girard can teach you about real Sales success*. New York: Amacom, 2006.

SCHOPENHAUER, Arthur. *A Vontade de Amar*. Tradução de: Aurélio de Oliveira. Rio de Janeiro: Tecnoprint, ____.

SEYMOUR, E.L.D. *American Home*. v.54. October, 1955.

SEYMOUR-SMITH, Martin. *Os 100 Livros que Mais Influenciaram a Humanidade*. A História do Pensamento dos Tempos Antigos à Atualidade. 4.ed. Tradução de Fausto Wolff. Rio de Janeiro: Difel, 2002.

SMALL, Collie. *Dale Carnegie: A Man With a Message*. Collier's for January 15, 1949.

SMELTZER, Suzanne C. e BARE, Brenda G. et. al. *Brunner/Suddarth: Tratado de Engermagem Médico-Cirúrgica*. 7.ed. v.2. Rio de Janeiro: Guanabara Koogan, 1994.

THOMAS, Lowell. *Rumo Certo à Distinção*. CARNEGIE, Dale. *Como Fazer Amigos & Influenciar Pessoas*. 48.ed. Tradução de: Fernando Tude de Souza. São Paulo: Companhia Editorial Nacional, 2000.

WILLIAMS, Mara Rose. *The Kansas City Star*. Monday, September 11, 2006, B2.

ZINGARELLI, Nicola. *Vocabolario della Língua Italiana*.12.ed. Bologna: Zanichelli, 1995.

## NEWSPAPERS AND MAGAZINES

CURRENT BIOGRAPHY YEARBOOK. New York: H.W. Wilson Co, 1941

*Nations Business*. December, 1988.

*The Belton Herald*. Belton, March 02, 1916.

*Collier's* January 15, 1949.

*Collier's* March 05, 1938.

*The Daily Star-Journal*. Warrensburg: Friday, October 22, 2004.

*The Kansas City Star*. Monday, September 11, 2006, B2.

*The Kansas City Times*. Thursday, December 3, 1981.

*The Student*. Warrensburg, Missouri, May 20, 1949. N. 22. Vol. XXXIX.

*The Saturday Evening Post*, August, 14, 193(7).

# NOTES

[1] LONGGOOD, William. *Talking Your Way to Success. The Story of the Dale Carnegie Course.* New York: Association Press, 1962. p.213-214.

[2] CARNEGIE, Dale. *Dale Carnegie's Biographical Roundup.* Highlights in the lives of Forty Famous People. New York: Greenberg, 1944, op. Cit. p.1-6.

[3] CARNEGIE, Dale. *Funny Fields.* A Five-Minute Biography.

[4] While the story is true, my friend's name has been changed to protect her privacy.

[5] DURANT, Philippe. *Jack Nicholson.* Tradução de Alexandra Maria Sousa Salgueiral. Lisboa: Pergaminho, 1990, p.133 and following

[6] DURANT, Philippe. Op. Cit. p.126.

[7] Mentioned in DURANT, Philippe. Op. Cit. p.08.

[8] DURANT, Philippe. Op. Cit. p.153.

[9] *Nations Business.* December, 1988, p.41.

[10] CURRENT BIOGRAPHY, 1941, p.139.

[11] HOCHENAUER, Kurt. *Carnegie Course Continues to Pass the Test of Time.* The Kansas City Times. Thursday, December 3, 1981.

[12] CARNEGIE, Dale. *Simple Secrets of Public Speaking.* Coronet Magazine. February, 1949, p.109.

[13] LONDON, Jack. *História de um soldado.* Tradução de Carlos Rizzi. São Paulo: Hemus,___.

[14] LONDON, Jack. *O Lobo do Mar.* São Paulo: Martin Claret, 1998.

[15] MELVILLE, Herman. *Moby Dick.* London: Penguin Books, 1994. The Brazilian edition is MELVILLE, Herman. *Moby Dick.* Tradução de: Berenice Xavier. Rio de Janeiro: Tecnoprint, 1981.

[16] The true story that may have inspired Melville to write *Moby Dick* is described in: PHILBRICK, Nathaniel. *No coração do mar: a história real que inspirou o Moby Dick de Melville.* Tradução de: Rubens Figueiredo. São Paulo: Martins Fontes, 1999.

[17] CHARRIÈRE, Henri. *Papillon: o homem que fugiu do inferno.* Tradução de: Círculo do Livro, s.d.

[18] DAVIS JR., Sammy; BOYAR, Jane; BOYAR, Burt. *Sim, eu posso.* Tradução de: Maria Antonieta Tróia. Rio de Janeiro: Bloch, 1968.

[19] BACILA, Carlos Roberto. *Estigmas: Um Estudo Sobre os Preconceitos.* 2.ed. Rio de Janeiro: Lumen Juris, 2008.

[20] CARNEGIE, Dale. *Como Fazer Amigos & Influenciar Pessoas.* 48.ed. Tradução de: Fernando Tude de Souza. São Paulo: Companhia Editorial Nacional, 2000, p.99-100.

[21] FOHLEN, Claude. *O Faroeste.* Tradução de: Paulo Neves. São Paulo: Companhia das Letras-Círculo do Livro, 1989, p.11.

[22] FOHLEN, Claude. *O Faroeste.* p.26.

[23] FOHLEN, Claude. *O Faroeste.* p.26.

[24] NEVINS, Allan e COMMAGER, Henry Steele. *História dos Estados Unidos.* Tradução de: Henrique Correa de Sá e Benevides. Rio de Janeiro: Bloch, 1967, p.232.

[25] HOBART, Steven B. *Dale Carnegie: Missourian Who Made Good – 1888-1955.* Warrensburg: Central Missouri State University, 1984, p.02.

[26] KAYE, Joseph. *A Youth's Timidity Led Him to World Influence.* The Kansas City Star. Sunday, July 24, 1955.

[27] KIRKLAND, Stephen E. *Dale Carnegie: The Man and His Ideas.* Detroit: Wayne State University, 1993, p.07.

[28] ABRÃO, Bernadette Siqueira. *História da Filosofia.* São Paulo: Nova Cultural, 1999, p.180.

[29] KIRKLAND, Stephen E. *Dale Carnegie: The Man and His Ideas.* Detroit: Wayne State University, 1993, p.08.

[30] CARNEGIE, Dale. *Five Minute Biographies.* Today – Carry Nation. A Cyclone in Petticoat Who Startled America. 1937.

[31] HOBART, Steven B. *Dale Carnegie: Missourian Who Made Good...* Op. cit. p.03.

[32] KIRKLAND, Stephen E. *Dale Carnegie: The Man and His Ideas.* Detroit: Wayne State University, 1993, p.08.

[33] MAROIS, André. *História dos Estados Unidos.* Tradução de: Godofredo Rangel. São Paulo: Companhia Editora Nacional, 1946, p.422.

[34] THOMAS, Lowell. *Rumo Certo à Distinção.* CARNEGIE, Dale. *Como Fazer Amigos & Influenciar Pessoas.* 48.ed. Tradução de: Fernando Tude de Souza. São Paulo: Companhia Editorial Nacional, 2000.

[35] HARRIMAN, Margaret Case. "He Sells Hope". The Saturday Evening Post, August, 14, 193(7), p.12

[36] LONDON, Jack. *Before Adam.* Serialized in *Everybody's Magazine,* 1907.

[37] Not his real name.

[38] Not his real name.

[39] THOMAS, Lowell. *Rumo Certo à Distinção.* CARNEGIE, Dale. *Como Fazer Amigos & Influenciar Pessoas.* 48.ed. Tradução de: Fernando Tude de Souza. São Paulo: Companhia Editorial Nacional, 2000.

[40] CARNEGIE, Dale. *Como Evitar Preocupações e Começar a Viver.* 37.edição. Tradução de Breno Silveira. São Paulo: Companhia Editora Nacional, 2003. p.235.

[41] CARNEGIE, Dale. *Como Evitar Preocupações e Começar a Viver.* Op. Cit. p.321-322.

[42] CARNEGIE, Dale. *Como Evitar Preocupações...op. cit.* p.116.

[43] CARNEGIE, Dale. *Como evitar preocupações e começar a viver.* 37.ed. Op. Cit. p.107.

[44] CROM, Rosemary. *Dale Carnegie as others saw him.* Op. cit. p.18.

[45] NELTON, Sharon. Nations *Business.* December, 1988, p.40.

[46] ABBOTT, Harold. *Dale Carnegie – As I Knew Him.* BELTON HISTORICAL SOCIETY. The First Hundred Years. 2.ed. Belton: Dodie Maurer Editor, 2006, p.18.

[47] THOMAS, Lowell. *Rumo Certo à Distinção.* Op. Cit. p.17-25.

[48] THOMAS, Lowell. *Rumo Certo à Distinção.* Op. Cit. p.17-25.

[49] KAYE, Joseph. Op. cit.

[50] KIRKLAND, Stephen E. *Dale Carnegie: The Man and His Ideas.* Detroit: Wayne State University, 1993, p.08 and HARRIMAN, Margaret Case. "He Sells Hope". The Saturday Evening Post, August, 14, 1938, p.12

[51] CARNEGIE, Dale. We Have With Us Tonight. *The Reader's Digest*. November 1936, v.29.

[52] THOMAS, Lowell. *Rumo Certo à Distinção*. Op. Cit. p.26.

[53] KEMP, Giles and CLAFLIN, Edward. *Dale Carnegie: the man who influenced millions*. New York: St. Martins, 1989, p.09.

[54] HOBART, Steven B. *Dale Carnegie: Missourian Who Made Good*...Op. cit. p.04.

[55] CARNEGIE, Dale. *Viva com Entusiasmo*. Dale Carnegie Training, p.03 e 04.

[56] CARNEGIE, Dale. *Viva com Entusiasmo*. Dale Carnegie Training, p.04.

[57] CARNEGIE, Dale. *Viva com Entusiasmo*. Dale Carnegie Training, p.05.

[58] SANT, Tom. *The Giants of Sales: what Dale Carnegie, John Patterson, Elmer Wheeler, and Joe Girard can teach you about real Sales success*. New York: Amacom, 2006, p.86-87.

[59] CARNEGIE, Dale. *Viva com Entusiasmo*. Dale Carnegie Training, p.05.

[60] THOMAS, Lowell. *Rumo Certo à Distinção*. Op. Cit. p.27.

[61] SANT, Tom. *The Giants of Sales...* Op. Cit. p.87.

[62] CARNEGIE, Dale. *Viva com Entusiasmo*. Dale Carnegie Training, p.06.

[63] THOMAS, Lowell. *Rumo Certo à Distinção*. Op. Cit. p.27.

[64] KIRKLAND, Stephen E. *Dale Carnegie: The Man and His Ideas*. Detroit: Wayne State University, 1993, p.12.

[65] SANT, Tom. *The Giants of Sales...* Op. Cit. p.88.

[66] Steele Mackaye and François Desarte are the mentors of some of these ideas (see KEMP, Giles and CLAFLIN, Edward. *Dale Carnegie: the man who influenced millions*. New York: St. Martins, 1989, p.46-55).

[67] CARNEGIE, Dale. *Dale Carnegie's Lifetime Plan for Success: How to Win Friends and Influence People and How to Stop Worrying and Start Living* New York, Galahad, 1998 P 376.

[68] The play debuted in 1907 and was made into a movie in 1932.

[69] THOMAS, Lowell. *Rumo Certo à Distinção*. Op. Cit. p.28.

[70] SANT, Tom. *The Giants of Sales...* Op. Cit. p.88.

[71] KEMP, Giles and CLAFLIN, Edward. Op. cit. p.116.

[72] Commemorative CD-ROM celebrating ninety years of the Dale Carnegie Training. It was kindly provided by Brenda Leigh Johnson.

[73] MAROIS, André. *História dos Estados Unidos*. Op. Cit. p.499.

[74] CARNEGIE, Dorothy. Interview to Biography.

[75] CARNEGIE, Donna Dale. Interview to Biography.

[76] LONDON, Jack. *O Chamado da Floresta*. Tradução de William Lagos. 2.ed. Porto Alegre: L & PM, 2008, p.05.

[77] KEMP, Giles and CLAFLIN, Edward. Op. cit. p.51-68.

[78] SANT, Tom. *The Giants of Sales...* Op. Cit. p.88-89.

[79] KIRKLAND, Stephen E. *Dale Carnegie: The Man and His Ideas*. Detroit: Wayne State University, 1993, p.13.

[80] CARNEGIE, Dale. Dale Carnegie's Plan for Success (op cit) p 242.

[81] KIRKLAND, Stephen E. *Dale Carnegie: The Man and His Ideas*. Detroit: Wayne State University, 1993, p.13.

[82] KEMP, Giles and CLAFLIN, Edward. Op. cit. p.72.

[83] THOMAS, Lowell. *Rumo Certo à Distinção*. Op. Cit. p.28.

[84] SANT, Tom. *The Giants of Sales...* Op. Cit. p.91.

[85] KIRKLAND, Stephen E. *Dale Carnegie: The Man and His Ideas*. Detroit: Wayne State University, 1993, p.18.

[86] Referred to in KIRKLAND, Stephen E. *Dale Carnegie: The Man and His Ideas*. Detroit: Wayne State University, 1993, p.19.

[87] KIRKLAND, Stephen E. *Dale Carnegie: The Man and His Ideas*. Detroit: Wayne State University, 1993, p.19.

[88] This subject will also be seen later.

[89] SEYMOUR, E.L.D. *American Home*. v.54. October, 1955, p.92.

[90] SEYMOUR, E.L.D. *American Home*. v.54. October, 1955, p.93.

[91] LONGGOOD, William. *Talking Your Way to Success*. The Story of the Dale Carnegie Course. New York: Association Press, 1962, p.41.

[92] LONGGOOD, William. Op. cit. p.62.

[93] Referred to in LONGGOOD, William. Op. cit. p.62.

[94] LONGGOOD, William. Op. cit. p.64.

[95] Referred to in LONGGOOD, William. Op. cit. p.68.

[96] LONGGOOD, William. Op. cit. p.104-105.

[97] LONGGOOD, William. Op. cit. p.106-108.

[98] SANT, Tom. *The Giants of Sales...* Op. Cit. p.93-94.

[99] LONGGOOD, William. Op. cit. p.109.

[100] HOBART, Steven B. *Dale Carnegie: Missourian Who Made Good...*Op. cit. p.06.

[101] LONGGOOD, William. Op. Cit. p.19.

[102] Some touching stories can be seen in: CARNEGIE, Dale. *Como Falar em Público e Influenciar Pessoas no Mundo dos Negócios*. 46.ed. Tradução de Carlos Evaristo M. Costa. Rio de Janeiro: Record, 2008, p.18.

[103] KEMP, Giles and CLAFLIN, Edward. Op. cit. p.73.

[104] KEMP, Giles and CLAFLIN, Edward. Op. cit. p.74.

[105] KIRKLAND, op. cit. p.21.

[106] SANT, Tom. *The Giants of Sales...* Op. Cit. p.92.

[107] KIRKLAND, op. cit. p.31.

[108] SMALL, Collie. *Dale Carnegie: A Man With a Message*. Collier's for January 15, 1949.

[109] SMALL, Collie. Op. cit.

[110] SMALL, Collie. Op. cit.

[111] SMALL, Collie. Op. cit.

[112] HOBART, Steven B. *Dale Carnegie: Missourian Who Made Good...*Op. cit. p.13.

[113] CROM, Rosemary. *Dale Carnegie as others saw him*. Op. Cit. p.12.

[114] CROM, Rosemary. *Dale Carnegie as others saw him*. Op. cit. p.26.

[115] LONGGOOD, William. Op. cit. p.28.

[116] LONGGOOD, William. Op.cit. p.44.

[117] KEROUAC, Jack. *On The Road*. Pé na Estrada. Tradução de Eduardo Bueno. Porto Alegre: L & PM, 2008, p.39.

[118] LONGGOOD, William. Op. cit. p.178.

[119] LONGGOOD, William. Op. cit. p.166.

[120] KEMP, Giles and CLAFLIN, Edward. Op. cit. p.121.

[121] PARKER, Gail Thain. *How to Win Friends and Influence People: Dale Carnegie and The Problem of Sincerity*. Burlington: The Johns Hopkins University Press, 1977, p.14.

[122] BELTON HISTORICAL SOCIETY. *The First Hundred Years*. 2.ed. Belton: Dodie Maurer Editor, 2006, p.16.

[123] KEMP, Giles and CLAFLIN, Edward. Op. cit. p.124-125.

[124] CARNEGIE, Dale. *Grab Your Bootstraps*. Op. cit. p.14.

[125] CROM, Rosemary. *Dale Carnegie as others saw him*. Op. cit. p.10.

[126] CARNEGIE, Dale. *Grab Your Bootstraps*. Op. cit. p.14.

[127] CARNEGIE, Dale. *Grab Your Bootstraps*. Op. cit. p.14.

[128] CARNEGIE, Dale. *Grab Your Bootstraps*. Op. cit. p.14.

[129] Referred to in CARNEGIE, Dale. *Grab Your Bootstraps*. Op. cit. p.15.

[130] Referred to in CARNEGIE, Dale. *Grab Your Bootstraps*. Op. cit. p.15.

[131] CARNEGIE, Dale. *Grab Your Bootstraps*. Op. cit. p.15.

[132] KIRKLAND, op. cit. p.38.

[133] KEMP, Giles and CLAFLIN, Edward. Op. cit. p.110-113.

[134] Phrase spoken by a graduate of the Dale Carnegie Course.

[135] LONGGOOD, William. Op. Cit. p.163-164.

[136] LONGGOOD, William. Op. Cit. p.164-165.

[137] LONGGOOD, William. Op. Cit. p.165-166.

[138] Mentioned in LONGGOOD, William. Op. Cit. p.159.

[139] LONGGOOD, William. Op. Cit. p.143-144.

[140] LONGGOOD, William. Op. Cit. p.136-159.

[141] A fictional name to protect his privacy.

[142] LONGGOOD, William. Op. Cit. p.152.

[143] The name is not really hers, but the story is true.

[144] CROM, Rosemary. *Dale Carnegie as others saw him*. op. cit. p.24.

[145] PARKER, Gail Thain. *How to Win Friends and Influence People: Dale Carnegie and The Problem of Sincerity*. Op. cit. p.507.

[146] BERNARDINHO. *Transformando Suor em Ouro*. 2.ed. Rio de Janeiro: Sextante, 2006, p.112.

[147] HANDAL, Peter. COMMEMORATIVE CD-ROM celebrating the ninetieth year of the *Dale Carnegie Training*.

[148] CHALITA, Gabriel. *Mulheres que Venceram Preconceitos: Mulheres Célebres que Trouxeram e Trazem Benefícios à Sociedade*. Rio de Janeiro: Imagem, 1996, p.106-107.

[149] Referred to in CHALITA, op. Cit. p.110.

[150] CHALITA, op. Cit. p.111.

[151] CHALITA, op. Cit. p.112.

[152] CHALITA, op. Cit. p.112.

[153] CHALITA, op. Cit. p.113.

[154] CHALITA, op. Cit. p.114.

[155] CHALITA, op. Cit. p.115.

[156] CHALITA, op. Cit. p.117.

[157] CHALITA, op. Cit. p.118.

[158] CHALITA, op. Cit. p.119.

[159] CHALITA, op. Cit. p.103-129.

[160] CHALITA, op. Cit. p.112.

[161] CHALITA, op. Cit. p.122.

[162] CHALITA, op. Cit. p.124.

[163] Referred to in CHALITA, op. Cit. p.128.

[164] Carnegie, Dale. *Como Evitar Preocupações...* op. cit. p. 157.

[165] LONGGOOD, William. Op. cit. p. 92 and 94.

[166] LONGGOOD, William. Op. cit. p. 46.

[167] ABBOTT, Harold. *Dale Carnegie – As I Knew Him. BELTON HISTORICAL SOCIETY. The First Hundred Years.* 2.ed. Belton: Dodie Maurer Editor, 2006. p.18.

[168] LEVINE, Stuart R. & CROM, Michael A. *O Líder em Você. Como Fazer Amigos, Influenciar Pessoas e Ter Sucesso em Um Mundo em Mutação.* 12.ed. Tradução de Ruy Jungmann. Rio de Janeiro-São Paulo: Record, 2004. p.44.

[169] ABBOTT, Harold. *Dale Carnegie – As I Knew Him. BELTON HISTORICAL SOCIETY. The First Hundred Years.* 2.ed. Belton: Dodie Maurer Editor, 2006, p.18.

[170] ABBOTT, Harold. Op. cit. p.18.

[171] KEMP, Giles and CLAFLIN, Edward. Op. cit. p.119.

[172] KEMP, Giles and CLAFLIN, Edward. Op. cit. p.120.

[173] LONGGOOD, William. Op. cit. p.105-106.

[174] LONGGOOD, William. Op. cit. p.108.

[175] KEMP, Giles and CLAFLIN, Edward. Op. cit. p.124.

[176] KEMP, Giles and CLAFLIN, Edward. Op. cit. p.125.

[177] KEMP, Giles and CLAFLIN, Edward. Op. cit. p.128.

[178] CARNEGIE, Dale. Dale Carnegie's Plan for Success, Op. Cit. p. 328.

[179] KEMP, Giles and CLAFLIN, Edward. Op. cit. p.162.

[180] CROM, Rosemary. *Dale Carnegie as others saw him.* Op. Cit..

[181] LONGGOOD, William. Op. cit. p.53.

[182] SMALL, Collie. Op. cit.

[183] ABBOTT, Harold. Op. cit. p.18.

[184] LONGGOOD, William. Op. cit. p.91 and 92.

[185] Referred to in LONGGOOD, William. Op. cit. p.133.

[186] SMALL, Collie. Op. cit.

[187] LONGGOOD, William. Op. cit. p.54.

[188] CROM, Rosemary. *Dale Carnegie as others saw him.* p.03.

[189] CD-ROM commemorating 90 years of the *Dale Carnegie Training.* Generously provided by Brenda Leigh Johnson.

[190] ABBOTT, Herald. *Dale Carnegie – As I Knew Him. BELTON HISTORICAL SOCIETY. The First Hundred Years.* 2.ed. Belton: Dodie Maurer Editor, 2006. p.18.

[191] LONGGOOD, William. Op. cit. p.129.

[192] LONGGOOD, William. Op. cit. p.131.

[193] CARNEGIE, Dale. *Little Known Facts About Well Known People.* Op. cit. p. 04.

[194] CARNEGIE, Dale. *Como Evitar Preocupações...*op. cit. p. 394.

[195] Carnegie, Dale. *Lincoln, the unknown*. D. Appletown-Century Company. New York: 1937.

[196] CARNEGIE, Dale. *Lincoln, the unknown* Op. Cit. p.vii.

[197] CARNEGIE, Dale. *Lincoln, esse deconhecido*. Op Cit, p. 9.

[198] CARNEGIE, Dale. *Lincoln, esse desconhecido*. 2.ed. Op. Cit. p.11.

[199] CARNEGIE, Dale. *Lincoln, the unknown*. Op Cit p viii.

[200] CARNEGIE, Dale. *Lincoln, esse desconhecido*. 2.ed. Op. Cit. p.11.

[201] CARNEGIE, Dale. *Lincoln, esse desconhecido*. 2.ed. Op. Cit. p.11.

[202] CARNEGIE, Dale. *Lincoln, the unknown*. Op. Cit. p. ix-x.

[203] CARNEGIE, Dale. *Lincoln, the unknown*. Op. Cit. p.36.

[204] CARNEGIE, Dale. *Lincoln, esse desconhecido*. 2.ed. Op. Cit. p.42.

[205] CARNEGIE, Dale. *Lincoln, the unknown*. Op. Cit. p.39-40.

[206] CARNEGIE, Dale. *Lincoln, esse desconhecido*. 2.ed. Op. Cit. p.44.

[207] CARNEGIE, Dale. *Lincoln, esse desconhecido*. 2.ed. Op. Cit. p.45-46.

[208] CARNEGIE, Dale. *Lincoln, esse desconhecido*. 2.ed. Op. Cit. p.61.

[209] CARNEGIE, Dale. *Lincoln, esse desconhecido*. 2.ed. Op. Cit. p.248.

[210] KEMP, Giles and CLAFLIN, Edward. Op. cit. p.132. According to the authors, the interview was supposedly given to the Saturday Evening Post, after Carnegie had spent a long period of time without talking about his first wedding.

[211] HUGO, Victor. *Les Miserables*. Trans. Norman Denny. London: Penguin Classics, 1982. Pg 497. .

[212] HUGO, Victor. *Os Miseráveis.* Traducao de: Frederico Ozanam Pessoa de Barros. São Paulo, Cosac & Naify, 2002   p.19.

[213] HUGO, Victor. *Os Miseráveis*. Op. Cit. p.17.

[214] CARNEGIE, Dale. *Lincoln, esse desconhecido*. 2.ed. Op. Cit. p.22.

[215] CARNEGIE, Dale. *Lincoln, esse desconhecido*. 2.ed. Op. Cit. p.28.

[216] CARNEGIE, Dale. *Lincoln, the unknown*. Op. Cit. p.21.

[217] CARNEGIE, Dale. *Lincoln, esse desconhecido*. 2.ed. Op. Cit. p.29.

[218] CARNEGIE, Dale. *Lincoln, esse desconhecido*. 2.ed. Op. Cit. p.37.

[219] CARNEGIE, Dale. *Lincoln, the unknown*. Op. Cit. p.37.

[220] CARNEGIE, Dale. *Lincoln, esse desconhecido*. 2.ed. Op. Cit. p.43.

[221] CARNEGIE, Dale. *Lincoln, the unknown*. Op. Cit. p.130.

[222] CARNEGIE, Dale. *Lincoln, the unknown*. Op. Cit. p.152-153.

[223] CARNEGIE, Dale. *Lincoln, esse desconhecido*. 2.ed. Op. Cit. p.165.

[224] CARNEGIE, Dale. *Lincoln, esse desconhecido*. 2.ed. Op. Cit. p.166.

[225] CARNEGIE, Dale. *Lincoln, esse desconhecido*. 2.ed. Op. Cit. p.166.

[226] CARNEGIE, Dale. *Lincoln, the unknown*. Op. Cit. p.194-5.

[227] CARNEGIE, Dale. *Lincoln, esse desconhecido*. 2.ed. Op. Cit. p.170-172.

[228] CARNEGIE, Dale. *Lincoln, the unknown*. Op. Cit. p. 201-203.

[229] CROM, Rosemary. *Dale Carnegie as others saw him*. Op. cit. p.18.

[230] CURRENT BIOGRAPHY YEARBOOK. New York: H.W. Wilson Co, 1941. p.140.

[231] On the subject of juries, I would like to recommend a fantastic book by Dr. Paulo Rangel, Public Prosecutor and Professor of Penal Process Law at the Universidade Estadual do Rio de Janeiro; Rangel explores the concept of Jury from various angles:

linguistic vision, history, society and dogma. He also brings his own dynamic experience with jury work in Rio de Janeiro (RANGEL, Paulo. *Tribunal do Júri: Visão Lingüística, Histórica, Social e Dogmática*. Rio de Janeiro: Lumen Juris, 2007).

[232] Professor Marcelo Motta Carneiro wrote wonderful books, some about public speaking, such as CARNEIRO, Marcelo Motta. *A expressão Verbal na Educação Permanente*. Curitiba: Vicentina, 1986, etc.

[233] Reinaldo Polito, for example, mentions three books by Carnegie and one by Dorothy Carnegie in his bibliography. POLITO, Reinaldo. *Assim é que se Fala: Como Organizar a Fala e Transmitir Idéias*. 5.ed. São Paulo: Saraiva, 1999. p.212.

[234] FERREIRA, Aurélio Buarque de Holanda. *Dicionário da Língua Portuguesa*. 3.ed. Rio de Janeiro: Nova Fronteira, 1993. p.569.

[235] HEMINGWAY, Ernest. *O Velho e o Mar*. 15.ed. Tradução de: Fernando de Castro Ferro. Rio de Janeiro: Civilização Brasileira, 1973. I discuss this title in my book: BACILA, Carlos Roberto. *Estigmas: Um Estudo Sobre os Preconceitos*. 2.ed. Rio de Janeiro: Lumen Juris, 2008. p.37 and onward.

[236] SMALL, Collie. *Dale Carnegie: A Man With a Message*. Collier's for January 15, 1949.

[237] SMALL, Collie. *Dale Carnegie: A Man With a Message*. Collier's for January 15, 1949.

[238] SMALL, Collie. *Dale Carnegie: A Man With a Message*. Collier's for January 15, 1949.

[239] CARNEGIE, Dorothy. Introdução de CARNEGIE, Dale. *Como Falar em Público e Influenciar Pessoas no Mundo dos Negócios*; revista por Dorothy Carnegie. 25.ed. Tradução de: Carlos Evaristo M. Costa. Rio de Janeiro: Record, 1993. p.11.

[240] For example: BYRNE, Rhonda. *The Secret – O Segredo*. Tradução de: Marcos José da Cunha, Alexandre Martins, Alice Xavier. Rio de Janeiro: Ediouro, 2007.

[241] SEYMOUR, E.L.D. American Home. v.54. October, 1955, p.93-94.

[242] CARNEGIE, Dale. *Simple Secrets of Public Speaking*. Op. Cit. p.108-110.

[243] Referred to in CARNEGIE, Dale. *Simple Secrets of Public Speaking*. Op. Cit. p.110-111.

[244] CARNEGIE, Dale. *Simple Secrets of Public Speaking*. Op. Cit. p.111.

[245] CARNEGIE, Dale. *Simple Secrets of Public Speaking*. Op. Cit. p.111.

[246] Referred to in ADAMS, Ian and DYSON, R. W. *Cinqüenta Pensadores Políticos Essenciais: da Grécia Antiga aos Dias Atuais*. Tradução de: Mario Pontes. Rio de Janeiro: Difel, 2006. p.186.

[247] CHARRIÈRE, op. cit., p.65.

[248] CHARRIÈRE, op. cit., p.75.

[249] CHARRIÈRE, op. cit., p.81.

[250] CHARRIÈRE, op. cit., p.72.

[251] CHARRIÈRE, op. cit., p.84.

[252] CHARRIÈRE, op. cit., p.205.

[253] CHARRIÈRE, op. cit., p.83.

[254] CHARRIÈRE, op. cit., p.85.

[255] BACILA, Carlos Roberto. *Estigmas: Um Estudo Sobre os Preconceitos*. 2.ed. Rio de Janeiro: Lumen Juris, 2008, p.211-212.

[256] CARNEGIE, Dale. *Como Falar em Público...* Op. cit. p.17.

[257] CARNEGIE, Dale. *Como Falar em Público...* Op. cit. p.70.

[258] CARNEGIE, Dale. *Como Falar em Público...* Op. cit. p.80.

[259] CARNEGIE, Dale. *Como Falar em Público...* Op. cit. p.88.

[260] CARNEGIE, Dale. *Como Falar em Público...*Op. cit. p.91.

[261] CARNEGIE, Dale. *Como Falar em Público...*Op. cit. p.92.

[262] CARNEGIE, Dale. *Como Falar em Público...*Op. cit. p.95-96.

[263] CARNEGIE, Dale. *Como Falar em Público...*Op. cit. p.96-98.

[264] CARNEGIE, Dale. *Como Falar em Público...*Op. cit. p.117.

[265] CARNEGIE, Dale. *Como Falar em Público...*Op. cit. p.130.

[266] CARNEGIE, Dale. *Como Falar em Público...*Op. cit. p.134-135.

[267] CARNEGIE, Dale. *Como Falar em Público...*Op. cit. p.138.

[268] CARNEGIE, Dale. *Como Falar em Público...*Op. cit. p.140.

[269] CARNEGIE, Dale. *Como Falar em Público...*Op. cit. p.141.

[270] CARNEGIE, Dale. *Como Falar em Público...*Op. cit. p.161.

[271] CARNEGIE, Dale. *Como Falar em Público...*Op. cit. p.165.

[272] CARNEGIE, Dale. *Como Falar em Público...*Op. cit. p.166.

[273] CARNEGIE, Dale. *Como Falar em Público...*Op. cit. p.182.

[274] CARNEGIE, Dale. *Como Falar em Público...*Op. cit. p.182.

[275] CARNEGIE, Dale. *Como Falar em Público...*Op. cit. p.184.

[276] The Zingarelli Dictionary of Italian defines 'sincèro' as: pure, genuine, unaltered, one who expresses with absolute truth what he or she feels or believes. (ZINGARELLI, Nicola. *Vocabolario della Língua Italiana.*12.ed. Bologna: Zanichelli, 1995. p.915).

[277] CARNEGIE, Dale. *Como Falar em Público...*Op. cit. p.37.

[278] CARNEGIE, Dale. *Como Falar em Público...*Op. cit. p.36.

[279] CARNEGIE, Dale. *Como Falar em Público...*Op. cit. p.135.

[280] CARNEGIE, Dale. *Como Falar em Público...*Op. cit. p.85.

[281] CARNEGIE, Dale. *Como Fazer Amigos & Influenciar Pessoas.* 48.ed. Tradução de: Fernando Tude de Souza. São Paulo: Companhia Editorial Nacional, 2000. This work which I analyze is the equivalent of the US release *How to Win Friends and Influence People*, and was expanded by Dorothy Carnegie. The book released with the title "How to Enjoy your Life and your Work" was organized from a selection from *How to Win Friends and Influence People* and *How to Avoid Worrying and Begin to Live.*

[282] LONDON, Jack. *The Call of the Wild.* New York: Viking, 1996.p. 53 .

[283] SAINT, op. cit. p.104-105.

[284] SAINT, op. cit. p.105.

[285] CARNEGIE, Dale. *Little Known Facts About Well Known People.* New York: Greenberg, 1934.

[286] CARNEGIE, Dale. *Little Known Facts About Well Known People.* Op. Cit. p.01.

[287] SEYMOUR-SMITH, Martin. *Os 100 Livros que Mais Influenciaram a Humanidade. A História do Pensamento dos Tempos Antigos à Atualidade.* 4.ed. Tradução de Fausto Wolff. Rio de Janeiro: Difel, 2002.

[288] SEYMOUR-SMITH, Martin. *Os 100 Livros que Mais Influenciaram a Humanidade.* Op. Cit. p.553-560.

[289] SAINT, op. Cit. p.105.

[290] CROM, Rosemary. *Dale Carnegie as others saw him.* Op. cit. p.25.

[291] CROM, Rosemary. *Dale Carnegie as others saw him*. Op. cit. p.25.

[292] SAINT, op. cit. p.106.

[293] LONGGOOD, William. *Talking Your Way to Success*. The Story of the Dale Carnegie Course. New York: Association Press, 1962, p.44.

[294] KEMP, Giles and CLAFLIN, Edward. Op. cit. p.141.

[295] HARRIMAN, Margaret Case. "He Sells Hope". *The Saturday Evening Post*, August 14, 193(7). p.12.

[296] HARRIMAN, Margaret Case. "He Sells Hope". *The Saturday Evening Post,* August 14, 193(7).

[297] CARNEGIE, Dorothy. Prefácio à Edição Revista de CARNEGIE, Dale. *Como Fazer Amigos & Influenciar Pessoas*. 48.ed. Tradução de: Fernando Tude de Souza. São Paulo: Companhia Editorial Nacional, 2000. p.13.

[298] KIRKLAND, op. cit. p.42.

[299] CARNEGIE, Dale. *Como Fazer Amigos & Influenciar Pessoas*. 48ªed. Op. Cit. p.1.

[300] CROM, Rosemary. *Dale Carnegie as others saw him*. Op. cit. p.05.

[301] CROM, Rosemary. *Dale Carnegie as others saw him*. Op. cit. p.26.

[302] CROM, Rosemary. *Dale Carnegie as others saw him*. Op. cit. p.14.

[303] CROM, Rosemary. *Dale Carnegie as others saw him*. Op. Cit. p.12.

[304] CROM, Rosemary. *Dale Carnegie as others saw him*. Op. cit. p.12.

[305] CROM, Rosemary. *Dale Carnegie as others saw him*. Op. cit. p.09.

[306] PARKER, op. cit. p.507.

[307] HOLLYMAN, Thomas B. *Success Amazes Even Carnegie*. Warrensburg: Daily Star-Journal, 28;01;1938.

[308] SMALL, Collie. *Dale Carnegie: A Man With a Message*. Collier's for January 15, 1949.

[309] SMALL, Collie. Op. cit.

[310] CROM, Rosemary. *Dale Carnegie as others saw him*. Op. cit. p.10.

[311] CROM, Rosemary. *Dale Carnegie as others saw him*. Op. cit. p.14.

[312] CROM, Rosemary. *Dale Carnegie as others saw him*. Op. cit. p. 19.

[313] ABBOTT, Harold. Op. Cit. p.18.

[314] ABBOTT, Harold. Op. Cit. p.18.

[315] CARNEGIE, Dale. *Dale Carnegie's Lifetime Plan for Success* op cit P. 59

[316] CARNEGIE, Dale. *Dale Carnegie's Lifetime Plan for Success* Op. Cit. P. 109.

[317] CARNEGIE, Dale. *Dale Carnegie's Lifetime Plan for Success* op cit p 182.

[318] CARNEGIE, Dale. *Dale Carnegie's Lifetime Plan for Success* op cit p 221.

[319] FOUCAULT, Michel. *Vigiar e Punir*. 9.ed. Tradução de: Lígia M. Ponde Vassalo. Petrópolis: Vozes, 1991. p.11.

[320] Vigilance is compared to the "Panopticon" system of prison design developed by Jeremy Bentham, in which a single tower allowed a single guard to maintain permanent, uninterrupted observation of the prisoners.

[321] FOUCAULT, Michel. *Discipline and Punish. The Birth of the Prison*. Trans. Alan Sheridan. New York: Pantheon Books, 1977. p. 216.

[322] FOUCAULT, Michel. *Microfísica do Poder*. 20.ed. Tradução de: Roberto Machado. Rio de Janeiro: Graal, 2004. p.106.

[323] Referred to in LONGGOOD, William. Op. cit. p.217.

[324] LONGGOOD, William. Op. cit. p.14 e 15.

[325] LONGGOOD, William. Op. cit. p.14.

[326] CROM, Rosemary. *Dale Carnegie as others saw him.* Op. cit. p.25.

[327] LONGGOOD, William. Op. cit. p.74.

[328] CROM, Rosemary. *Dale Carnegie as others saw him.* Op. cit. p.21.

[329] CARNEGIE, Dale. *Grab Your Bootstraps.* Op. Cit. p.14.

[330] COBRA, Nuno. *A Semente da Vitória.* 91 ed. São Paulo: Senac, 2008, p.45.

[331] COBRA, Nuno. Op. Cit. p.79.

[332] CARNEGIE, Dale. *Como Evitar Preocupações e Começar a Viver.* Op. Cit. p.316-324.

[333] SMALL, Collie. Op. Cit.

[334] Carnegie does not use this expression, but I use it to try to explain the essence of his subject.

[335] CARNEGIE, Dale. *Como Evitar Preocupações*...op. cit. p.149-150.

[336] CARNEGIE, Dale. *Como Evitar Preocupações*...op. cit. p.150.

[337] CARNEGIE, Dale. *Como Evitar Preocupações*...op. cit. p.177-178.

[338] A fictitious name, according to Carnegie, given to protect her family's privacy.

[339] CARNEGIE, Dale. *Como Evitar Preocupações e Começar a Viver.* Op. Cit. p.258-259.

[340] CARNEGIE, Dale. *Como Evitar Preocupações e Começar a Viver.* Op. Cit. p.261.

[341] CARNEGIE, Dale. *Como Evitar Preocupações e Começar a Viver.* Op. Cit. p.273.

[342] CARNEGIE, Dale. *Dale Carnegie's Formula for Success* Op Cit p 430

[343] CARNEGIE, Dale. *Dale Carnegie's Formula for Success* Op cit p 427.

[344] KIRKLAND, op. cit. p.26.

[345] MEYER, Adolph E. *How Dale Carnegie Made Friends*, Etc. p.47.

[346] CARNEGIE, Dale. *Dale Carnegie's Lifetime Plan for Success* Op. cit. p.64.

[347] CARNEGIE, Dale. *Como Evitar Preocupações...* op. cit. p.157.

[348] KEMP, Giles and CLAFLIN, Edward. Op. cit. p.132.

[349] MEYER, Adolph E. *How Dale Carnegie made friends....* p.44.

[350] MEYER, Adolph E. *How Dale Carnegie made friends....* Op. Cit. p.47.

[351] KEMP, Giles and CLAFLIN, Edward. Op. cit. p.66-67.

[352] MEYER, Adolph E. *How Dale Carnegie made friends....* Op. Cit. p.46.

[353] KEMP, Giles and CLAFLIN, Edward. Op. cit. p.66-67.

[354] See KIRKLAND, op. cit. p.22.

[355] KIRKLAND, op. Cit. p.26.

[356] "Father Forgets" by W. Livingstone Larned appears on pages 30 and 31 of CARNEGIE, Dale. *How to Win Friends & Influence People.* New York: Galahad Books, 1998.

[357] CARNEGIE, Dale. *Dale Carnegie's Lifetime Plan for Success.* Op. cit. p.31.

[358] CARNEGIE, Dale. *Dale Carnegie's Lifetime Plan for Success.* Op. cit. p.31.

[359] SANT, Tom. *The Giants of Sales.* Op. Cit. p.94.

[360] SANT, Tom. The Giants of Sales. Op. Cit. p.96-97.

[361] CARNEGIE, Dale. Como Fazer Amigos e Influenciar Pessoas. 48a ed. Op. cit. p. 107.

[362] CARNEGIE, Dale. *Como Fazer Amigos e Influenciar Pessoas.* 48.ed. Op. cit. p.112.

[363] CARNEGIE, Dale. *Como Fazer Amigos e Influenciar Pessoas.* 48.ed. Op. cit. p.113.

[364] SANT, Tom. *The Giants of Sales.* Op. Cit. p.97.

[365] LONGGOOD, William. Op. cit. p.64-65.

[366] LONGGOOD, William. Op. cit. p.66.

[367] LONGGOOD, William. Op. cit. p.103.

[368] KEROUAC, Jack. On The Road. Op. cit. p. 254-255.

[369] LONGGOOD, William. Op. cit. p.64.

[370] MARSHALL, Margaret. *Dale Carnegie. Columnists on Parade.* The Nation, March 14, 1938, p.325-328.

[371] LONGGOOD, William. Op. cit. p.67.

[372] Referred to in LONGGOOD, William. Op. cit. p.67 and 68.

[373] LONGGOOD, William. Op. cit. p.70.

[374] PARKER, op. cit. p.507.

[375] PARKER, op. cit. p.511.

[376] PARKER, op. cit. p.517.

[377] PARKER, op. cit. p.517.

[378] CARNEGIE, Dale. *Como Falar em Público...*Op. cit. p.85.

[379] PARKER, op. cit. p.517.

[380] LONGGOOD, William. Op. Cit. p.34 and 35.

[381] BACILA, Carlos Roberto. *ESTIGMAS: Um Estudo Sobre os Preconceitos.* 2.ed. Rio de Janeiro: Lúmen Júris, 2008. p.25.

[382] CARNEGIE, Dale. *Como Evitar Preocupações...*op. cit. p.151-153.

[383] CROM, Rosemary. *Dale Carnegie as others saw him.* Op. cit. p.09.

[384] CARNEGIE, Dale. *Como Evitar Preocupações...* Op. cit. p.153-156.

[385] CARNEGIE, Dale. *Como Evitar Preocupações...* Op. cit. p.156.

[386] Apud CONDE, Francisco Muñoz. *Edmund Mezger e o Direito Penal do Seu Tempo. Estudos Sobre o Direito Penal no Nacional-Socialismo.* 4.ed. Tradução de Paulo César Busato. Rio de Janeiro: Lumen Juris, 2005. p.180.

[387] CONDE, Francisco Muñoz. *Edmund Mezger e o Direito Penal do Seu Tempo.* Op. Cit. p.227.

[388] CARNEGIE, Dale. *Como Evitar Preocupações...* op. cit. p.156.

[389] Referred to in CARNEGIE, Dale. *Como Evitar Preocupações...* op. cit. p.156.

[390] CARNEGIE, Dale. *Como Evitar Preocupações...* op. cit. p.192-194.

[391] CARNEGIE, Dale. *Como Evitar Preocupações...* op. cit. p.157.

[392] CARNEGIE, Dale. *Como Evitar Preocupações...* op. cit. p.158.

[393] CARNEGIE, Dale. *Como Evitar Preocupações...* op. cit. p.172-173.

[394] Referred to in CARNEGIE, Dale. *Como Evitar Preocupações...* op. cit. p.175.

[395] CARNEGIE, Dale. *Como Evitar Preocupações...* op. cit. p.204-206.

[396] CARNEGIE, Dale. *Como Evitar Preocupações...* op. cit. p.207-208.

[397] LONDON, Jack. *História de um soldado.* Tradução de Carlos Rizzi. São Paulo: Hemus,___, p.21-46. My book *ESTIGMAS: Um Estudo Sobre os Preconceitos.* 2.ed contains a commentary on the works of Jack London (BACILA, Carlos Roberto. ESTIGMAS: Um Estudo Sobre os Preconceitos. 2.ed. Rio de Janeiro: Lúmen Júris, 2008, p.229-231).

[398] CARNEGIE, Dale. *Como Evitar Preocupações...* op. cit. p.208.

[399] CARNEGIE, Dale. *Como Evitar Preocupações...*op. cit. p.211.

[400] OBAMA, Barack. *A Origem dos Meus Sonhos*. Tradução de Irati Antonio, Renata Laureano e Sonia Augusto. São Paulo: Editora Gente, 2008. p.43-44.

[401] CARNEGIE, Dale. *Como Evitar Preocupações*...op. cit. p.214-233.

[402] CARNEGIE, Dale. *Como Evitar Preocupações*...op. cit. p.296.

[403] CARNEGIE, Dale. *Como Evitar Preocupações*...op. cit. p.225-226.

[404] CARNEGIE, Dale. *Como Evitar Preocupações*...op. cit. p.195-196.

[405] BACILA, Carlos Roberto. *ESTIGMAS: Um Estudo Sobre os Preconceitos*. 2.ed. Rio de Janeiro: Lúmen Júris, 2008. p.33-43.

[406] CARNEGIE, Dale. *Como Evitar Preocupações*... op. cit. p.197.

[407] Referred to in JAMES, William. *Pragmatismo*. Op. Cit. p.100.

[408] For example, see the excellent treatment of this subject in KIRKLAND, Stephen E. Dale *Carnegie: The Man and His Ideas*. Detroit: Wayne State University, 1993. p.02.

[409] CARNEGIE, Dale. *Como Evitar Preocupações e Começar a Viver*. Op. Cit. p.325-328.

[410] CARNEGIE, Dale. *Como Evitar Preocupações e Começar a Viver*. Op. Cit. p.329.

[411] CARNEGIE, Dale. *Como Evitar Preocupações e Começar a Viver*. 37.ed. Op. Cit. p.30.

[412] CARNEGIE, Dale. *Como Evitar Preocupações e Começar a Viver*. Op. Cit. p.235-238.

[413] Referred to in CARNEGIE, Dale. *Como Evitar Preocupações e Começar a Viver*. Op. Cit. p.238.

[414] CARNEGIE, Dale. *Como Evitar Preocupações e Começar a Viver*. Op. Cit. p.239.

[415] CARNEGIE, Dale. *Como Evitar Preocupações e Começar a Viver*. Op. Cit. p.240.

[416] CARNEGIE, Dale. *Como Evitar Preocupações e Começar a Viver*. Op. Cit. p. 247-248.

[417] CARNEGIE, Dale. *Como Evitar Preocupações e Começar a Viver*. Op. Cit. p.240.

[418] CARNEGIE, Dale. *Como Evitar Preocupações e Começar a Viver*. Op. Cit. p. 240.

[419] NEWTH, Eirik. *Breve Soria della Scienza*. La Ricerca della Verità. Firenze: Salani, 1998.

[420] POPE, Alexander.

[421] CARNEGIE, Dale. *Como Evitar Preocupações e Começar a Viver*. Op. Cit. p. 393.

[422] CARNEGIE, Dale. *Como Evitar Preocupações e Começar a Viver*. Op. Cit. p.395-396.

[423] CARNEGIE, Dale. *Como Evitar Preocupações e Começar a Viver*. Op. Cit. p.163-164.

[424] CARNEGIE, Dale. *Como Evitar Preocupações e Começar a Viver*. Op. Cit. p.279-297.

[425] CARNEGIE, Dale. *Como Evitar Preocupações e Começar a Viver*. Op. Cit. p.298.

[426] CARNEGIE, Dale. *Como Evitar Preocupações e Começar a Viver*. Op. Cit. p.329.

[427] CARNEGIE, Dale. *Little Known Facts About Well Known People*. Op. Cit. p.01

[428] CARNEGIE, Dale. *Dale Carnegie's Biographical Roundup*. Highlights in the lives of Forty Famous People. New York: Greenberg, 1944, p.1

[429] CARNEGIE, Dale. *Dale Carnegie's Biographical Roundup*. Op. Cit. p.2.

[430] CARNEGIE, Dale. *Como Evitar Preocupações e Começar a Viver*. Op. Cit. p.301-302.

[431] DAVIS JR., Sammy e BOYAR, Jane e Burt. *Sim, Eu Posso. A História de Sammy Davis Jr*. Tradução de Maria Antonieta Tróia. Rio de Janeiro: Bloch, 1968.

[432] CHARRIÈRE, Henri. Papillon. *O Homem que Fugiu do Inferno*. Tradução de Círculo do Livro. São Paulo: Círculo do Livro, _____.

[433] CARNEGIE, Dale. "We Have With Us Tonight". *The Reader's Digest*. November 1936, v.29.

[434] CARNEGIE, Dale. "We Have With Us Tonight". *The Reader's Digest*. November 1936, v.29.

[435] CARNEGIE, Dale. "We Have With Us Tonight". *Reader's Digest*. November 1936, v.29.

[436] CARNEGIE, Dale. *Biographical Roundup*. Op. Cit. p.02.

[437] CARNEGIE, Dale. *Como Evitar Preocupações e Começar a Viver*. Op. Cit. p.308-309.

[438] CARNEGIE, Dale. *Como Evitar Preocupações e Começar a Viver*. Op. Cit. p.315.

[439] CARNEGIE, Dale. *Como Evitar Preocupações e Começar a Viver*. Op. Cit. p.311.

[440] CARNEGIE, Dale. *Simple Secrets of Public Speaking*. Op. Cit. p.109.

[441] HOBART, Steven B. *Dale Carnegie: Missourian Who Made Good...*Op. cit. p.08.

[442] LONGGOOD, William. Op. cit. p.46-47.

[443] LONGGOOD, William. Op. cit. p.47.

[444] LONGGOOD, William. Op. cit. p.47.

[445] KEMP, Giles and CLAFLIN, Edward. Op. cit. p.116-117.

[446] KEMP, Giles and CLAFLIN, Edward. Op. cit. p.116-117.

[447] LONDON, Jack. *Caninos Brancos*. Tradução de: Antivan Guimarães Mendes. São Paulo: Melhoramentos, 2002. p.07 e segs.

[448] LONDON, Jack. *Caninos Brancos*. Op. Cit. p.236.

[449] LONDON, Jack. *O Chamando da Floresta*. Op. Cit. p.06.

[450] LONDON, Jack. *O Chamando da Floresta*. Op. Cit. p.05.

[451] STONE, Irving. *A Vida Errante de Jack London*. Tradução de Genolino Amado e Geraldo Cavalcanti. 3a Ed. Rio de Janeiro: José Olympio, 1952, p. 204 and 205.

[452] JAMES, William. *Pragmatism. And Four Essays from The Meaning of Truth*. New York: Meridian Books, 1969. Pg:167

[453] On this topic: CALDER, GIDEON. *Rorty e a Descricao*. Traducao de Luiz Henrique de Arauio Dutra. São Paulo: UNESP, 2006, p 5.

[454] Ibid., CALDER, p. 21

[455] HOBART, Steven B. *Dale Carnegie: Missourian Who Made Good – 1888-1955*. Warrensburg: Central Missouri State University, 1984, p.01-02.

[456] DRUCKER, Peter. *O homem que inventou a Administração*. Tradução de Alessandra Mussi Araujo. Rio de Janeiro: Elsevier, 2006, introdução.

[457] CARNEGIE, Dale. *Como Evitar Preocupações e Começar a Viver*. Op. Cit. p.158 e seguintes.

[458] GAARDER, Jostein. *O Mundo de Sofia. Romance da História da Filosofia*. 17ª reimpressão. Tradução de João Azenha Jr. São Paulo: Companhia das Letras, 1995. p.147.

[459] GAARDER, Jostein. *O Mundo de Sofia*. Op. Cit. p.147.

[460] ABRÃO, Bernadette Siqueira. *História da Filosofia*. São Paulo: Nova Cultural, 1999. p.75.

[461] ABRÃO, Bernadette Siqueira. *História da Filosofia*. Op. Cit. p.75.

[462] GAARDER, Jostein. *O Mundo de Sofia*. Op. Cit. p.148-149.

[463] AURÉLIO, Marco. *Meditações*. Tradução de: Alex Marins. São Paulo: Martin Claret, 2001. p.40.

[464] AURÉLIO, op. Cit. p.90.

[465] ABRÃO, Bernadette Siqueira. Op. Cit. p.87.

[466] CARNEGIE, Dale. *Como Evitar Preocupações*. Op. Cit. p.128.

[467] ABRÃO, Bernadette Siqueira. *História da Filosofia*. Op. Cit. p.76.

[468] SCHOPENHAUER, Arthur. *A Vontade de Amar*. Tradução de: Aurélio de Oliveira. Rio de Janeiro: Tecnoprint, ____, p.101.

[469] SCHOPENHAUER, Arthur. *A Vontade de Amar*. Op. Cit. p.100-101.

[470] CARNEGIE, Dale. *Como evitar preocupações e começar a viver*. 37.ed. Op. Cit. p.143.

[471] COCHRAN, Fred Lloyd. *O Vôo dos Gansos*. Coordenação de CANFIELD, Jack e HANSEN, Mark Victor. *Histórias para Aquecer o Coração*. Tradução de Marilena Moraes. Rio de Janeiro: Sextante, 2003. p.106-107.

[472] MARTELL, Hazel Mary. *O mundo antigo*. 5.ed. Tradução de: Antivan Guimaraens Mendes. São Paulo: Melhoramentos, 2001. p.56.

[473] MARTELL, op. cit. p.61.

[474] FAZOLI FILHO, Arnaldo. *História Geral*. São Paulo: Editora do Brasil, 1981. p.49.

[475] Carnegie credits Sir William Osier for the origins of this phrase (CARNEGIE, Dale. *Como Evitar Preocupações e Começar a Viver*. 37.ed. Op. Cit. p.34).

[476] The reader may note the influence of Carnegie's dramatic training in his books.

[477] CARNEGIE, Dale. *Como Evitar Preocupações e Começar a Viver*. 37.ed. Op. Cit. p.40.

[478] CARNEGIE, Dale. *Como Falar em Público e Influenciar Pessoas no Mundo dos Negócios;* revista por Dorothy Carnegie. 25.ed. Tradução de: Carlos Evaristo M. Costa. Rio de Janeiro: Record, 1993. Originally published in the US under the title *The Quick and Easy Way to Effective Speaking*.

[479] ABRÃO, Bernadette Siqueira. Op. Cit. p.164-165.

[480] FRANKLIN, Benjamin. *The Autobiography of Benjamin Franklin*. . New Haven: Yale University Press, 1964 p. 62.

[481] CARNEGIE, Dale. *Como Fazer Amigos...* Op. Cit. p.206.

[482] FRANKLIN, Benjamin. Op. Cit. p.65.

[483] FRANKLIN, Benjamin. Op. Cit. p.65.

[484] BLIVEN, Bruce. *O Incomparável Talento de Benjamin Franklin*. FRANKLIN, Benjamin. *Autobiografia*. Op. Cit. p.205.

[485] FRANKLIN, Benjamin. Op. Cit. p.82.

[486] FRANKLIN, Benjamin. Op. Cit. p.149

[487] FRANKLIN, Benjamin. Op. Cit. p.149-150

[488] FRANKLIN, Benjamin. Op. Cit. p.154.

[489] FRANKLIN, Benjamin. Op. Cit. p.113 and 114.

[490] BLIVEN, Bruce. Op. Cit. p.205.

[491] FRANKLIN, Benjamin. Op. Cit. p. 242.

[492] CARNEGIE, Dale. *Como Evitar Preocupações e Começar a Viver*. 37.ed. Op. Cit. p.62.

[493] CARNEGIE, Dale. *Como Evitar Preocupações e Começar a Viver.* 37.ed. Op. Cit. p.45, 75, 117, 159, 162, 198, 211, 238, 242, 243, 247, 254 and 258.

[494] GHIRALDELLI JR., Paulo. *O que é Pragmatismo.* São Paulo: Brasiliense, 2007. p.26- 27.

[495] GHIRALDELLI JR., Paulo. Op. Cit. p.24-25.

[496] GHIRALDELLI JR., Paulo. Op. Cit. p.31.

[497] GHIRALDELLI JR., Paulo. Op. Cit. p.37.

[498] HAY, Louise L. *Você Pode Curar a Sua Vida.* Tradução de Evelyn Kay Massako. 13.ed. Rio de Janeiro: BestSeller, 2009. p.83.

[499] JAMES, William. *Pragmatismo.* Tradução de: Jorge Caetano Silva. São Paulo: Nova Cultural, 1989. p. 09.

[500] JAMES, William. *Pragmatismo.* Op. Cit. p.18.

[501] JAMES, William. *Pragmatismo.* Op. Cit. p.27.

[502] JAMES, William. *Pragmatismo.* Op. Cit. p.30.

[503] JAMES, William. *Pragmatismo.* Op. Cit. p.60.

[504] JAMES, William. *Pragmatismo.* Op. Cit. p.18.

[505] NEVINS, Allan and COMMAGER, Henry Steele. *História dos Estados Unidos.* Op. Cit. p.347.

[506] JAMES,William. *Pragmatismo.* Op. cit. p.99.

[507] LONGGOOD, William. Op. Cit. p.46.

[508] EMERSON, Ralph Waldo. Coordenação de CANFIELD, Jack e HANSEN, Mark Victor. *Histórias para Aquecer o Coração.* Tradução de Marilena Moraes. Rio de Janeiro: Sextante, 2003. p.102.

[509] Quoted by Dale Carnegie in *Biographical Roundup.* Op. Cit. p.06.

[510] Information obtained from the Central University of Missouri.

[511] *The Daily Star-Journal.* Warrensburg: Friday, October 22, 2004, p.01.

[512] WILLIAMS, Mara Rose. The *Kansas City Star.* Monday, September 11, 2006, B2.

[513] *The Student.* Warrensburg, Missouri, May 20, 1949. N. 22. Vol. XXXIX.

[514] LONGGOOD, William. Op. cit. p.55.

[515] CROM, Rosemary. *Dale Carnegie as others saw him.* Op. cit. p.24.

[516] CROM, Rosemary. *Dale Carnegie as others saw him.* Op. cit. p.08.

[517] ANDREOLI, Thomas E. *et. al. Medicina Interna Básica.* Op. Cit. p.752.

[518] LONGGOOD, William. Op. cit. p.55.

[519] LONGGOOD, William. Op. cit. p.56.

[520] The Kansas City Star. Monday, September 11, 2006, B2.

[521] ANDREOLI, Thomas E. *et. al. Medicina Interna Básica.* 3.ed. Rio de Janeiro: Guanabara Koogan, 1994, p.334-335. SMELTZER, Suzanne C. and BARE, Brenda G. *et. al. Brunner/Suddarth: Tratado de Engermagem Médico-Cirúrgica.* 7.ed. v.2. Rio de Janeiro: Guanabara Koogan, 1994. p.687.

[522] ANDREOLI, Thomas E. *et. al. Medicina Interna Básica.* Op. Cit. p.335.

[523] ANDREOLI, Thomas E. *et. al. Medicina Interna Básica.* Op. Cit. p.336. According to this medical manual, "Risk of infection is an important problem with Hodgkin's Disease. *Immunological anomalies, in particular those involving T-cell dysfunction, may be detected even before the patient receives any treatment, which explains the frequent co-occurence of Herpes Zoster with Hodgkin's Disease. These patients are also subsceptible to fungal*

infections, such as cryptoccocus. Bacterial infections, primarily pneumococcus and meningococcus, principally affect patients submitted to laparascopy and splenectomy." (ANDREOLI, op. Cit. p.336). SMELTZER and BARE inform that "...patients frequent[ly] develop esophagitis, anorexia, loss of taste, dry mouth, nausea and vomiting, diarrhea, skin reactions and lethargy as a result of radiotherapy. Great creativity is needed in helping patients deal with unpleasant side effects." (SMELTZER e BARE, op. Cit. p.688) KIRKLAND names Carnegie's cause of death as uremia, op. cit. p.45.

[524] CROM, Rosemary. *Dale Carnegie as others saw him*. Op. cit. p.15.

[525] CROM, Rosemary. *Dale Carnegie as others saw him*. Op. Cit. p.07.

[526] CROM, Rosemary. *Dale Carnegie as others saw him*. Op. cit. p.07.

[527] CROM, Rosemary. *Dale Carnegie as others saw him*. Op. cit. p.03.

[528] BELTON HISTORICAL SOCIETY. *The First Hundred Years*. 2.ed. Belton: Dodie Maurer Editor, 2006. p.16.

[529] BELTON HISTORICAL SOCIETY, op. cit. p.16.

[530] ABBOTT, Harold. Op. Cit. p. 18.

[531] SEYMOUR, E.L.D. *American Home*. v.54. October, 1955.

Made in the USA
San Bernardino, CA
13 February 2019